Softwa
A Standards-Based Guide

by
Carma McClure

IEEE
COMPUTER
SOCIETY

Los Alamitos, California

Washington • Brussels • Tokyo

Library of Congress Cataloging-in-Publication Data

McClure, Carma L.
   Software reuse: a standards-based guide / Carma McClure
      p.   cm.
   ISBN 0-7695-0874-X
   1. Computer software—Reusability   I. Title.
   QA76.76.R47 M32 2001
   005—dc21

                                                                    2001002634
                                                                        CIP

IEEE Computer Society Press Order Number BP00874
Library of Congress Number 2001002634
ISBN 0-7695-0874-X

Additional copies may be ordered from:

IEEE Computer Society
Customer Service Center
10662 Los Vaqueros Circle
P.O. Box 3014
Los Alamitos, CA 90720-1314
Tel: +1-714-821-8380
Fax: +1-714-821-4641
http://computer.org/
csbooks@computer.org

IEEE Service Center
445 Hoes Lane
P.O. Box 1331
Piscataway, NJ 08855-1331
Tel: +1-732-981-0060
Fax: +1-732-981-9667
http://shop.ieee.org/store/
customer-service@ieee.org

IEEE Computer Society
Asia/Pacific Office
Watanabe Building
1-4-2 Minami-Aoyama
Minato-ku, Tokyo 107-0062
JAPAN
Tel: +81-3-3408-3118
Fax: +81-3-3408-3553
tokyo.ofc@computer.org

Publisher: Angela Burgess
Group Managing Editor, CS Press: Deborah Plummer
Advertising/Promotions: Tom Fink
Production Editor: Denise Hurst
Cover photo provided by Bill Frymire / Masterfile
Printed in the United States of America

IEEE
COMPUTER
SOCIETY

Contents

Part 1. Overview

List of Figures

List of Tables

Foreword

Software reuse is an important software attribute which permits individual software components from one software system to be incorporated into other software systems to perform a reusable function. Like all key software attributes such as security, testability, quality, and maintainability, software reuse features must be built into the software from the beginning.

This book, *Software Reuse: A Standards-Based Guide*, is part of the IEEE Software Engineering Standards series that will serve as a companion to the IEEE's software engineering standards. All of the books in the series are standards-based guides to provide the reader with a discussion of how the IEEE software engineering standards may be applied to various software projects and issues. Each book will relate a specific topic (project management, quality assurance, requirements, etc) and its associated IEEE Software Engineering standard to the IEEE/EIA 12207.0 lifecycle process standard. These new standards based books will:

➢ Interpret the standard, including analysis of the intent and meaning of each part of the standard
➢ Provide examples of the application to different industry sectors
➢ Provide techniques, methods, and examples for implementing the standard,
➢ Relate the specific IEEE software engineering standard that is the subject of the book to the IEEE/EIA 12207.0 Standard for Technology — Software Life Cycle Processes
➢ Provide sample exercise problems (where possible), and
➢ Enable the reader with reference material and discussion to understand and implement the IEEE Software Engineering standard that is the subject of the book.

Further, each book in the IEEE Software Engineering Standards series will focus on a key software life cycle process or software attribute. The books planned for the series include the following:

➢ Software Life Cycle Processes
➢ Software Project Management

- ➢ Software Quality Assurance
- ➢ Software Requirements
- ➢ Software Configuration Management
- ➢ Software Verification and Validation
- ➢ Software Testing
- ➢ Software Risk Management
- ➢ Software Reuse

Each book in the series will be formatted to make it easy for the reader to find relevant topics and discussion. The chapters/sections of the book will be organized along the software life cycle processes as defined by IEEE/EIA 12207.0 Standard for Technology — Software Life Cycle Processes. Material relevant to specific life cycle processes can be found quickly and the relevant discussion is easily available. Each book will cross reference topics to the other software processes and attributes so the reader may easily find related topics in other books in the series. It is the objective of the Software Engineering Standards book series to provide the reader with introductory tutorial material as well as serve as a reference text.

The author of this title, Carma McClure, has a Ph.D. in Computer Science from Illinois Institute of Technology. While specializing in the area of software engineering she has taught classes in the Computer Science department of I.I.T. as well as the Kellogg Graduate School of Management at Northwestern University. She has published nine software engineering books, and, was the chair and principal writer of the IEEE Std. 1517 Reuse Processes.

Roger U. Fujii
IEEE Software Engineering Standards Book Series Editor
San Pedro, California
May 2001

Preface

Reuse is one of the most basic software concepts. It is simply the idea of using a previously developed software part, such as a data structure or logic function, rather than developing a new one when building a software application or system.

Although a simple concept, reuse is a powerful software practice that can deliver significant improvements in software productivity and quality, as well as substantially lower software development and maintenance costs. Unfortunately, few companies have been able to capitalize on the tremendous benefits that reuse offers. A major reason is that their software life cycle models do not adequately address reuse. Even when using "reuse-pro" technologies such as object-orientation and component-based development, not much reuse is likely to be achieved in a project if it relies on a software life cycle model with only an implicit mention of reuse. *IEEE Std. 1517—Standard for Information Technology—Software Life Cycle Processes—Reuse Processes* was created to address this deficiency.

As explained in this standard, "Unless software reuse is explicitly defined in the software life cycle processes, an organization will not be able to repeatedly exploit reuse opportunities in multiple software projects or software products. Without this repetition, the improvement to the software life cycle and the software products that result from reuse will be limited and perhaps disappointing."

The purpose of the IEEE Std. 1517 is to provide to the software community a well defined approach for practicing systematic reuse within the context of the software life cycle. It is a collection of the best reuse practices recognized by the software industry. It organizes this collection into a set of reuse processes and activities fit into the context of the software life cycle. It covers both the life cycle of a software product developed with reusable assets and the life cycle of reusable assets.

IEEE Std. 1517 was the work product of the Working Group on Information Technology—Software Life Cycle Processes—Reuse Processes. Their work was coordinated with the IEEE Computer Society Software Engineering Standards Committee's Reuse Steering Committee. The SESC sponsored this standard. The SESC and the ISO/IEC JTC1/SC7 are the only two credited standards bodies chartered to develop software engineering standards. Their standards are recognized in US government policy, European Union policy, and world trade organization treaties. The IEEE Computer Society has global membership and is completely independent of any government or industry group.

Membership in the IEEE Std. 1517 Working Group represented a cross section of the software industry—academics, industry practitioners, researchers, members of the government, and members of organizations authoring *de facto* standards (such as the Carnegie Mellon Software Engineering Institute's Capability Maturity Model).

The history of IEEE Std. 1517 began in 1995 with the SESC's formation of the Reuse Planning Group. The purpose of the Reuse Planning Group was to define a statement of direction for IEEE standards with respect to software reuse. The Reuse Planning Group consisted of 36 members from ten countries. Its focus was on standardizing the engineering practice of software reuse, the life cycle processes that involve and enable reuse, and the infrastructure that supports reuse processes and practices.

In 1996, the Reuse Planning Group produced an Action Plan that reported their recommendations for the development of the following reuse standards:[2]

- **Principles of Software Reuse**
- **Definition of Domain Analysis**
- **Software Reuse Life Cycle Processes**

The Reuse Planning Group proposed the development of a software reuse life cycle process standard to explain how reuse processes may be incorporated into the software life cycle. It was their position that most reuse processes are not distinct and independent of the software life cycle and therefore should be integrated into the software life cycle. They recommended that a reuse processes standard should be created to supplement the existing ISO and IEEE 12207 Standard for Information Technology–Software Life Cycle Processes.[3]

The following procedure is used for the development of IEEE standards, such as IEEE Std. 1517:

1. A Study Group is formed
2. The Study Group writes a Project Authorization Request (PAR) to obtain approval to work on the development of the standard
3. The PAR is approved by the sponsor of the standard and the IEEE Standards Board
4. A Working Group is formed; writes the draft of the standard
5. The Working Group sends its completed draft to the Sponsor
6. The Sponsor forms a Balloting Group to vote on the draft(s) of the standard
7. The Sponsor or the Working Group revises the draft based on comments from the Balloting Group
8. The final draft of the standard is approved by the IEEE Standards Board
9. The standard is published by IEEE

Table 1 shows the time line for the development of the IEEE Std. 1517.

Table 1. Time Line for Development of IEEE Std. 1517

Date Step Completed	Step
April 1997	1. Study Group formed
May 1997	2. PAR written
June 1997	3. PAR approved
July 1997	4. Working Group formed
May 1998	5. Working Group completes draft
September 1998	6. Balloting Group formed
November 1998	7. Draft revised
June 1999	8. Final draft approved
July 1999	9. Standard published by IEEE

In accordance with the IEEE standard procedure, IEEE Std. 1517 was developed by consensus and openly reviewed and commented upon by the software industry at large. Each draft of the standard was distributed via the Web. Based on their own research and experience, and the feedback they obtained from review comments, the working group developed several draft versions of the standard. The final draft was approved by the IEEE and accepted as an IEEE standard. IEEE Std. 1517 was approved by the IEEE-SA Standards Board in June 1999 and was published by the IEEE in July 1999.

IEEE Std. 1517 is intended to be used as a requirements specification for practicing software reuse. It identifies the process, activity, task, and deliverable requirements of a software life cycle model that enables the practice of software reuse. However, the standard does not recommend a specific software life cycle model. The user of the standard may map these requirements to the software life cycle that is being developed or acquired to determine its capability to support the practice of software reuse. In the case of developing or redeveloping a life cycle to support reuse, the standard may be used to specify how to extend the life cycle to explicitly include reuse practices. In the case of acquiring or selecting a life cycle, the standard may be used to evaluate how well the life cycle supports reuse practices.

In general, the purpose of IEEE Std. 1517 is to provide the basis for the incorporation of reuse into the software life cycle. More specifically, its purposes are to:

- Establish a framework for practicing reuse within the software life cycle
- Specify the minimum set of processes, activities, and tasks to enable the practice of reuse when developing or maintaining software applications and systems
- Define the input and output deliverables required and produced by these reuse processes
- Explain how to integrate reuse processes, activities, and tasks into the ISO/IEC & IEEE/EIA 12207 Std software life cycle framework
- Improve and clarify communication between software producers and consumers regarding reuse processes and reuse terminology
- Promote and control the practice of software reuse to develop and maintain software products.

Some reasons to conform to this standard are to:

- Improve the software life cycle processes used to develop and maintain software applications and systems
- Adopt the best software reuse practices
- Adopt a component-based development (CBD) approach
- Improve the quality of software applications and systems developed
- Decrease the costs of developing and maintaining software applications and systems
- Decrease the time to develop and maintain software applications and systems
- Understand software reuse terminology
- Increase competitive advantage with respect to software applications and systems
- Extend a software life cycle model to include reuse processes, activities, and tasks.

Also, the reader should be aware of the following limitations of the standard. First, the primary focus of the standard is on the software processes—not the software product. Therefore, the standard does not address software quality or software asset quality in detail. The subject of software quality is covered in other software engineering standards. Second, although the standard generally applies to all types of assets, only commercial off-the-shelf (COTS) assets specifically designed for reuse are addressed by this standard. In this special case, COTS assets are treated by the standard like any another type of asset. Third, based on the recommendation of the IEEE Reuse Steering Committee, domain engineering is not addressed in detail because it will be addressed in a separate IEEE software engineering standard.

Purpose of the Book

Like IEEE Std. 1517, this book is written for both managers and technical personnel involved in acquiring, supplying, or developing software applications and systems or reusable assets.

The purposes of this book are to:
1. Aid the reader in interpreting the meaning of the standard
2. Guide the reader in implementing the standard
3. Guide the reader in applying the standard

Since the standard is written as a high-level, succinct specification of the reuse requirements for the software life cycle, the reader may find it somewhat difficult to determine the meaning of each requirement. This book attempts to clarify the meaning of each requirement by explaining the meaning intended by the authors of the standard. The author of this book was the principal writer of the standard.

Also, since the standard is written as a supplement to the *IEEE/EIA Std. 12207.0-1996—Standard for Information Technology—Software Life Cycle Processes*, the reader must understand IEEE/EIA Std.12207 to interpret IEEE Std. 1517. Whereas IEEE Std. 1517 is specific to reuse, IEEE/EIA Std. 12207 is a general requirements specification for software life cycle processes. IEEE Std. 1517 adds to the IEEE 12207 life cycle framework those processes, activities, tasks, and deliverables that are necessary to support and enable the practice of software reuse. This book begins the discussion of IEEE Std. 1517 by explaining the structure and content of the IEEE/EIA Std. 12207. With this background information about IEEE/EIA Std. 12207, the reader is prepared to learn about IEEE Std. 1517.

The second purpose of the book is to provide the reader suggestions on how to implement the standard. The standard is intended for use with virtually any software life cycle model. The book discusses each requirement and then offers suggested ways to implement the requirement in a software life cycle model.

The third purpose of the book is to advise the reader about how to apply the standard. For instance, the text explains some common ways the standard is expected to be used. Ways to achieve compliance with this standard are discussed. The book also discusses how IEEE Std. 1517 relates to and may be used with *de jure* as well as important industry *de facto* standards addressing software reuse.

Structure of the Book

The book is divided into three parts:
1. Overview
2. Interpretation and Implementation
3. Application

Part 1: Overview

The first part (Chapters 1, 2, and 3) provides an overview of the standard and supporting background information.

Chapter 1 introduces IEEE Std. 1517. Software Reuse and its benefits are defined. The need for a reuse process standard is explained. The purposes and uses of IEEE Std.1517 are presented.

Chapter 2 discusses IEEE/EIA Std. 12207.0—the foundation for IEEE Std. 1517. An overview of IEEE Std. 12207 is presented. The software life cycle framework (used by IEEE Std. 12207.0 to organize life cycle processes and also used by IEEE Std. 1517) is presented. Each life cycle process specified in the framework is described. These same life cycle processes are used in the IEEE Std. 1517 when specifying the requirements for practicing software reuse.

Chapter 3 describes the organization of the IEEE Std. 1517. Systematic reuse, an organization-level formalized type of reuse, is defined. IEEE Std. 1517 is described as the process standard for systematic reuse. The software life cycle framework for systematic reuse is presented. The four process categories that compromise this framework are discussed.

Part 2: Interpretation and Implementation

Part 2 of the book (Chapters 4, 5, 6, and 7) provides a detailed interpretation of each IEEE Std. 1517 requirement as well as suggestions for implementing the requirement. First, the requirement, presented in the standard in the form of a task, is described. Next, a discussion of the meaning of the requirement is given. This is followed by suggested procedures that may be used to implement the requirement.

Chapter 4 discusses how to extend the primary processes defined in the IEEE/EIA Std. 12207.0 software life cycle framework to support the development, operation, and maintenance of software applications and systems with the use of reusable software parts. The primary processes include: acquisition, supply, development, operation, and maintenance.

Chapter 5 discusses the Asset Management Process. This is a new process defined by IEEE Std. 1517 and added to the IEEE/EIA Std. 12207.0 life cycle process framework in the supporting process category. The purpose of this process is to handle the special requirements that reuse of software parts places on software management, storage, retrieval, version control, change control, and distribution.

Chapter 6 discusses the Reuse Program Administration Process. This is a new process defined by IEEE Std. 1517 and added to the IEEE/EIA Std. 12207.0 life cycle process framework in the organizational process category. It specifies the requirements for a formal reuse program that operates at the organizational or enterprise level and addresses the management aspects of practicing reuse.

Chapter 7 presents the domain engineering process. This is a new process defined by the IEEE Std. 1517 and added to the IEEE Std. 12207.0 life cycle framework in the new category called cross-project processes. The purpose of this process is to provide through acquisition or development the reusable software parts to be used by the primary processes in the development, operation, and maintenance of software applications and systems.

Part 3: Application

Chapter 8 discusses the expected users and uses of IEEE Std. 1517. It also discusses the various ways in which compliance with this standard may be achieved.

Chapter 9 explores the relationship of IEEE Std. 1517 to the Capability Maturity Model from the Software Engineering Institute. CMM is used to evaluate the quality of a software life cycle process model. Reuse is one software life cycle quality characteristic measured by CMM.

Chapter 10 discusses the Object Management Group's Unified Modeling Language (UML). The UML is an analysis and design notation used to model component-based systems. The use of UML to implement IEEE Std. 1517 reuse requirements is examined.

References

1. *IEEE Std. 1517 Standard for Information Technology—Software Life Cycle Processes—Reuse Processes*, Institute of Electrical and Electronic Engineers, Inc., Piscataway, N.J., 1999.

2. *Action Plan, Version 1*, Reuse Planning Group, Software Engineering Standards Committee, IEEE Computer Society, 17 September 1996.

3. Ibid.

Acknowledgements

I would like to thank the members of the IEEE Computer Society Working Group on Information Technology—Software Life Cycle Processes—Reuse Processes for the many lively discussions we had while exploring and debating industry reuse practices. Through these discussions, I gained a much better understanding of the reuse requirements for the software life cycle.

I would also like to thank the IEEE Computer Society's Reuse Steering Committee for guiding the efforts of the Working Group. Thank you as well to the Software Engineering Standards Committee for sponsoring the Working Group. In particular, I would like to thank James W. Moore of the MITRE Corporation for serving as my guide during my first trip into the software standards world.

Finally, I would like to thank William B. McClure for encouraging me to bring this project to conclusion.

Part 1.
Overview

Chapter 1.
Introduction to IEEE Std. 1517—
Software Reuse Processes

1.1 Reuse is Boring!

Software reuse is the process of building or assembling software applications and systems from previously developed software parts designed for reuse. Software reuse is practiced to save time and money, and to improve quality.

Although a potentially powerful technology, reuse has never been counted among the most interesting software topics. In truth, most software professionals consider reuse downright boring. After all, who would find a worn-out subject as old as programming itself interesting? For years, we have been hearing about the benefits reuse offers, but have yet to see them realized in practice. Even when the popularity of object-oriented development (OOD) brought the notion of reuse to the forefront, the software community was disappointed because less object reuse was achieved than expected. Reuse, it seems, is not an automatic byproduct of OOD.

1.2 The Next Form of Reuse

In the future, however, reuse is likely to elicit a very different reaction. The next form of reuse will be the key enabler of the world trade of software via the World Wide Web. Reuse via the Web has already captured the imagination of the software industry and business community at large. After all, who would not be interested in the primary enabler of an emerging multi-billion dollar industry that promises to turn the traditional software development approach upside down?

The next form of reuse centers on components and component-based development. Figure 1-1 shows the projected growth for the component industry over the next few years.[1] Components are expected to be the primary driver of the dramatic changes about to take place in software development.

Components lie at the very heart of the future vision of computing. Corporations expect that they soon will be running their businesses using Web-enabled, enterprise business applications composed from predefined, reusable, and replaceable components distributed over networks. Although part of the application may run on a client, part on the middle-tier, and another part on a backend database server, its comprising components—written in different languages and supplied from multiple sources—will work together to perform the application's services.

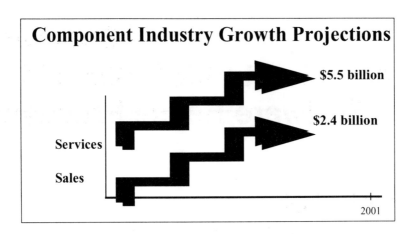

Figure 1-1. Between 1998 and 2001, component sales are
predicted to increase from $1.1 billion to $2.4 billion, and
related services from $2.2 billion to $5.5 billion.

Component-based applications offer the advantages of being both easily customized to meet current business needs and easily modified to meet changing business needs over time. Also, they leverage a corporation's investment in its legacy systems by containing valuable existing functionality wrapped into reusable components. Thus, component-based applications are likely to be composed of an interacting mixture of pre-developed components that preserve the business' core functionality and new components that take advantage of the newest technologies, such as the Internet. Today, examples of components include objects written in languages such as Smalltalk, C++, and Java, and other software parts such as Active X controls and design frameworks.

1.3 Components

A *component* may be thought of as an independent module that provides information about what it does and how to use it through a public interface, while hiding its inner workings. The interface identifies the component, its behaviors, and interaction mechanisms.

The idea of components is not new. Fundamental to the component concept are the predecessor software engineering concepts of program modularization, structured programming, and information hiding, which were introduced in the 1960s by Edgar Dijkstra, David Parnes, and others.

Although as of yet there is no industry consensus on the definition of a component, there is some agreement on the properties that a component is expected to have. For instance, a component should provide a set of common functionality that may be used as a self-contained building block in the construction of software applications. In addition, a component should have a well-defined interface, hide implementation details, fit into an architecture, be easily replaced, and have the ability to inter-operate with other components. Finally, a component should be reusable in many different software applications and systems.

Szyperski's definition of a component emphasizes the importance of the interface and context specification of a component as well as its independent nature:

> *A software component is a unit of composition with contractually specified interfaces and explicit context dependencies only. A software component can be deployed independently and is subject to composition by third parties.*[2]

Table 1-1 is a list of components compiled from several recent software publication articles on the topic. The components listed include examples of small-grained, desktop-bound visual components (e.g., GUI widgets), as well as large-grained components that capture a complete business function (e.g., a shipping component that includes order entry and shipment functionality).

The list of components illustrates how the industry's notion of components has evolved over the last decade. At first, the term *component* typically was used to refer to compound documents (e.g., OpenDoc components and Microsoft's Object Linking and Embedding (OLE) components), and then also to refer to binary and source code components (e.g., Active X Controls and CORBA components). Later, due to the market's drive to expand component technology beyond the desktop to the server, the concept of components was enlarged to include more abstract and larger-grained components, such as design templates, frameworks, and even application packages. In contrast to earlier components, most of which were visual and client-based, these types of components (e.g., Enterprise JavaBeans, SAP AG's R/3 Package, IBM's San Francisco Project, VISIX Software's Galaxy, Template Software's SNAP) are often non-visual, backend, and server-based. They implement infrastructure services such as event notification, backend services such as transaction processing, and business functions such as shipping.

1.3.1 Beyond Objects

Today, components are seen as a step beyond objects. Like objects, components use contractually specified interfaces to implement the requirement of plug-compatibility with other components. But they go beyond objects by better addressing the requirement for replaceability and by enabling the reuse of software parts that are larger-grained and at higher levels of abstraction.

A noted shortcoming of objects is that they do not scale up well when used to build large, complex application systems because they are too fine-grained and at too low an abstraction level. Another shortcoming is that system modification, maintenance, and testing can be difficult because of inheritance and behavior overriding. Replacement of an object with a new object that implements changes to the business may impact all other objects that inherit properties of the replaced object and thus may lead to extensive re-testing.

In contrast to objects, components can be large-grained as well as small-grained software parts. Large-grained components (enterprise components) encapsulate major chunks of an application's functionality in an independent, reusable, and easily replaceable unit. Because of their size, fewer enterprise components are needed to construct an application than objects. This solves the scaling problem with fine-grained components where integration and assembly become very tedious because of the number of parts needed to construct a large application.

Enterprise components maximize the potential benefits that reuse can deliver by making reuse practical in large-scale system projects. Also, because they are independent units that encapsulate a complete function, enterprise components also solve the replaceability problem. When changes in the business occur, the old component can be easily pulled out and replaced with a new component that satisfies the new business requirements with little or no impact on other parts of the system.

Table 1-1. Examples of Components

- Calendars: On screen widget
- Button for a user screen: List Box, Dialog Box
- Order entry process (full application)
- CICS transaction call
- Customer service screen
- Customer management component
- Validation component that interacts with multiple DB2 tables
- Customer management component
- Workflow component
- Shipping component (order entry and shipment specification)
- Charge amount
- Business Associates
- Container type
- Unit of measure
- Event notification (infrastructure service)
- User interface controls
- Inter-application communication protocols
- Customer component
- Invoice component
- Order component
- Security
- General ledger
- Asset depreciation component
- Letter-of-credit
- Manufacturing work-in-process module
- Inventory tracking application

1.4 Component-Based Development

So strong is the software community's belief in components, that it may be simply a matter of time before component-based development becomes the dominant software development approach. Component industry projections are that 61 percent of all new applications will be developed using components by the year 2001.[3]

Component-based development (CBD) is the latest embodiment of reuse. It is an assembly approach to software development in which software applications are constructed by means of assembling components. Some of these components may be predefined components housed in libraries or supplied by other sources such as external vendors, some may be harvested from existing systems and applications, and others may be developed anew for the project at hand. CBD may also be described as an architecture-driven software development approach, where an *architecture* is a generic structure or high-level design that is intended to be used to build a set of related software products or systems. The architecture provides a framework for assembling the components into a software application.

The strategy underlying CBD is to use predefined software components and architectures to eliminate redesigning and rebuilding the same software structures over and over again. Because of this underlying strategy, not only does the CBD approach imply reuse, it demands reuse to deliver any significant gains in software productivity, quality, and development speed. Since reuse lies at the very heart of the CBD approach, this development method must be guided by the principles of reuse.

1.4.1 Benefits of Component-Based Development

It has long been recognized that reuse is a powerful technology that potentially can deliver tremendous benefits. Exploiting component-based development can provide very significant software productivity, quality, and cost improvements to an organization. Table 1-2 lists the benefits of component-based development, which are really just a repeat of the benefits that have always been promised by reuse.

1.4.2 Delivering Quality

One of the most important benefits that reuse delivers is quality. Among all the powerful software technologies available today, software reuse is the best way to accelerate the production of high quality software. What sets reuse apart is its ability to provide the benefits of faster, better, and cheaper without compromise. With the exception of reuse, all other software technologies require a trade-off of possible benefits (e.g., faster software development at the expense of software quality). According to the Gartner Group's findings, reuse is the only technology that allows a company to simultaneously address software cost, time-to-market, flexibility, and quality.[6] Reuse enables a company to achieve both higher quality systems and lower costs, hence gaining a competitive advantage in the marketplace.

Table 1-2. Benefits of Component-Based Development[4,5]

- Deploy critical software applications more quickly
- Simplify large-scale software development
- Encapsulate business services into reusable application logic
- Shorten software development cycles
- Reduce the amount of new code to write
- Allow software applications to share functionality
- Make software applications more adaptable; easier to change
- Decrease software complexity
- Increase software reliability and overall quality
- Increase software productivity by reducing costs

1.4.3 Exploiting Reuse Benefits

Not only are there tremendous benefits to be gained from reuse, but also there are tremendous opportunities to employ reuse in software projects. Analysis of software applications and systems has shown that they are composed of similar parts. In general, it is reasonable to expect that 60 to 70 percent of a software application's functionality is similar to the functionality in other software applications, that 40 to 60 percent of its code is reusable in other software applications, and that 60 percent of its design is reusable in other software applications.[7] Therefore, the majority of almost any software application can be assembled from predefined components, provided those components were designed to be "plug compatible."

Components are the software industry's latest attempt to capitalize on this similarity. Backed by advances in technologies and tools, components offer the best chance yet to achieve a significant level of reuse in industrial-strength application development projects.

1.5 Components and Standards

However, there is one catch. *Standards*. The success of the components industry is totally dependent on standards. For example, it is obvious that interoperability standards are a basic necessity. Interoperability standards are necessary to be able to assemble components from different sources into working applications and systems.

Components are expected to communicate with one another and to use each other to provide their services or functionality. A standard component interoperability model assures components written in different languages, located in different places, and running on different platforms and on different machines or address spaces can be used together, sharing data and capabilities.

There currently are three *de facto* standards for component specification, interoperability, and distributed computing:

1. Object Management Group's Common Object Request Broker Architecture/Internet Interoperability Protocol (OMG's CORBA/IIOP): for CORBA components that are written in different languages such as C++, Visual Basic, and Java and run on multi-

ple distributed platforms

2. Microsoft's Component Object Model/Distributed Component Object Model (COM/DCOM): for ActiveX controls that can be built in different languages such as C++, Smalltalk and Java, and run on a Windows environment

3. Java/JavaBeans/Enterprise JavaBeans: for JavaBeans that are built in Java and run on all environments that support the Java virtual machine

IIOP is the CORBA message protocol used to provide component communication over the Internet or an Intranet. Remote Method Invocation (RMI) is used to enable distributed Java components to communicate with one another.

The fact that there are three such interoperability models rather than one is not considered a problem by companies attempting to implement component technology because the three models are quite similar and are bridged by tools.[8]

1.6 Process Standards

Although interoperability standards ensure that components will fit together, they are not enough to ensure the success of a global components industry. Software developers also need process standards that detail how to identify, analyze, design, implement, test, deploy, maintain, and evolve high-quality components and component-based applications.

Process standards serve two important functions to enable the world trade of software components:

1. Establishment of a common understanding of the software process between software producers and software consumers

2. Assurance of the quality of software components and component-based applications

1.6.1 Improving Communication

First, consider the issue of understanding between software producers and software consumers. In this context, a software producer refers to a software developer or vendor who provides software products (e.g., software systems, applications, or components) to a software consumer (e.g., user or software developer who uses the software product to build a new software product). Software producers and software consumers often do not speak the same language. When they enter into a relationship where one agrees to provide software to the other, it is very difficult to communicate product and project requirements unless the process to be used is well understood by all parties involved. The world trade of software complicates this problem because software producers and software consumers may not know of one another. Also, they may be members of different organizations and can be located in different places around the world.

A standard can foster an improved understanding between software consumers, software producers, and everyone else involved in the life cycle of software products, regardless of these complications. As an example, consider the user (or manager) who wants a CBD approach employed to develop a software product. Having a standard that specifies what is required in a software life cycle model to enable CBD can clarify for the user (or manager) and the developer what is entailed in such an approach. The standard specification of what is required in the life cycle model can even be used as the basis for an informal or legally binding contractual agreement between the parties.

1.6.2 Assuring Quality

Second, quality has always been an important software issue. The world trade of software makes quality an even more important software issue. The business of global reuse of components via the World Wide Web cannot succeed unless the quality of components can be assured. Component consumers will demand quality assurance from component producers. Interface standards are not enough to guarantee component quality.

Historically, the software industry has followed the Deming school of total quality management which espouses using a better quality process to produce a better quality product. Empirical evidence has shown that the quality of the software life cycle process used directly affects the quality of the software it produces.[9,10] In other words, software quality follows from software process quality. Process standards that capture the best-known software practices are considered the best means available to assure the quality of the software life cycle process and, hence, the quality of the software product. Like any software user, component consumers will demand that component producers use software processes and practices that result in high quality software components and component-based applications. The components industry must rely on process standards and product quality standards as important means to assure the quality of components and component-based applications.

1.7 IEEE Std. 1517—Reuse Processes

IEEE Std. 1517—Standard for Information Technology—Software Life Cycle Processes—Reuse Processes is the process standard for reuse and for CBD.[11] It is a requirements specification for practicing reuse and CBD on an enterprise-wide basis. IEEE Std. 1517 identifies the processes involved in practicing software reuse and describes, at a high level, how the processes operate and interact during the software life cycle. Also, it defines reuse terminology. Because IEEE Std. 1517 addresses both the development and maintenance of software with the use of predefined reusable software parts and the development and maintenance of reusable software parts, it is applicable to CBD. In this standard, reusable software parts are called *assets*.[12]

1.7.1 Purpose of IEEE Std. 1517

In general, the purpose of IEEE Std. 1517 is to provide the basis for the incorporation of reuse into the software life cycle. More specifically, its purposes are to:

- Establish a framework for practicing reuse within the software life cycle
- Specify the minimum set of processes, activities, and tasks to enable the practice of reuse when developing or maintaining software applications and systems

- Define the input and output deliverables required and produced by these reuse processes

- Explain how to integrate reuse processes, activities, and tasks into the ISO/IEC & IEEE/EIA 12207 Standard software life cycle framework

- Improve and clarify communication between software producers and software consumers regarding reuse processes and reuse terminology

- Promote and control the practice of software reuse to develop and maintain software products

It is important to emphasize that this standard does not define one specific, rigid software life cycle that must be adhered to. Instead, IEEE Std. 1517 is more correctly viewed as simply a specification of the minimum requirements that a software life cycle must meet to include reuse. In other words, it provides the software community with a clear and explicit specification as to what is required in a software life cycle to accomplish the practice of reuse and to enable CBD.

Software developers will shy away from a standard that dictates one specific process and rightly so, because this is not a one-size-fits-all situation. It is a well-known fact that different software projects and different organizations have very different software life cycle requirements and preferences. However, going to the other extreme where there is no reuse process standard whatsoever leaves the software industry without any guidance as to what is needed to practice reuse or any means to evaluate and choose among software products and service providers that claim to enable and support reuse. The result of having no clear idea of what is needed to practice reuse is a history of little reuse.

Because this standard is a requirements specification rather than an implementation of reuse processes, IEEE Std. 1517 is open and can be used with virtually any software life cycle offered by a vendor or developed in-house by an organization. Organizations and developers who do not want a specific set of reuse processes forced upon them have nothing to fear and much to gain from IEEE Std. 1517.

1.7.2 Uses of IEEE Std. 1517

Like all IEEE standards, the use of this standard is voluntary. An individual organization may choose to adopt IEEE Std. 1517 as a means of improving its software processes. For example, an organization that desires to use the software reuse practices that have been deemed by consensus to represent the "best of breed" may choose to adopt this standard.

Alternatively, an organization may decide to adopt this standard as a way to assert that its software development process conforms to the best-known software reuse practices. Some reasons to conform to this standard include:

- Improve the software life cycle processes used to develop and maintain software applications and systems

- Adopt the best software reuse practices

- Adopt a CBD approach

- Improve the quality of software applications and systems developed

- Decrease the costs of developing and maintaining software applications and systems
- Decrease the time required to develop and maintain software applications and systems
- Understand software reuse terminology
- Increase competitive advantage of software applications and systems
- Extend a software life cycle model to include reuse processes, activities, and tasks

1.7.3 Application of IEEE Std. 1517

IEEE Std. 1517 is written for both managers and technical personnel that are involved in acquiring, supplying, or developing software applications and systems or reusable assets. IEEE Std. 1517 applies to:

1. the acquisition of software and software services
2. the acquisition of assets
3. the supply, development, operation, and maintenance of software applications and systems using a CBD approach
4. the supply, development, management, and maintenance of assets
5. the establishment of a systematic reuse program and components strategy at the organization or enterprise level

1.8 Placement of IEEE Std. 1517 in the IEEE Software Engineering Standards Collection

As Table 1-3 shows, software engineering standards have been produced by several organizations.[13] At the time of writing, IEEE Std. 1517 is one of more than 300 software engineering standards that have been developed and maintained by more than 50 different standards organizations. The IEEE Computer Society is responsible for the creation and maintenance of approximately 50 standards. IEEE Std. 1517 is a member of the IEEE Computer Society Software Engineering Standards Committee (SESC) collection of standards. IEEE Std. 1517 has been designed to fit into the SESC standards collection as a practice standard; i.e., a description of the best software reuse practices. It provides the reuse processes requirements to be met by a software life cycle model that claims reuse support.

1.8.1 SESC

The IEEE Software Engineering Standards Committee (SESC) was formed in 1976.[14] Its mission is to plan, improve, and coordinate a collection of software engineering standards whose function is to prescribe the norms of software engineering practice.

Software engineering is: (1) The application of a systematic, disciplined, quantifiable approach to the development, operation, and maintenance of software; that is, the application of engineering to software. (2) The study of approaches as in (1).[15]

Since its formation, the number of SESC software engineering standards has grown from one to nearly 50.[16] Software engineering standards cover the various software life cycle processes such as design, testing, and maintenance; the various aspects of software quality such as quality assurance, performance monitoring, and reliability; and supporting functions such as training, project management, and configuration management.

To better manage and make standards easier to use, the SESC is reorganizing its standards collection. The reorganization is based on an architecture comprised of five classes of objects: customer, process, agent, resource, and product.[17] This object-oriented view represents software engineering as being performed by a project that consists of a set of agents. The agent interacts with the customer and uses resources to perform a process that produces a product.

Table 1-3. Examples of Organizations that Produce Software Engineering Standards

ORGANIZATION	ORGANIZATION'S NAME
US National Standards	
ASTM	American Society for Testing and Materials
EIA	Electronic Industries Association
ANS	American National Standard
IEEE	Institute of Electrical and Electronics Engineers
US Government Standards	
NIST	National Institute of Standards and Technology
DoD	Department of Defense
NASA	National Aeronautics and Space Administration
International Standards	
ISO	International Organization for Standardization
IEC	International Electrotechnical Commission

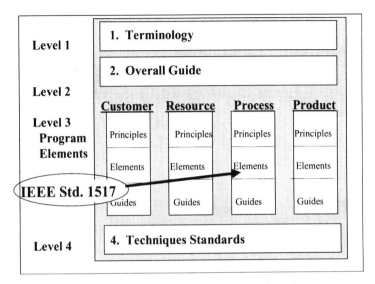

Figure 1-2. The SESC Standards Architecture

1.8.2 SESC Standards Architecture

The SESC Standards Architecture is depicted in Figure 1-2.[18] The first level of the SESC standards architecture contains software engineering terminology standards and the taxonomy of the standards.

The second level contains an overall guide to the SESC collection of standards. It describes the relationships among the SESC standards.

The third level consists of four three-layer stacks (or the program elements). The four stacks contain standards regarding the customer, process, product, and resource objects of software engineering. Each stack is divided into three layers representing three types of standards:

- Layer 1: *Principles*—Principle or policy standards describe objectives for standards that belong to a stack

- Layer 2: *Elements*—Element standards provide high-level guidelines of software engineering activities that belong to a stack

- Layer 3: *Application Guides and Supplements*—Guides provide guidance on how to apply Element Standards that belong to a stack

The fourth level of the standards architecture contains the Techniques Standards. These standards describe software-engineering techniques that are broadly applicable (e.g., can be used by several life cycle processes or activities).

IEEE Std. 1517 is classified as a *process elements* standard. As shown in Figure 1-2, it belongs at Level 3 and in Layer 2 of the Process Stack in the SESC Standards Architecture.

1.9 Supplement to ISO 12207

IEEE Std. 1517 is a supplement to the ISO and IEEE 12207 Standard for Information Technology—Software Life Cycle Processes.[19] IEEE Std. 1517 identifies the reuse processes and explains how they are integrated into the ISO 12207 life cycle process framework. (Note that the ISO 12207 framework and the IEEE 12207 framework are the same. Therefore, when reference is made to the ISO 12207 framework, it refers to both versions of the standard.)

A 24 September 1997 meeting letter of the IEEE Software Engineering Standards Committee states: "The ISO 12207 framework is considered the strategic definition of the software life cycle model." (See Chapter 2, Figure 2-2 for the 12207 Life Cycle Framework.) However, the ISO 12207 Standard is not sufficient by itself to enable and support the practice of reuse because it does not explicitly define reuse process requirements for the software life cycle. IEEE Std. 1517 was created to make reuse an explicit part of the software life cycle. (See Chapter 3, Figure 3-1 for the 1517 Life Cycle Process Framework.)

The writers of IEEE Std. 1517 designed it as a supplement that is integrated into the ISO 12207 specification. Desiring to practice what they preached, the writers of IEEE Std. 1517 reused the life cycle framework and process descriptions from the ISO 12207 Standard, rather than recreate a new framework to show how to augment the software life cycle with reuse processes. (See Chapter 8, Figure 8-1 for the 1517 Framework and Processes.) This means that compliance with IEEE Std. 1517 also results in compliance with the ISO (and IEEE) 12207 Standard. This also means that it is impossible to understand or apply the IEEE Std. 1517 without also understanding the ISO 12207 Standard—both its framework and its contents. For this reason, Chapter 2 is devoted to a detailed explanation of the ISO 12207 Standard.

1.10 References

1. D. Kara, "Build vs. Buy: Maximizing the Potential of Components," *Component Strategies,* July 1998, pp. 22–35.

2. Szyperski, *Component Software: Beyond Object-Oriented Programming,* Addison Wesley Longman, 1998, P. 34.

3. B. Ambler and S. Venkat, "Large-Grained Components & Standards: Perfect Together," *Component Strategies,* Oct. 1998, pp. 32–46.

4. R. Levin, "Components on Track," *Information Week,* 5 June1998, pp. 93–98.

5. M. Buchheit and B. Hollunder, "Building and Assemblying Components," *Object Magazine,* Nov. 1997, pp. 62–64.

6. *Software Reuse Report,* Gartner Group, Stanford, Conn., 1995, p.7.

7. W. Tracz, *Tutorial: Software Reuse: Emerging Technology,* IEEE Computer Society Press, Los Alamitos, Calif., 1988.

8. N. Ward-Dutton, "Componentware Turns the Corner," *Application Development Trends,* July 1998, pp. 18–19.

9. P. Lawlis et al., "A Correlation Study of the CMM and Software Development Processes," *CrossTalk,* Sept. 1995, pp. 21–25.

10. *CMM Summary*, Software Engineering Institute, Carnegie Mellon University, Pittsburgh, Pa., SEI Web page: sei.cmu.edu.

11. *IEEE 1517, Standard for Information Technology—Software Life Cycle Processes—Reuse Processes*, IEEE, Piscataway, N.J., 1999.

12. Ibid.

13. J. Moore, *Software Engineering Standards*, IEEE Computer Society, 1998, pp. 267–276.

14. Ibid., 1998, pp. 34–57.

15. *IEEE Std. 610.12, Standard Glossary of Software Engineering Terminology*, IEEE, Piscataway, N.J., 1990.

16. J. Moore, *Software Engineering Standards*, pp.34–57.

17. Ibid., p. 23.

18. Ibid., p. 23.

19. *ISO/IEC 12207—1996 Standard for Information Technology—Software Life Cycle Processes*, International Organization for Standardization and International Electrotechnical Commission, Geneva, Switzerland, 1996.

Chapter 2.
The ISO/IEC & IEEE/EIA Standard 12207— Standard for Information Technology— Software Life Cycle Processes

2.1 Overview of 12207

Standards are essential not only to the growth of the components industry but also to the advancement of software engineering practices. To encourage their use in practice, the standards must be integrated through a common set of software engineering terminology and a common view of the software life cycle. To this end, the IEEE Software Engineering Standards Committee adopted the software life cycle process framework defined in the ISO/IEC Std. 12207, as the cornerstone in the SESC standards collection. As the title suggests, *ISO/IEC Std.12207.0—Standard for Information Technology—Software Life Cycle Processes* is about the life cycle of a software product. As defined by this standard, a software product is "the set of computer programs, procedures, and possibly associated documentation and data."[1] ISO/IEC Std. 12207 specifies the minimum set of processes that must be included in the software life cycle.

ISO/IEC 12207 bases its representation of the software life cycle on the general principles and basic components of system engineering: analysis, design, fabrication, evaluation, testing, integration, manufacturing, and distribution.[2]

2.1.1. Two Versions of 12207

There are actually two versions of the12207 software life cycle standard:

1. ISO/IEC 12207—the international version[3]
2. IEEE/EIA 12207—the U.S./IEEE version[4]

There are only minor differences between the ISO and IEEE versions. For example, the IEEE version includes a few additions to the ISO version, such as an annex that explains the basic concepts underlying the software life cycle. Another difference is that the IEEE version tightens the compliance requirements in the area of tailoring. Tailoring of the life cycle is included in the 12207 Standard to allow an organization to adapt the life cycle requirements to suit its particular needs. For example, tailoring can be used to delete processes, activities, or tasks from the standard for use in a specific software project. Tailoring is also allowed in the IEEE version, but is more restricted than in the ISO version.

One of the reasons for creating the IEEE version was to incorporate the best-known U.S. software engineering practices and experiences.[5]

Finally, it is important to note that compliance with IEEE 12207 also implies compliance with ISO 12207, since the IEEE version is fully compliant with the ISO version. For the purpose of discussion in this chapter, "12207 Standard" will be used to refer to both versions of this standard.

2.1.2 Purpose

The major purposes of the 12207 Standard are to:

- Establish a common framework for software life cycle processes
- Improve communication among all parties involved in the life cycle of a software product by providing a common terminology
- Define the processes that are applied during the complete life cycle of a software product beginning with acquisition through retirement
- Enable the world trade of software products

The 12207 Standard has been written to serve both the acquirer and the supplier of software, both of whom may be either internal or external to an organization. In the context of this standard, an acquirer (i.e., consumer) is the party that desires to acquire a software product from a supplier; and the supplier (i.e., producer), on the other hand, is the party that desires to provide the software product to the acquirer. The standard provides the means to construct a contract between these two parties to define how the software project, which supplies the software product, will be carried out. The 12207 Standard is normally applied at the software project level. However, the IEEE version also includes application at the enterprise level, which is particularly important for practicing systematic reuse and CBD.

In the 12207 Standard, software life cycle processes are described at a high-level to enable the standard to have the broadest possible applicability. The standard does not specify a particular software life cycle model or methodology. It can be applied with any type of software life cycle model (including the waterfall, rapid prototyping, and iterative models) and can be used to guide traditional, object-oriented, and component-based software development.

2.1.3 A Requirements Specification

The 12207 Standard is written in the form of a requirements specification for the processes that should be included in a software life cycle model. This requirements specification is expressed as a set of activities that comprise the process and a set of tasks that comprise the activity. However, the 12207 Standard does not describe how a software life cycle model must implement the activity and task specifications. Nor does the standard specify the details of the deliverables that must be produced by a software life cycle model. The implementation particulars are left to the specific model selected by the user of the standard.

For example, task 5.3.7.3 from the 12207 Standard reads:

The developer shall update the user documentation as necessary.[6]

The language used to specify the tasks (i.e., in particular, the use of the word "shall" tells the users of the standard that this task is required for compliance (Table 2-1.). It also tells the user that the agent responsible for updating user documentation is the developer. And finally, it tells the user that the deliverable produced is user documentation, in this case an updated version of the user documentation. How the documentation is produced (e.g., automatically generated by software tools) is not covered by the standard. Nor are the contents or format of the user documentation described by the standard. These details are the prerogative of the implementation model selected.

Table 2-1. Use of Language to Indicate 12207 Standard Requirements[7]

> *"Will"* denotes purpose or intent by one party
>
> *"Shall"* denotes a binding provision between two or more parties
>
> *"Should"* expresses a recommendation among other possibilities
>
> *"May"* denotes a permitted action

2.2 Structure of the 12207 Standard

The developers of the 12207 Standard used the Basili process abstraction architecture to describe software life cycle processes and to structure the standard. The Basili architecture is important to understanding the content and implementation of the 12207 Standard.

2.2.1 Basili Architecture for Process Abstraction

In his component factory, Basili defined the following three levels of abstraction at which processes can be represented:[8]

- Level 1—*Reference*: At this level, a process is represented in terms of a single agent that is responsible for performing the process. The process consists of a set of activities that may be performed by this single agent.

- Level 2—*Conceptual*: At this level, a process is represented in terms of flow of control and flow of data that may occur between process agents. Logical relationships among the process agents are defined.

- Level 3—*Implementation*: At this level, the process agent is mapped to the organizational structure of the organization that is responsible for implementing the process. The roles of the process agent are assigned to specific organizational units within this structure.

Based on the Basili architecture, the 12207 Standard is a *level-1 reference* standard. For this reason, definitions for software processes in the 12207 Standard do not contain procedural details, time sequence relationships between the processes, or process implementation guidance.

In accordance with the Basili architecture, each 12207 Standard process is assigned to a single agent who is responsible for performing this process. According to Moore, "from this point of view, the 12207 Standard is a list of agents and their minimum responsibilities."[9] For example, the agent responsible for the *Development Process* is the *developer*. Also, from this point of view, a process is a set of assignments of continuing agent responsibilities that persist for the duration of the life cycle of a software product.

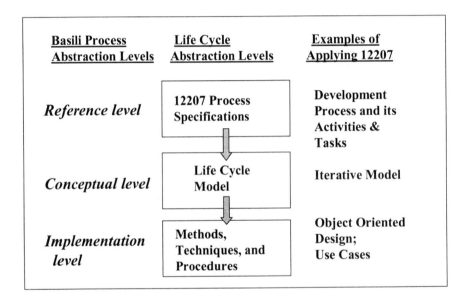

Figure 2-1. Using the 12207 Standard as a Requirements Specification for the Software Life Cycle

As we have seen, a reference-level standard can be described as a requirements specification for process. In general, to implement a requirements specification, the specification is first transformed into a design, and then the design is implemented in an executable form. To implement a reference-level standard, the requirements specification is first represented as a model that describes it at a conceptual level, and then the model is mapped to the organizational units and procedures that implement the model. In the case shown in Figure 2-1, the 12207 Standard provides the requirements specification for the life cycle; a particular life cycle model, such as the waterfall or spiral model, provides the design; and the supporting life cycle methods, procedures, and techniques provide the implementation.

2.3 Software Life Cycle Framework of 12207

The SESC has organized its software process standards according to the software life cycle framework specified in the 12207 Standard. *IEEE Std. 1517—Reuse Processes* is also structured in accordance with the 12207 software life cycle framework.

The 12207 software life cycle framework is used to organize software processes and, as Figure 2-2 shows, is composed of three categories of software processes:

- *Primary:* A primary process serves a primary party. A primary party is an agent who performs development, operation, or maintenance of a software product.

- *Supporting:* A supporting process supports another process with a distinct purpose and contributes to the success of the software project.

- *Organizational:* An organizational process is employed by an organization to establish and implement an underlying support structure for the software life cycle.

There are two requirements that the standard imposes on qualification as a process:

1. The process is a conceptually cohesive unit

2. One agent can be assigned responsibility for the process

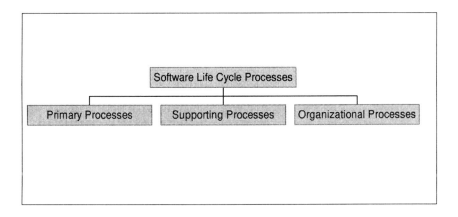

Figure 2-2. 12207 Standard Software Life Cycle Framework

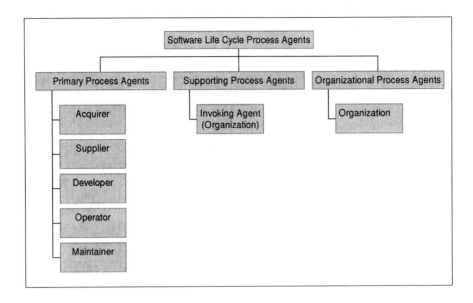

Figure 2-3. 12207 Standard Software Life Cycle Process Agents

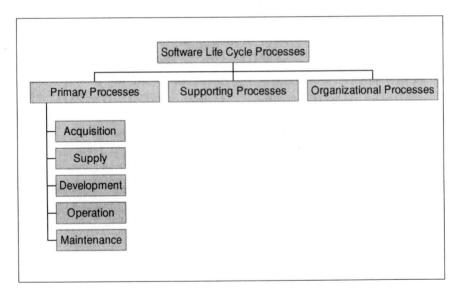

Figure 2-4. 12207 Standard Primary Processes

Each software process in the framework is subdivided into a set of activities and the requirements for each activity, in turn, are specified as a set of tasks for that activity. The responsibility for performing each process is assigned to a single agent, referred to in the standard as a "party" or an "organization." According to the 12207 Standard, an organization "is a body of persons organized for some specific purpose, such as a club, union, corporation, or society," and "when an organization, as a whole or a part, enters into a contract, it is a party."[10] Figure 2-3 shows the agents defined in the 12207 Standard.

2.4 Primary Life Cycle Processes

The activities that are fundamental to the creation, use, and maintenance of software products are grouped into the primary process category. Primary processes are mainly concerned with the technical and contractual aspects of the life cycle of an individual system or software product.

As shown in Figure 2-4, the 12207 Standard defines five primary processes:

- *Acquisition*: A set of activities for acquiring a system, software product, or software service from a supplier

- *Supply:* A set of activities for supplying a system, software product, or software service to an acquirer

- *Development:* A set of activities related to the development portion of the life cycle of a software product

- *Operation:* A set of activities related to the operation of a software product

- *Maintenance:* A set of activities related to the maintenance portion of the life cycle of a software product

The 12207 Standard distinguishes between a system, software product, and software services with the definitions shown in Table 2-2.[11]

Table 2-2. 12207 Standard Definitions for System,
Software Product, and Software Service

- *System*: An integrated composite that consists of one or more of the processes, hardware, software, facilities and people, that provides a capability to satisfy a stated need or objective
- *Software product*: The set of computer programs, procedures, and possibly associated documentation and data
- *Software service*: Performance of the activities, work, or duties connected with a software product, such as its development, maintenance, and operation

Note that software is one element of a system. Although this standard is mainly concerned with software, it does recognize that software is integrated into a larger entity, namely a system. When acquiring software, especially when defining the terms of a request for proposal (RFP), or a contract, it is important to consider the requirements of the software with respect to the system.

In accordance with the object-oriented model discussed above, the 12207 Standard defines one primary party, or agent, that is responsible for performing the activities of each primary process. The five primary agents corresponding to the five primary processes are:

- *acquirer*
- *supplier*
- *developer*
- *operator*
- *maintainer*

2.4.1 Acquisition Process

According to the 12207 Standard, the Acquisition Process specifies the activities for acquiring a system, software product, or software service. The Acquisition Process begins with the creation of the RFP and concludes with the acceptance of the software. Software can be acquired by means of development of the software or purchase of off-the-shelf software, as in the case of an application package.

The *acquirer* is the agent responsible for performing the Acquisition Process. For example, a user, customer, owner, or buyer may take on the role of acquirer.

The Acquisition Process (Section 5.1 in the 12207 Standard) consists of the following five activities:

1. *Initiation:* System requirements and the software requirements are analyzed and defined; an acquisition plan is created

2. *Request for Proposal Preparation:* The acquisition requirements are documented

3. *Contract Preparation and Update:* A procedure for selecting a supplier is defined, a supplier is selected, and an acquisition contract is created, agreed to, and updated as needed

4. *Supplier Monitoring:* The supplier activities are monitored by the acquirer

5. *Acceptance and Completion:* Acceptance review and testing procedures of the delivered system, software, or service are developed and performed to assure that the acquirer's requirements are satisfied

The major types of deliverables produced by the Acquisition Process follow:

- Acquisition Plan including:
    o Acquisition Needs Description
    o System Requirements
    o Software Requirements

- Request for Proposal
- Supplier Selection Procedure
- Contract
- Contract Change Control Mechanism
- Acceptance Procedure including:
  - o Acceptance Test Data
  - o Acceptance Test Cases
  - o Acceptance Test Procedure
  - o Acceptance Test Environment

2.4.2 Supply Process

While the Acquisition Process is from the point of view of an organization that wishes to acquire software, the Supply Process is from the point of view of an organization that wishes to provide software. The Supply Process includes entering into a contractual relationship between the acquirer and the supplier, and establishing and executing a supply procedure to deliver the desired software to the acquirer. The *supplier* is the agent responsible for performing the Supply Process. For example, a vendor, producer, seller, or contractor may take on the role of supplier. The Supply Process (Section 5.2 of the 12207 Standard) consists of the following seven activities:

1. *Initiation:* The RFP is reviewed and a decision regarding the supply of the system, software product, or software service requested is made
2. *Preparation of Response:* A response to the RFP is prepared
3. *Contract*: A contract between the supplier and the acquirer is agreed upon
4. *Planning:* The acquisition requirements are reviewed, a software life cycle model considered appropriate for the project is selected, the requirements for a software supply plan are defined, and a project management plan is developed
5. *Execution and Control:* The supplier implements the project management plan, monitors the project progress, and controls the software product or software service quality
6. *Review and Evaluation:* The supplier performs reviews, testing, and audits to demonstrate that the software product or software service meets the acquirer's requirements
7. *Delivery and Evaluation:* The software product or service is delivered to the acquirer according to the terms of the contract

The major types of deliverables produced by the Supply Process are:

- Response to the Request for Proposal
- Software Life Cycle Process Model Selection
- Project Management Plan

- Problem Report
- Project Status Report
- Evaluation Report
- Review Report
- Audit Report

2.4.3 Development Process

The Development Process contains the activities related to the development portion of the software life cycle. These activities cover requirements analysis, design, coding, integration, testing and installation of a software product; and can be applied within any type of life cycle, such as waterfall, iterative, or rapid prototyping. The *developer* is the agent responsible for performing the Development Process.

Table 2-3 lists the definitions of important software terms used to describe various types of software parts recognized in the 12207 Standard.

Table 2-3. 12207 Standard Development Process Terminology[12]

- **Software item:** A piece in the software portion of the system architecture
- **Software component:** A piece in the architecture of a software item
- **Software unit:** A separately compilable piece of code

The Development Process (Section 5.3 of the 12207 Standard) consists of 13 activities:

1. *Process Implementation:* Appropriate software life cycle models, standards, methods, tools, and programming languages are chosen for the project

2. *System Requirements Analysis:* The system requirements specification, describing the system functions and capabilities, is defined, evaluated, and documented

3. *System Architectural Design:* A high-level architecture specifying the hardware, software, and manual operations of the system is defined, evaluated, and documented

4. *Software Requirements Analysis:* For each software item in the system architecture, a software requirements specification describing the software item's function and capabilities is defined, evaluated, and documented

5. *Software Architectural Design:* For each software item in the system architecture, the software requirements are transformed into a high-level software architecture

6. *Software Detailed Design:* For each software item specified in the software architecture, (1) a detailed design of the components comprising the software item, (2) a detailed design of the external interfaces, (3) a detailed design of the data base, and (4) the test requirements and schedule are developed, evaluated, reviewed, and documented

7. *Software Coding and Testing:* For each software item specified in the software architecture, (1) each unit and data base included in the software item are coded, evaluated, and tested; and (2) the documentation, test requirements, and schedule are updated

8. *Software Integration:* For each software item, a software unit and software component integration plan is developed, and software units and components are integrated, tested, reviewed, and evaluated according to the plan

9. *Software Qualification Testing:* For each software item in the software architecture, qualification tests are performed, documented, reviewed, and evaluated

10. *System Integration:* The software items are integrated with other elements of the system architecture into the system, and the system is tested

11. *System Qualification Testing:* System qualification testing is performed, evaluated, and documented

12. *Software Installation:* A software product installation plan is developed and documented, and the software product is installed

13. *Software Acceptance Support:* The software product is completed and delivered, and training is provided

The major types of deliverables produced by the Development Process follow:

- Software Life Cycle Model Selection
- Development Process Plan
- System Requirements Specification
- System Requirements Specification Evaluation Report
- System Architecture
- System Architecture Evaluation Report

For each Software Item in the System Architecture:

- o Software Requirements Specification
- o Software Architecture Evaluation Report
- o Preliminary Test Requirements
- o High-Level Interface Design
- o Preliminary User Documentation

- Software Architecture and High-Level Design Evaluation Reports

For each Component in each Software Item:

- o Software Detailed Design
- o Detailed Database Design
- o Detailed Interface Design
- o Updated User Documentation

- o   Test Requirements
- Software Detailed Design and Test Requirements Evaluation Report

For each Software Unit and Data Base:

- o   Code
- o   Updated User Documentation
- o   Code Evaluation and Test Results Report

For each Software Item:

- o   Integration Plan
- Integrated and Tested Software Product
- Integration and Test Results Report
- Software Qualification Tests, Test Cases, Test Procedure Requirements
- Integration Plan, Design, Code, Tests, Test Results and User Documentation
- Evaluation Reports

For each Software Item:

- o   Qualification Testing Results Report
- o   Audit Results Report
- Integrated, Tested System
- Integration Evaluation and Testing Results Report
- System Qualification Testing Results Report
- System Evaluation Report
- System Audit Report
- Software Product Installation Plan
- Software Product Installation Report
- Acceptance Review and Testing Report

2.4.4 Operation Process

The Operation Process includes the activities for operating the software, within the context of operating the system into which the software is integrated, and the activities for providing software user support. The *operator* is the agent responsible for performing the Operation Process. The Operation Process (Section 5.4 of the 12207 Standard) consists of the following four activities:

1. *Process Implementation:* An operation plan that includes problem tracking, problem resolution, and test procedures is defined and executed

2. *Operation Testing:* Operation testing is performed for each new release of the software product

3. *System Operation:* The system is operated in its target environment(s)

4. *User Support:* User assistance, including problem tracking and problem resolution, through the maintenance process, is provided

The major types of deliverables produced by the Operation Process are:

- Operation Plan
- Operation Procedures Definition
- User Request
- Problem/Request Resolution Report

2.4.5 Maintenance Process

The Maintenance Process concerns changes made to software after it is delivered to the acquirer. Maintenance changes are made for different reasons, such as to correct defects or to meet changes in requirements related to functionality, performance, or operating environments. In addition, the Maintenance Process is concerned with replacing or retiring delivered software.

The *maintainer* is the agent responsible for the Maintenance Process. The Maintenance Process (Section 5.5 of the 12207 Standard) consists of the following six activities:

1. *Process Implementation:* A maintenance plan is developed and executed

2. *Problem and Modification Analysis:* Problem reports and modification requests are analyzed, and a modification option is selected and approved

3. *Modification Implementation:* Approved modifications are made to the affected software units and associated documentation

4. *Maintenance Review and Acceptance:* The modified system is reviewed and modification approval is obtained

5. *Migration:* When a system or software product is to be migrated to a different software environment, a migration plan is developed and executed

6. *Software Retirement:* When support of the operation and maintenance of a system or software product is to be removed, a retirement plan is developed and executed

The major types of deliverables produced by the Maintenance Process are:

- Maintenance Process Plan
- Problem/Request Report
- Maintenance Analysis Report
- Test and Evaluation Criteria Definition Test Results Report
- System or Software Product Migration Plan
- Migration Notice
- Post-Operation Review Report

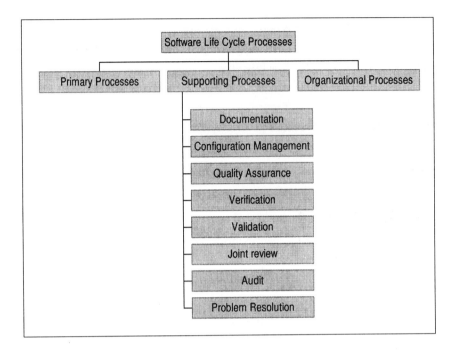

Figure 2-5. 12207 Standard Supporting Life Cycle Processes

- System or Software Product Retirement Plan
- Retirement Notice

2.5 Supporting Life Cycle Processes

The 12207 primary processes employ the supporting life cycle processes for assistance in performing the fundamental software life cycle activities. The 12207 Standard supporting processes provide various activities, such as documentation and auditing, to support the creation, use, and maintenance of software products. In addition, a particular supporting life cycle process may employ other supporting processes for assistance in performing its activities. For example, the Quality Assurance Process uses the Verification Process, Validation Process, Joint Review Process, Audit Process, and Problem Resolution Process to carry out its activities.

As Figure 2-5 shows, the 12207 Standard defines the following eight supporting life cycle processes:

1. *Documentation*: A set of activities for documenting software process activities and software products

2. *Configuration Management:* A set of activities for performing configuration management of products produced by the life cycle process

3. *Quality Assurance:* A set of activities for demonstrating that software processes and products conform to their requirements

4. *Verification:* A set of activities for verifying software products

5. *Validation:* A set of activities for validating the products produced by the software life cycle processes

6. *Joint Review:* A set of activities for evaluating the status of a software process or product

7. *Audit:* A set of activities for determining compliance to software process and product requirements, plans, and contracts

8. *Problem Resolution:* A set of activities for resolving problems that occur during the execution of software life cycle processes

Table 2-4 lists the definitions of terms used by the 12207 Standard to describe supporting processes.

Table 2-4. 12207 Supporting Process Terminology

- *Audit:* Conducted by an authorized person for the purpose of providing an independent assessment of software products and processes in order to assess compliance with requirements
- *Quality Assurance:* All the planned and systematic activities implemented within the quality system, and demonstrated as needed, to provide adequate confidence that an entity will fulfill requirements for quality
- *Validation:* Confirmation by examination and provision of objective evidence that the particular requirements for a specific intended use are fulfilled
- *Verification:* Confirmation by examination and provision of objective evidence that specified requirements have been fulfilled

2.5.1 Documentation Process

The Documentation Process contains all the activities related to producing software product or system documents by the software life cycle processes. The Documentation Process (Section 6.1 of the 12207 Standard) consists of the following four activities:

1. *Process Implementation:* A documentation plan for the software product is developed, documented, and implemented

2. *Design and Development:* Documentation items are designed in accordance with the organization's standards and are prepared, documented, reviewed, and approved

3. *Production:* Documentation items are produced in accordance with the documentation plan

4. *Maintenance:* Documentation items are maintained and modified as required

The major types of deliverables produced by the Documentation Process are software process and product documents.

2.5.2 Configuration Management Process

The Configuration Management Process applies procedures throughout the software life cycle to identify, baseline, and manage versions, releases, modifications, and storage of software items in a system. The Configuration Management Process (Section 6.2 of the 12207 Standard) consists of six activities:

1. *Process Implementation:* A configuration management plan is developed, documented, and implemented

2. *Configuration Identification:* Each software configuration item is identified and baselined

3. *Configuration Control:* Change requests for a configuration item are identified, recorded, analyzed, and approved

4. *Configuration Status Accounting:* Management record and status reports for configuration items are prepared

5. *Configuration Evaluation:* The functional and physical completeness of software configuration items are determined

6. *Release Management and Delivery:* The release and delivery of the software product is controlled

The major types of deliverables produced by the Configuration Management Process are:

- Configuration Management Plan
- Configuration Scheme of a Software Configuration Item
- Change Request for a Software Configuration Item
- Audit Trail of a Software Configuration Item
- Management Record for a Software Configuration Item
- Status Report for Software Configuration Item

2.5.3 Quality Assurance Process

The Quality Assurance Process provides assurance that the software products and the software life cycle processes conform to their respective requirements and plans. The Quality Assurance Process (Section 6.3 of the 12207 Standard) consists of the following four activities:

1. *Process Implementation:* The quality assurance process plan is developed, documented, and implemented

2. *Product Assurance:* It is assured that software products comply to contract requirements and are acceptable to the acquirer

3. *Process Assurance:* It is assured that software process complies to contract requirements

4. *Assurance of Quality Systems:* It is assured that quality management activities are in accordance with the ISO 9003 Standard, as specified in the contract

The major types of deliverables produced by the Quality Assurance Process are:

- Quality Assurance Process Definition
- Quality Assurance Plan
- Problem Report
- Records of Quality Assurance

2.5.4 Verification Process

The Verification Process determines whether software products produced throughout the life cycle meet their respective requirements. The Verification Process (Section 6.4 of the 12207 Standard) consists of the following two activities:

1. *Process Implementation:* The project is analyzed to determine whether it requires a verification effort. If yes, the organization that will conduct the verification is selected and a verification plan is defined and established.

2. *Verification:* The project contract, software life cycle model, system and software product requirements, software design, software code, software product integration, and documentation are verified.

The major types of deliverables produced by the Verification Process are:

- Verification Process Definition
- Verification Plan
- Verification Report

2.5.5 Validation Process

The Validation Process determines whether the completed system or software product meets its usability requirements; that is, operates as intended. The Validation process (Section 6.6 of the 12207 Standard) consists of the following two activities:

1. *Process Implementation:* The project is analyzed to determine whether it requires a validation effort. If yes, a validation plan is defined and established.

2. *Validation:* Test cases and test specifications are prepared and tests of the software product are executed in its target environment(s) to demonstrate that the software product operates as intended.

The major types of deliverables of the Validation Process are:

- Validation Process Definition
- Validation Plan
- Validation Report

2.5.6 Joint Review Process

The Joint Review Process performs a project management evaluation of the project status and a technical evaluation of the software products produced throughout the software life cycle. The Joint Review Process consists of three activities:

1. *Process Implementation:* Periodic software project and product reviews are performed and results are documented at project milestones
2. *Project Management Reviews:* Project status is evaluated
3. *Technical Reviews:* Software products and services are evaluated

The major types of deliverables produced by the Joint Review Process are:

- Report of Problems Detected during the Review
- Review Results

2.5.7 Audit Process

The Audit Process determines project process and software product compliance with the project requirements, plans, and contract. The Audit Process (Section 6.7 of the 12207 Standard) consists of two activities:

1. *Process Implementation:* Periodic audits are performed at project milestones by an independent party (i.e., a party not directly responsible for the development of the software product)
2. *Audit:* An audit of the software process and the software product is performed

The major types of deliverables produced by the Audit Process are:

- Report of Problems Detected during the Audit
- Audit Report

2.5.8 Problem Resolution Process

The Problem Resolution Process analyzes, documents, and resolves any project process or product problems that are detected during the software life cycle.

The Problem Resolution Process (Section 6.8 of the 12207 Standard) consists of two activities:

1. *Process Implementation:* The problem resolution process is defined and established

2. *Problem Resolution:* When a software process or software product problem is detected, the problem resolution process is executed

The major type of deliverable produced by the Problem Resolution Process is the Problem Report.

2.6 Organizational Life Cycle Processes

The organizational life cycle processes provide the underlying structure needed to effectively and successfully execute software life cycle processes such as Development, Operation, Maintenance, and Documentation. Organizational processes include activities for process and project management, infrastructure setup, process measurement and improvement, and training.

Because these activities have application to possibly multiple projects in an organization, (e.g., the same infrastructure can be used by more than one project, or trained personnel can utilize the same set of skills in more than one project), organizational processes transcend the project level, and more appropriately belong at the organizational or enterprise level. According to Moore, "the organizational processes of 12207 are expected to be inherent in the responsible organization; instances of those processes are instantiated for the execution of a specific project."[13]

Figure 2-6 shows four organizational life cycle processes specified in the 12207 Standard:

1. *Management Process:* A set of activities related to managing a software life cycle process

2. *Infrastructure Process:* A set of activities to establish and maintain a support infrastructure for a software life cycle process

3. *Improvement Process:* A set of activities to assess and improve a software life cycle process

4. *Training Process:* A set of activities to provide trained personnel who can effectively apply software life cycle processes

The agent responsible for performing the organizational life cycle processes is the *organization.*

2.6.1 Management Process

The Management Process provides process management, project management, and task management activities for use by the other software life cycle processes.

The Management Process (Section 7.1 of the 12207 Standard) consists of the following five activities:

1. *Initiation and Scope Definition:* The requirements of the Management Process are defined; and the feasibility of executing the process is evaluated

2. *Planning:* The management plan is developed

3. *Execution and Control:* The management plan is executed, monitored, and reported upon

4. *Review and Evaluation:* The management plan and the software product are evaluated

5. *Closure:* The process is evaluated to determine if it is complete; and its associated records are archived

The major types of deliverables produced by the Management Process are as follows:

- Process Requirements

- Management Plan

- Process Progress Report

- Process Problem Report

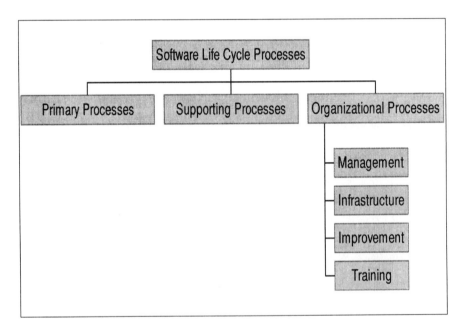

Figure 2-6. 12207 Standard Organizational Life Cycle Processes

2.6.2 Infrastructure Process

The Infrastructure Process establishes and maintains an infrastructure, including elements such as hardware, software, tools, techniques, and standards, that provide support for executing the primary life cycle processes.

The Infrastructure Process (Section 7.2 of the 12207 Standard) consists of the following three activities:

1. *Process Implementation:* An infrastructure, that meets the requirements of the processes employing it, is defined, planned, and documented

2. *Establishment of the Infrastructure:* The infrastructure is installed

3. *Maintenance of the Infrastructure:* The infrastructure is maintained

The major types of deliverables produced by the Infrastructure Process are as follows:

- Infrastructure Documentation
- Infrastructure Configuration Plan

2.6.3 Improvement Process

The Improvement Process is used to assess, measure, and improve the software life cycle processes.

The Improvement Process (Section 7.3 of the 12207 Standard) consists of the following three activities:

1. *Process Establishment:* Organizational processes are established for all software life cycle processes. A process control mechanism is established to assess, measure, and improve software life cycle processes.

2. *Process Assessment:* A software life cycle assessment procedure is developed, documented, and applied to the life cycle.

3. *Process Improvement:* Based on an evaluation of the findings and recommendations of the assessment procedures, improvements are made to the life cycle processes.

The major types of deliverables produced by the Improvement Process are as follows:

- Organizational Process Documentation
- Process Control Mechanism Definition
- Process Assessment Procedure

2.6.4 Training Process

The Training Process defines the activities for providing trained personnel for software projects. The Training Process (Section 7.4 of the 12207 Standard) consists of the following three activities:

1. *Process Implementation:* A personnel training plan is developed and documented

2. *Training Material Development:* Training material is developed

3. *Training Plan Implementation:* The training personnel plan is implemented

The major types of deliverables produced by the Training Process follow:

- Training Personnel Plan
- Training Material
- Training Record

2.7 Uses and Users of 12207

The 12207 Standard is for use by all parties involved in the software life cycle. These parties include (1) technical personnel such as software developers, software maintainers, operators, and quality assurance personnel; (2) management personnel, such as project managers and quality assurance managers; (3) software owners; and (4) software users.

Uses of the standard may be grouped into the following categories:

1. Software Acquisition and Supply
2. Software Development, Operation, and Maintenance
3. Software Process Management

For each use category, there are different users as well as different uses of the standard. In the Acquisition and Supply category, the standard is used to specify a two-party view of the software life cycle. One view is that of the acquirer who wishes (1) to obtain software through purchase of an off-the-shelf software product or development of a new software product, (2) to re-engineer an existing software product, or (3) to acquire a software service. The second view is that of the supplier who wishes to provide the software product or service. The software life cycle standard is used to provide terminology that is commonly understood by both parties and used as a basis for negotiating a contract between these two parties.

In the Development, Operation, and Maintenance category, the standard is used to guide technical personnel who produce, operate, and maintain software products. It is also used to guide technical personnel who are responsible for assuring and managing the quality of the software product and its associated deliverables, such as documentation and test data. Examples of these users include software developers, software maintainers, software operators, quality assurance managers and staff, configuration management managers and staff, software testers, software auditors, joint review leaders.

In the Process Management category, the standard is used to plan, control, review, evaluate, and improve any of the software life cycle processes. Since this category covers all software life cycle processes, it applies to all types of users. For example, a software maintainer may use the standard to manage the Maintenance Process.

The 12207 Standard is intended to be applied at the software project-level or organization-level. Also, it is intended to be applied by one organization internally, or by two or more organizations contractually. It can be used in software projects that involve embedded or stand-alone software products written in any programming language.

2.8 Compliance to 12207

According to the ISO 12207 Standard:

> *Compliance with this standard is defined as the performance of all the processes, activities, and tasks selected from this standard in the tailoring process for the software project. The performance of a process or an activity is complete when all its required tasks are performed in accordance with the pre-established criteria and the requirements specified in the contract as applicable.* [14]

As described in the IEEE version of the 12207 Standard, compliance may be claimed for an organization or for a project as absolute or tailored.[15] Absolute compliance is claimed when all the processes, activities, and tasks that the standard specifies as required are performed by the organization or project.

When an organization claims tailored compliance, it must provide a public document describing how the standard is tailored and how the standard interprets the contract. When a project claims tailored compliance, the project plans and contract must describe how the standard is tailored and how the standard interprets the contract.

2.9 Tailoring of 12207

Because software projects vary greatly in terms of their size, type, requirements, criticality, and so forth, the software life cycle should be configured to meet the needs of a particular organization or a particular project. The 12207 Standard may be tailored for a particular application. According to the IEEE 12207 Standard, tailoring of the standard may be performed at two levels: 1. Business area or organization and 2. Project or contract.

Tailoring the 12207 Standard may entail deleting required processes, activities, and tasks from the standard, as well as adding additional processes, activities, and tasks to the standard. Some factors to consider when deleting requirements from the standard include:

- *Risk:* Increasing the risk of project failure may result from deleting tasks, such as those concerned with testing or quality assurance

- *Cost:* Increasing the long-term cost of the software may result from deleting required software development tasks, such as those that concern detailed design documentation, to decrease short-term software development cost

- *Size:* Including all the required processes, activities, and tasks may be overkill in a small, straightforward project

- *Control:* Deleting tasks that concern planning, process and project management, reviews, and audits may decrease the ability to properly manage and control a project

According to the IEEE 12207 Standard:

> *The standard contains only a set of well-defined building blocks (processes); the user of this standard should select, tailor, and assembly those processes*

and their activities and tasks that are cost-effective for the organization and the project. [16]

2.10 References

1. *ISO/IEC 12207—1996 Standard for Information Technology—Software Life Cycle Processes,* International Organization for Standardization & International Electrotechnical Commission, Geneva, Switzerland, 1996.

2. Ibid., Annex E, p. 59.

3. Ibid.

4. *IEEE/EIA 12207.0-1996 Standard for Information Technology—Software Life Cycle Processes,* IEEE, Piscataway, N.J., 1996.

5. J. Moore, *Software Engineering Standards,* IEEE CS Press, Los Alamitos, Calif., 1998, p.190.

6. *IEEE/EIA 12207.0-1996 Standard for Information Technology—Software Life Cycle Processes,* p. 19.

7. Ibid., Annex E, p. 59.

8. V. Basili et al., "A Reference Architecture for the Component Factory," *ACM Trans. S.E. and Methodology,* vol. 1, no. 1, Jan. 1992, pp. 53–80.

9. J. Moore, *Software Engineering Standards,* p.193.

10. *IEEE/EIA 12207.0-1996 Standard for Information Technology—Software Life Cycle Processes,* Annex D, p. 56.

11. Ibid., pp. 3–5.

12. Ibid., pp. 3–5.

13. J. Moore, *Software Engineering Standards,* p. 261.

14. *IEEE/EIA 12207.0-1996 Standard for Information Technology—Software Life Cycle Processes,* p 2.

15. Ibid., Annex F, pp. 64–65.

16. Ibid., Annex E, p.62.

Chapter 3.
Organization of IEEE Std. 1517

3.1 The Failure of Ad Hoc Reuse

Because they are well aware of the impressive productivity and quality benefits it can provide, most companies want to incorporate reuse into their software life cycle processes. However, the type of reuse that companies typically practice is not likely to lead to the benefits they seek. Most companies practice an *ad hoc* form of reuse where reuse is an unplanned, implicit byproduct of their software life cycle processes. With ad hoc reuse, software parts are scavenged from previously built software systems and applications for use as building blocks to construct new systems, applications, or enhancements. Because reuse is an afterthought, these parts were probably not designed for reuse. Often, they must be force-fitted into the new software system or application, leading to compromise of the software requirements, possible performance problems, and maintenance complications down the road. Disappointing results from ad hoc reuse experiences have caused many companies to abandon the whole reuse concept as simply too much trouble for too little gain.

Companies that have abandoned the practice of ad hoc reuse have made the right decision. However, they should not give up entirely on the reuse concept. The benefits that reuse promises are real and achievable. However, to achieve these benefits, a company must recognize and implement the special requirements that reuse places on software life cycle processes.

3.2 Reuse Life Cycle Process Requirements

First, reuse requires a broader application of the software life cycle processes. The processes must be applied at the organization level for a family of related software systems and applications, rather than only at the project level for an individual system or application. At the organization level, it becomes possible to identify which software parts have the greatest reuse potential and to plan for their reuse in upcoming software development, maintenance, and enhancement projects. Also, at the organization level, there is more opportunity to use software parts in multiple software projects and in multiple software systems or applications; and therefore a better chance to get payback from a company's investment in designing and preparing the software parts for reuse.

Second, reuse requires a restructuring of the software life cycle itself, splitting it into two related and intertwined, but different, life cycles:

- Development and maintenance of reusable software parts
- Development and maintenance of software systems or applications composed from reusable software parts

Third, reuse requires support from the software infrastructure. The software life cycle models and methodologies, software tools, software standards, software measurements, software training, the structure of the software organization, and the software-related management directives all must explicitly include support for reuse.

Fourth, reuse requires an organization-level standardization of software methodologies and software tools. These standards provide the foundation for repeatedly using software methodologies, software tools, and reusable software parts in multiple software projects and software systems and applications.

To implement these reuse requirements, an organization must be ready, willing, and able to make some substantive changes. Process, technology, management, and organizational changes are likely to be necessary to support reuse. For example, the software organization, which is frequently structured on a project basis, should be restructured on an organizational basis, and the roles of reuse producer and reuse consumer should be added. The reuse producer role is concerned with the reusable software part life cycle, while the reuse consumer role is concerned with the software system or application life cycle. Reuse producers must operate at the organizational level to identify and provide software parts that have the potential to be reused in multiple software projects. Reuse consumers operate at the project level where they utilize the software parts in the construction of new systems and applications.

Another example of the changes that reuse requires concerns the software organization's reward structure. To encourage the practice of reuse, software developers and maintainers must be rewarded—not penalized—for reusing previously developed software parts to build software systems and applications rather than building them from scratch.

3.3 Systematic Reuse

Furthermore, reuse requires recognition as an integral, explicit part of the software life cycle, not as an implicit byproduct. This means that the practice of reuse must be formalized at the project and organizational levels. In contrast to ad hoc reuse, this type of formalized reuse is called *systematic reuse*.

> *Systematic reuse is the practice of reuse according to a well-defined repeatable process.*[1]

Systematic reuse provides the foundation for coordinating reuse efforts within and across software project teams, and across software organizations within an enterprise. Systematic reuse lifts the practice of reuse to the enterprise level to enable a company to reach the highest possible reuse levels (e.g., in the 90 percent range) when building new software systems and applications and to achieve the maximum possible reuse benefits.

3.3.1 Removing the Barriers to Practicing Systematic Reuse

Even though a company's management and software developers are in favor of adopting systematic reuse and the resources needed to implement systematic reuse are available, there still may be stumbling blocks to institutionalizing the practice of systematic reuse across an enterprise. No industry guidelines for systematic reuse exist. Even worse, there are no industry-agreed-upon definitions for reuse terminology. There is only a vague understanding of what reuse is and how it should be practiced.

The purpose of the IEEE Std.1517 is to provide to the software industry a common, well-defined approach for practicing systematic reuse within the context of the software life cycle.[2] It addresses both the development and maintenance of software systems and applications with the use of predefined, reusable software parts and the development and maintenance of reusable software parts. In IEEE Std. 1517, software systems and software applications are called *software products,* and reusable software parts are called *assets.*

3.4 Structure of IEEE Std. 1517

IEEE Std. 1517 is a collection of the best reuse practices, as recognized by the software industry. It organizes this collection into a comprehensive set of reuse processes, activities, and tasks that must be included within the software life cycle to enable and support systematic reuse. These reuse processes, activities, and tasks cover the acquisition, supply, development, operation, and maintenance of software products built with assets; and the acquisition, supply, development, and maintenance of assets. In addition, they cover the definition, control, and improvement of the software life cycle.

In the standard, each reuse process is defined as a set of activities and each reuse activity is defined as a set of reuse tasks. However, the details of how to implement or perform the activities and tasks are not included because IEEE Std. 1517 is intended to serve only as a reuse requirements specification. How a particular software life cycle model or software methodology implements the reuse specifications is left entirely to the user of the standard. For example, the following task is included in the System Requirements Analysis Activity of the Development Process in IEEE Std. 1517:

> *5.3.2.2 The developer shall select and reuse applicable system requirements specifications, if any exist, before writing new requirements specifications. When writing new requirements specifications, the developers shall use the language and concepts of the domain models to which this system belongs.[3]*

Notice that although the developer is required to reuse applicable existing system requirements specifications rather than write new ones, no details of how to select, reuse, or write requirements specifications are given. Also, notice that the developer is required to write specifications that are consistent with the domain model. However, the format for the domain model is unspecified.

3.5 Reuse Process Framework

As Figure 3-1 shows, IEEE Std.1517 organizes the life cycle processes, activities, and tasks into a framework (or architecture) consisting of four process categories:

1. *Primary*

2. *Supporting*

3. *Cross-Project*

4. *Organizational*

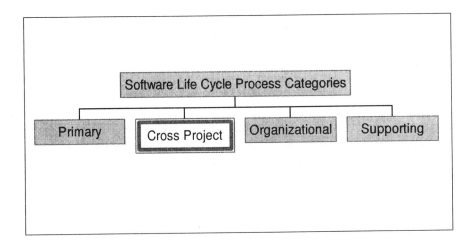

Figure 3-1. IEEE Std. 1517 Software Life Cycle Process Framework

This framework is based upon and expands the software life cycle framework specified in *IEEE/ISO/IEC Std. 12207—Standard for Information Technology—Software Life Cycle Processes.*[4] Recall that the 12207 Standard framework, which was discussed in detail in Chapter 2, includes only three process categories: primary, supporting and organizational processes. To extend the practice of systematic reuse beyond single software project boundaries, IEEE Std. 1517 adds the new process category—Cross-Project—to the 12207 Standard framework.

Also, IEEE Std. 1517 extends the 12207 Standard framework by identifying the reuse processes, activities, and tasks, and by integrating them into the 12207 framework. In this way, IEEE Std. 1517 makes reuse an explicit, rather then implied, part of the life cycle.

IEEE Std. 1517 not only reuses the 12207 Standard software life cycle framework, but also the format and language style of the 12207 Standard to specify software life cycle requirements. Recall that according to the language style used in the 12207 Standard (Chapter 2, Table 2-1) the words "will" and "shall" indicate that a requirement is required for compliance, while the word "should" indicates that a requirement is optional.

3.5.1 Primary Life Cycle Processes

Whereas in the 12207 Standard, the primary processes are concerned with developing, operating, and maintaining a software system or application, in IEEE Std. 1517 the primary processes are concerned with using assets to develop, operate, and maintain a software system or application. IEEE Std. 1517 specifies reuse requirements for five primary processes:

1. *Acquisition*: a process used to define the need to acquire a system, software product, or asset, prepare a request-for-proposal, select a supplier, and manage the acquisition process, using the appropriate, available assets to produce the process deliverables

2. *Supply*: a process used to prepare a response to a request-for-proposal for a system, software product, or asset, prepare a contract to provide a system, software product, or asset to an acquirer, and define a software project to develop and deliver the system, software product, or asset to the acquirer, using the appropriate, available assets to produce the process deliverables

3. *Development*: a process to used to analyze, design, implement, and install a system, software product, or asset, using the appropriate, available assets to produce the process deliverables

4. *Operation*: a process used to operate a system, software product, or asset, using the appropriate, available assets to produce the process deliverables

5. *Maintenance*: a process used to perform system, software product, or asset problem and modification analysis; and to perform modification, migration, and retirement of a system, software product or asset, using the appropriate, available assets to produce the process deliverables

All five primary processes were originally defined in the 12207 Standard. As a group, they cover the entire life cycle of a system or software product beginning with the definition of a need and concluding in the retirement of a software system (application). In IEEE Std.1517, each primary process includes all the activities and tasks specified in the 12207 Standard and in addition, includes new reuse-related tasks to specify the use of assets in the production of the process deliverables. Assets include domain models, domain architectures, and other types of assets such as requirements specifications, code, and test suites.

3.5.2 Consumer Reuse

In the software industry, the approach of using assets to develop software life cycle deliverables is often referred to as *application assembly* or *consumer reuse*. The most recent software development approach, called component-based development, is a form of consumer reuse.

Consumer reuse is concerned with taking every opportunity to build the deliverables of each software life cycle process from assets. To assure that creating deliverables from scratch is done only as a last resort, consumer reuse makes the practice of reuse an explicit, required part of each software life cycle process. As shown in Figure 3-2, consumer reuse is made explicit in each primary process by specifying tasks to:

- Search for available assets

- Select appropriate assets

- Incorporate assets into the deliverables

- Evaluate the value and impact of assets

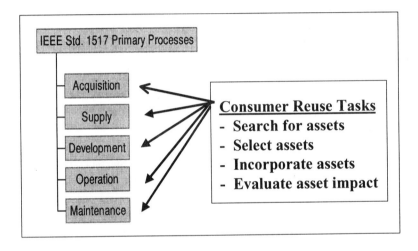

Figure 3-2. Adding Consumer Reuse to Each IEEE Std. 1517 Primary Process

For example, in the Planning Activity of the Supply Process in IEEE Std. 1517, the following task is specified to assure that a search for assets is performed:

5.2.1.4 The supplier shall gather existing candidate software products and assets that may be used to develop a software product that satisfies the requirements specifications from sources including:

- *Domain engineering deliverable*

- *Internal and external suppliers*

- *Organization's reuse libraries*

- *Other on-going projects in the organization*

- *Off-the-shelf software products and assets*

The supplier shall document this information in the project plans... [5]

In the Software Requirements Analysis Activity in the Development Process in IEEE Std. 1517, the following task is specified to assure that assets are incorporated into the production of the software requirements analysis deliverables:

> *5.3.4.3 The developers shall write new requirements using an applicable requirements template, if any exists, and using the language and concepts from the domain models of the domains to which this software product belongs. The developer shall define and document new software requirements to include, but not be limited to, reusability characteristics. (This task defines reuse-related requirements in addition to those requirements specified in IEEE/EIA Std 12207.0-1996, task 5.3.4.1)[6]*

Also, notice that IEEE Std. 1517 task 5.3.4.3 references IEEE/EIA Std. 12207.0 task 5.3.4.1 to indicate exactly how and where the software life cycle should be extended to support the practice of reuse. Task 5.3.4.1 in the IEEE/EIA Std. 12207.0 reads as follows:

> *5.3.4.1 The developer shall establish and document software requirements, including the quality characteristics specifications, described below. Guidance for specifying quality characteristics may be found in ISO/IEC 9126.*
>
> a) *Functional and capability specifications...*
>
> b) *Interfaces external to the software item*
>
> c) *Qualification requirements*
>
> d) *Safety specifications ...*
>
> e) *Security specifications...*
>
> f) *Human factors engineering ...*
>
> g) *Data definition and database requirements*
>
> h) *Installation and acceptance requirements of the delivered software product*
>
> i) *User documentation*
>
> j) *User operation and execution requirements*
>
> k) *User maintenance requirements.[7]*

IEEE Std. 1517 follows this referencing practice wherever its specifications extend the 12207 software life cycle specifications.

As another example, in the Software Architectural Design Activity in the Development Process in IEEE Std. 1517, the following task is specified to assure that the reuse value of assets used to produce the software architectural design is evaluated:

> *5.3.5.6 The developer shall evaluate the software architecture, the interface, and database designs according to reusability criteria. The results of the*

evaluation shall be documented. Note: reusability criteria may include, but are not limited to:

    a)   Compliance with the organization's reuse standards

    b)   Usability and reusability of the software architecture and database designs

    c)   Reuse potential of the software architecture and its components to be used in multiple contexts.[8]

3.5.3 Cross-Project Life Cycle Processes

In IEEE Std. 1517, the cross-project life cycle process category includes processes that span more than one software project in the sense that they meet the requirements for multiple projects and/or produce deliverables that can be used by multiple software projects.

In IEEE Std. 1517, domain engineering is the only process categorized as a cross-project life cycle process. As Figure 3-3 shows, the Domain Engineering Process provides the assets that can be used by the primary life cycle processes to acquire, supply, develop, operate, and maintain systems and software products. In this respect, domain engineering enables the practice of consumer reuse.

3.5.4 Producer Reuse

Domain engineering is also referred to as *producer reuse*. Whereas consumer reuse covers the life cycle of a software product, domain engineering covers the life cycle of an asset. Consumer reuse is applied at the project level for a single software product; producer reuse is applied at the domain level for a set of assets that belong to the domain and are intended for use in multiple software projects. A *domain* is simply defined in the standard as "a problem space."[9] Examples of a domain are a product line (e.g., printers) or a business process (e.g., sales). The purpose of domain engineering is to produce assets, including domain models and domain architectures, for use in developing and maintaining software products in the domain.

The domain engineering process defined in IEEE Std. 1517 consists of five activities:

1. *Process Implementation*: to develop the domain engineering plan
2. *Domain analysis*: to produce the definition of the domain, the domain vocabulary, and the domain models
3. *Domain Design*: to produce the domain architecture and asset design specifications
4. *Asset Provision*: to develop or acquire domain assets
5. *Asset Maintenance*: to maintain domain assets

3.5.6 Organizational Life Cycle Processes

IEEE Std. 1517 organizational processes are concerned with the management aspects of the software life cycle for both a software product and an asset. They are used to establish an integrated structure of processes and personnel that can be managed and improved. IEEE Std. 1517 includes the following five processes in this category:

1. *Management:* a process used to perform software project and product management

2. *Infrastructure:* a process used to establish and maintain the technical and organizational infrastructures needed to perform software life cycle processes

3. *Improvement:* a process used to evaluate/improve software life cycle processes

4. *Training:* a process used to provide training to those responsible for performing software life cycle processes, activities, and tasks

5. *Reuse Program Administration*: a process used to plan, establish, and manage a reuse program

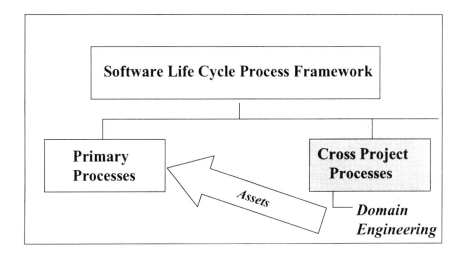

Figure 3-3. Domain Engineering is a Cross Project Process in IEEE Std. 1517

The first four processes listed above are defined in the 12207 Standard. They are used by IEEE Std. 1517 to provide project management support during the life cycle of a software product developed with assets and during the life cycle of assets.

The fifth process, Reuse Program Administration, is newly defined by IEEE Std. 1517. Its purpose is to enable the practice of systematic reuse and CBD at the organization or enterprise level. To reap the maximum benefits that reuse offers, an environment in which assets can be shared and reused across software projects must by established. The most effective way to establish such an environment is with a formal reuse program. The reuse program must be endorsed by management, adequately funded, and properly staffed. In addition, the reuse program must address both the technical and organizational aspects of implementing the practice of systemic reuse and/or CBD on an organization-wide basis.

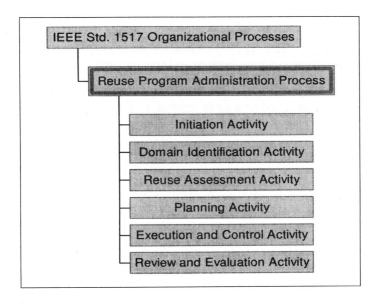

Figure 3-4. Reuse Program Administration is an
Organizational Life Cycle Process in IEEE Std. 1517

As Figure 3-4 shows, the Reuse Program Administration Process addresses the requirements for a formal reuse program by including activities to:

- Define the organization's reuse strategy

- Perform an reuse assessment to determine the organization's capability to practice systematic reuse

- Define and implement a reuse program implementation plan

- Establish a management and organizational support structure for the reuse program

- Monitor, evaluate, and improve the reuse program

3.5.7 Supporting Life Cycle Processes

In IEEE Std. 1517, supporting processes assist other processes in the development and maintenance of a software product or asset by performing functions that are essential to ensuring the quality, completeness and currency of the software product or asset. In IEEE Std. 1517, the following nine processes are included in this category:

1. *Documentation*: a process used to document the software product, an asset, and the software life cycle

2. *Configuration Management*: a process used to manage versions of and control changes to the software product or asset during the stages of its life cycle

3. *Quality Assurance:* a process used to assure that the software product, an asset, or the software life cycle processes conform to their requirements

4. *Verification*: a process used to verify a software product or asset

5. *Validation*: a process used to validate the deliverables produced by the software life cycle processes

6. *Joint Review:* a process used to review and evaluate the status and quality of the software project and software product or asset during its life cycle

7. *Audit*: a process used to determine whether a software project, software product, or asset conforms to its requirements

8. *Problem Resolution*: a process used to analyze and correct software project, software product, or asset problems

9. *Asset Management:* a process used to manage assets, including domain models and domain architectures

With the exception of Asset Management, all of the supporting processes are defined in the 12207 Standard. The Asset Management Process is newly specified in IEEE Std. 1517 to handle the special requirements that reuse places on management, storage, retrieval, version control, change control, and distribution functions. The Asset Management Process assures that potential consumers of an asset can know of its existence, can easily locate the current version of the asset, and can easily understand its purpose, status, and quality. A shown in Figure 3-5, the Asset Management Process in IEEE Std. 1517 includes activities to:

- Create and implement an asset management plan

- Implement and maintain an asset storage and retrieval mechanism (e.g. reuse library)

- Create and maintain an asset classification scheme and certification procedures

- Evaluate and accept new candidate assets and updated or new versions of assets into the asset storage and retrieval mechanism

- Manage asset storage, usage tracking, and problem reporting and resolution

3.6 Summary

This chapter introduced IEEE Std. 1517 by providing the reader with an overview of the content and structure of the standard. *IEEE Std. 1517—Reuse Processes* is a requirements specification for practicing systematic reuse at the enterprise level. It provides an organization with a clear description of what is needed to succeed with software reuse. It addresses both the technical and management aspects of adopting reuse. On the technical side, it defines the requirements for adding the practice of reuse to the software life cycle, covering both the life cycle of a software product and the life cycle of an asset. On the management side, it defines the requirements for managing software projects that practice reuse and for managing a formal reuse program at the enterprise level, as well as procedures for managing assets.

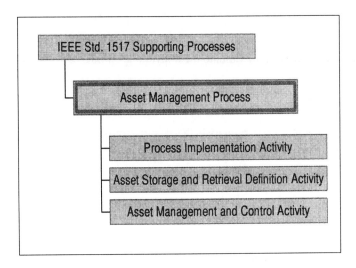

Figure 3-5. Asset Management is a Supporting Life Cycle
Process in IEEE Std. 1517

3.7 References

1. *IEEE 1517 Standard of Information Technology—Software Life Cycle Processes—Reuse Processes*, IEEE, Piscataway, N.J., 1999.

2. Ibid.

3. Ibid.

4. *IEEE/EIA 12207.0-1996 Standard for Information Technology—Software Life Cycle Processes*, IEEE, Piscataway, N.J., 1996.

5. *IEEE 1517 Standard of Information Technology—Software Life Cycle Processes—Reuse Processes.*

6. Ibid.

7. *IEEE/EIA 12207.0-1996 Standard for Information Technology—Software Life Cycle Processes.*

8. *IEEE 1517 Standard of Information Technology—Software Life Cycle Processes—Reuse Processes.*

9. Ibid.

Part 2.
Interpretation and
Implementation

Chapter 4.
IEEE Std. 1517 Primary Processes: Adding Reuse to Software Development, Operation, and Maintenance

4.1 Add Consumer Reuse to the Software Life Cycle

4.1.1 Consumer Reuse

To support and enable the practice of reuse, the software life cycle must implement reuse from two perspectives:

1. *Consumer reuse:* using assets to build or assemble software products
2. *Producer reuse:* building assets

This portion of IEEE Std. 1517 mainly addresses the software life cycle requirements for practicing consumer reuse. Consumer reuse focuses on the use of assets to develop all types of software life cycle process deliverables. For example, deliverables such as software project plans, software requirements, or software designs are developed reusing appropriate, existing assets.

The primary reuse strategy addressed by consumer reuse is to develop software life cycle deliverables from existing assets as the first development choice, rather than from scratch. By practicing consumer reuse, software development and maintenance can be accelerated. Other reasons for practicing consumer reuse are:

- improved software quality
- reduced software life cycle costs
- reduced risk of software project failures

4.1.2 Changing the Software Life Cycle to Support Consumer Reuse

Adding consumer reuse to the software life cycle changes each phase of the life cycle because the deliverables produced during each phase can be assembled from assets. This is true regardless of the type of software life cycle model (e.g., waterfall, rapid prototyping, spiral). Furthermore, adding consumer reuse changes each life cycle phase in essentially the same way. To develop software life cycle deliverables with the use of assets, a *consumer reuse mini life cycle* must be added to each life cycle phase.

As Figure 4-1 shows, the consumer reuse mini life cycle includes the following steps:

1. A search is made for candidate assets that may be used to produce the life cycle phase deliverables

2. Appropriate assets are selected for reuse

3. The software life cycle phase deliverables are built using the selected assets

4. Use of assets to build software life cycle deliverables and the reusability of the deliverables produced are evaluated

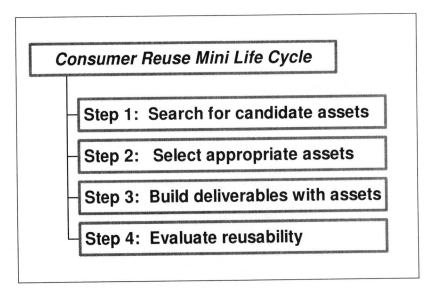

Figure 4-1. Consumer Reuse Mini Life Cycle

Table 4-1 lists some common sources to search for assets to use to develop software project deliverables. Table 4-2 lists some common asset selection criteria.

Table 4-1. Asset Sources

- Existing legacy software systems
- Application package and application template vendors
- Object class library and framework vendors
- Other concurrent projects in the organization
- Reuse catalogs and reuse libraries in the organization
- Strategic systems plans and enterprise models and architectures
- Assets available on the Internet or corporate intranets
- Marketing reports, trade press, customer/user surveys
- Software developers and maintainers
- Domain engineering groups

Table 4-2. Asset Selection Criteria

- Asset cost (the cost to build or acquire and maintain the asset)
- Asset quality (e.g., reliability, compliance to organization's standards)
- Asset domain
- Asset availability
- Asset constraints (e.g., licensing restrictions, target operating environment, performance limitations)
- Asset usage requirements (e.g., software tools, software training)
- Benefits expected from using the asset to build a project deliverable

To ensure that reuse is practiced throughout the life cycle, the consumer reuse mini life cycle should be integrated into each software life cycle primary process specified in the 12207 Standard (see Figure 4-2.) Although the general steps of the consumer reuse mini life cycle are the same for each primary process, the specific tasks will vary depending on the process. For example, during the development process, assets such as generic architectures should be reused to develop the software product design.

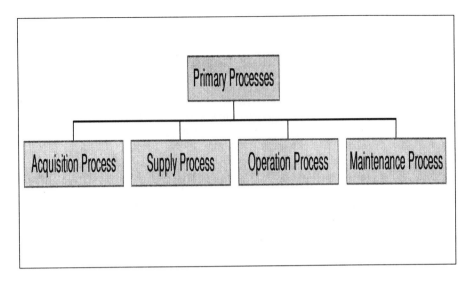

Figure 4-2. IEEE/EIA Std. 12207.0-1996 Primary Processes

IEEE Std. 1517 describes consumer reuse requirements for the software life cycle by extending the IEEE/EIA Std. 12207.0-1996 primary processes with the addition of reuse-related tasks that implement the steps of the consumer reuse mini life cycle.[1] For example, IEEE Std. 1517 task 5.1.1.1 is added to the Initiation Activity in the 12207 Standard Acquisition Process to serve as an explicit requirement to search for assets before developing new software:

> *5.1.1.1 Before acquiring software, the acquirer shall review current, available, and soon to-be-available assets to determine if what is needed exists or can be assembled to develop the needed software. The acquirer may ask the supplier, domain engineer, or asset manager to identify assets for consideration.[2]*

4.1.3 Adding Consumer Reuse Requirements to the Primary Processes

The Primary Processes are the category of processes defined in the 12207 Standard software life cycle framework to cover the acquisition, supply, development, operation, and maintenance of a system or software product (i.e., phases of the software life cycle). As Figure 4-2 shows, the 12207 Standard defines five primary processes:[3]

1. Acquisition
2. Supply
3. Development
4. Operation
5. Maintenance

Each primary process and its composing activities were discussed in Chapter 2. No additional processes or activities are added by IEEE Std. 1517 to the 12207 Standard framework to support and enable the practice of consumer reuse in the software life cycle.

The remainder of this chapter is devoted to a discussion of the reuse-related tasks that IEEE Std. 1517 adds to each 12207 primary process.

Throughout the chapter, one company's in-house methodology is used as an example to illustrate how to extend a methodology to meet the various IEEE Std. 1517 requirements for practicing consumer reuse. The company is referred to by the fictitious name INVESCO. INVESCO's in-house methodology is an object-oriented methodology based on the Fusion method developed by HP.[4] The methodology is described using a deliverable-driven format, meaning that the methodology consists of a set of phases, as shown in Figure 4-3, and each phase is described in terms of a set of deliverables that are produced during that phase. Figure 4-4 is the deliverable description template used by the INVESCO methodology.

Project Definition Phase	16 deliverables
Analysis Phase	30 deliverables
Design Phase	28 deliverables
Construction Phase	16 deliverables
Implementation Phase	11 deliverables

Figure 4-3. INVESCO In-House Object-Oriented Methodology

4.2 Reuse Requirements for the Acquisition Process

The 12207 Standard Acquisition Process specifies the requirements for acquiring a software product (system or software service). The main functions of the Acquisition Process are to create a request-for-proposal (RFP) for the desired software product and to select a supplier who agrees to provide the desired software product according to the terms of a contract. IEEE Std. 1517 extends the 12207 Standard Acquisition Process to also apply to an asset.

IEEE Std. 1517 pushes reuse requirements right up to the beginning of the software life cycle by adding consumer reuse tasks to the Acquisition Process. The *acquirer*, whom the standard names as the party responsible for performing the Acquisition Process, is required to search for software that is currently available in the organization and that may be able to meet the acquirer's needs, before acquiring new software.

DELIVERABLE DESCRIPTION TEMPLATE

Deliverable Name:

Deliverable Description:

Required or Optional:

Supporting Techniques:

Applicable Standards:

Relationship to Other Deliverables:

Life of Deliverable:

Review Audiences:

Approval for Deliverable:

Producer of Deliverable:

Custodian of Deliverable:

Suggested Tools:

Tasks/Procedure to Create Deliverable:

Figure 4-4. INVESCO In-House Object-Oriented Methodology
Deliverable Description Template

The 12207 Standard Acquisition Process includes the following five activities:

1. Initiation
2. Request for Proposal Preparation
3. Contract Preparation and Update
4. Supply Monitoring
5. Acceptance and Completion

As Figure 4-5 shows, IEEE Std. 1517 adds reuse-related tasks to the Initiation, Request for Proposal Preparation, and Acceptance and Completion Activities to specify the consumer reuse requirements for the Acquisition Process.

4.2.1 Adding Consumer Reuse Requirements to the Initiation Activity

The Initiation Activity is performed to define the requirements of the system, software product, or software service to be acquired.

IEEE Std. 1517 adds five new tasks to the 12207 Initiation Activity to support consumer reuse. Each of these reuse-related tasks is discussed below.

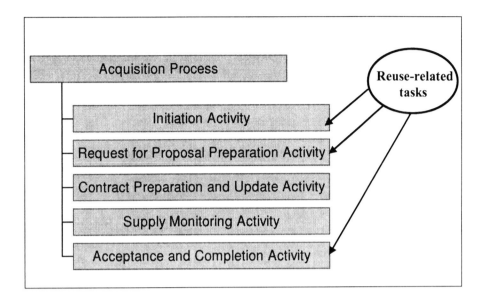

Figure 4-5. IEEE Std. 1517 Extensions to the IEEE/EIA Std. 12207
Acquisition Process to Support Consumer Reuse

4.2.1.1 Identify Candidate Assets

To practice consumer reuse to the fullest possible extent in a software project, assets should be identified as early as possible. Therefore, IEEE Std. 1517 implements the search step of the consumer reuse mini life cycle in the Initiation Activity of the Acquisition Process, which kicks off the process of acquiring software. IEEE Std. 1517 includes the following requirement to search for assets during the Initiation Activity:

> 5.1.1.1 Before acquiring software, the acquirer shall review current, available, and soon-to-be-available assets to determine if what is needed exists or can be assembled to develop the needed software. The acquirer may ask the supplier, domain engineer, or asset manager to identify assets for consideration.[5]

Discussion

IEEE Std. 1517 recognizes that a software acquirer may not be in a position to be knowledgeable or aware of assets that could be used to create the software product being requested. For this reason, the Standard suggests in this task that the parties or organizations responsible for performing the role of software supplier, domain engineer, or asset manager be enlisted to help identify assets that may be appropriate for use in this project.

4.2.1.2 Require Assets to be Reusable

IEEE Std. 1517 implements the selection step in the consumer reuse mini life cycle in the Acquisition Process by adding the requirement that assets are reusable and compatible with the domain architecture and domain models:

> *5.1.1.2 The acquirer shall require assets to:*
>
> *a) be reusable;*
>
> *b) have interfaces compatible with the domain architecture;*
>
> *c) be compatible with the domain models.*[6]

Discussion

With the addition of this requirement, IEEE Std. 1517 draws attention to the importance of domain models and domain architectures early in the software life cycle. They are the foundation for developing *with* assets, also known as consumer reuse. If there are no domain models or domain architectures, the project runs the risk of being able to use only a small number of assets and achieve only limited reuse benefits because of difficulties encountered when attempting to fit assets together.

To use assets to build a software product, the assets must be reusable. A reusable asset is designed for use in multiple contexts. However, it is also necessary that the assets are designed to fit together. Requiring that asset interfaces are compatible with the domain architecture assures that the assets will fit together and work together when assembled into a software product. According to IEEE Std. 1517, the domain architecture "provides a framework for configuring assets within individual software systems."[7]

The domain model is used to describe common concepts shared by software systems and products in the domain. According to IEEE Std. 1517, it "provides a representation of the requirements of the domain."[8] The domain model is essential to the selection of assets that are appropriate for use in acquiring the software system or product that is desired.

4.2.1.3 Consider Reuse as an Acquisition Option

As expressed in task 5.1.1.6 in IEEE/EIA Std 12207.0-1996, there typically have been only two options to consider when acquiring software:[9]

- Build the software

- Buy the software

With reuse, a third acquisition option is added. The software can be acquired by assembling it from existing assets. IEEE Std. 1517 makes this option explicit by adding it to the software acquisition choices an acquirer must seriously consider.

IEEE Std. 1517 implements the integration step of the consumer reuse mini life cycle in task 5.1.1.3 in the Acquisition Process' Initiation Activity :

> *5.1.1.3 The acquirer shall consider and document reuse as an option for acquisition as part of the acquirer's analysis of risk, cost, and benefits criteria. The acquirer shall compare software requirements with asset capabilities and, if proper, evaluate and document costs and benefits of modifying software requirements to enable or increase the reuse of assets. (This task defines reuse-related requirements in addition to those requirements specified in IEEE/EIA Std 12207.0-1996, task 5.1.1.6)* [10]

Discussion

Adding this requirement to the Acquisition Process accomplishes two important things. First, it makes the acquirer think about reuse at the beginning of the process where it is easiest to take the fullest possible advantage of reusing assets. Identifying assets that are available and accessible early in the software life cycle sets the direction for practicing reuse in subsequent life cycle activities. Second, it makes reuse a legitimate option in a software project. To avoid reuse, the acquirer must dismiss the reuse option with documented reasons to justify why reuse was not chosen.

Implementation Considerations

To illustrate how IEEE Std. 1517 reuse requirements defined in this task may be implemented in a methodology, the INVESCO OO methodology is extended in Figures 4-6 and 4-7. Figure 4-6 shows the reuse extensions added to the Risk Analysis Deliverable from the Project Definition Phase of the INVESCO methodology. Figure 4-7 shows the reuse extensions added to the Cost Analysis Deliverable from the Project definition Phase of the INVESCO methodology. The extensions are illustrated in italic type.

4.2.1.4 Require Assets to Meet Organization's Standards

Practicing consumer reuse requires software deliverables to be produced from assets. Much of the success of consumer reuse depends upon the general quality and, of course, the reusability of the assets from which the deliverables are produced. If poor quality assets are used, then the quality of the deliverables will be jeopardized. If the assets are not safe and easy to reuse, then the benefits sought from reuse will be greatly diminished.

IEEE Std. 1517 defines reusability as follows:

> *Reusability: (A) The degree to which an asset can be used in more than one software system, or in building other assets. (B) In a reuse library, the characteristics of an asset that make it easy to use in different contexts, software systems, or in building different assets.* [13]

RISK ANALYSIS DELIVERABLE DESCRIPTION

Deliverable Description: The risk analysis defines the top ten risks associated with not delivering the project as they relate to technology, architecture, staffing, and complexity of the project.

Required or Optional: Required

Supporting Techniques: Review the risk analysis sections of other planning documents.

Applicable Standards:

Relationship to Other Deliverables:

     Deliverables which contribute to this deliverable: High Level Project Description; Hardware Architecture Diagram; System Controls; Project Machine Interfaces

     Deliverables which this deliverable contributes to: Cost/Benefit Analysis; Development Approach; Project Definition Report; Analysis Report; Technical Design Document; *Reuse Project Evaluation*

Life of Deliverable: Project duration

Review Audience: Reviewed as part of the Project Definition Report, Analysis Report, and Design Document review.

Producer of Deliverable: Project team

Custodian of Deliverable: Project team

Suggested Tools: Word Processor

Tasks to Produce this Deliverable:

1. List all the risks you can think of. *Include any risks (e.g., such as lengthening project schedule, reusable components to be used in project are not available when needed) of practicing reuse in the project).*
2. Rank them to obtain the "top ten" (involve the project Team).
3. Document a plan to manage each of the top ten risks.

Figure 4-6. Example of Adding IEEE Std. 1517 Reuse Requirements to the INVESCO Methodology Risk Analysis Deliverable

COST/BENEFIT ANALYSIS DELIVERABLE DESCRIPTION

Deliverable Description: The cost/benefit analysis contains the comparison of the cost of the project based on the high level estimate to the projected benefits of the project to the company. Both business and technical costs and benefits should be included.

Required or Optional: Required

Supporting Techniques: Review previous projects' cost/benefit analysis documents. *If reuse is to be practiced, reference the Reuse Cost/benefit Analysis Technique.*

Relationship to Other Deliverables:

Deliverables which contribute to this deliverable:
High Level Estimates and Estimate Assumptions;
Risk Analysis
Deliverables which this deliverable contributes to:
Project Definition Report; *Reuse Project Evaluation*

Life of Deliverable: Project duration

Review Audience: Reviewed as part of the Project Definition Report review

Producer of Deliverable: Project team

Custodian of Deliverable: Project team

Suggested Tools: Word Processor, Spreadsheet

Tasks to Produce this Deliverable:

1. Ballpark development costs based on a high-level estimate.
2. Estimate training costs *and include reuse training costs.*
3. Estimate hardware software costs *and include reuse tool costs.*
4. Document benefits to company *and cite those related to practicing reuse.*
5. Estimate support costs, citing *those related to practicing reuse such as reuse consulting.*
6. *Note any expenses related to developing reusable assets that will have later payback using the Reuse Cost/Benefit Analysis Technique.*[12]

Figure 4-7. Example of Adding IEEE Std. 1517 Reuse Requirements to the INVESCO Methodology Cost/Benefit Analysis Deliverable

To assure quality of the software product that is acquired, IEEE Std. 1517 adds a task to the Acquisition Process Initiation Activity to require the selection of assets that meet the organization's reusability criteria and standards:

> *5.1.1.4 When an off-the-shelf software product or asset is to be acquired, the acquirer should select products or assets that meet the standards and criteria for reusability of the acquirer's organization. (This task defines reuse-related requirements in addition to those requirements specified in IEEE/EIA Std 122207.0-1996, task 5.1.1.7.)*[14]

Implementation Considerations

Task 5.1.1.4 is an example of an application of the selection step of the consumer reuse mini life cycle. The characteristics that should be included in reusability criteria for assets are listed in Table 4-3.

Table 4-3. Reusability Criteria

- Generalized
- Encapsulated: details are hidden to minimize the effects of change
- Widely applicable: able to be used in multiple contexts
- Adaptable/extensible
- Well-documented
- Reliable
- Testable
- Maintainable

4.2.1.5 Use Acquisition Plan Template

The 12207 Standard requires that an acquisition plan is created as one of the initiation activities in the Acquisition Process. In addition, IEEE Std. 1517 extends this requirement by specifying that an acquisition plan template shall be used to create the acquisition plan:

> *4.5.1.5 The acquirer shall create and document an acquisition plan, reusing an applicable acquisition plan template, if any exists, to define the resources and procedures to acquire software. The acquirer may use the acquisition plan template in Annex B of IEEE Std 1062, 1998 Edition. (This task defines reuse-related requirements in addition to those requirements specified in IEEE/EIA Std 12207.0-1996, task 5.1.1.8.)*[15]

Discussion

This task implements the search, select, and build steps in the consumer reuse mini life cycle. In this application of consumer reuse, the deliverable is the acquisition plan and the asset to be used is an acquisition plan template. Typically, a plan template is an outline with the standard portions of the plan document already filled in. Using a plan template offers the advantages of reducing the time needed to produce the plan, ensuring that the plan meets organization's standards, and improving the overall quality and completeness of the plan.

Implementation Considerations

In this case, the standard suggests the reuse of an acquisition plan template that was developed by another IEEE standard.

4.2.2 Adding Consumer Reuse Requirements to the RFP Preparation Activity

The purpose of the 12207 Standard RFP Preparation Activity is to produce a request-for-proposal for acquiring a software product, system, or software service. IEEE Std. 1517 adds one new task to this activity to assure that the request for proposal specifies the reuse requirements for the supplier.

4.2.2.1 Include Reuse Requirements in Acquisition Documentation

If the acquirer has chosen reuse as the development approach to be used for the requested software, then candidate suppliers of the software should be informed of this request to enable the supplier to properly respond with how reuse requirements will be addressed when supplying the software product. IEEE Std. 1517 adds the following task to the RFP Preparation Activity in the Acquisition Process to ensure that reuse requirements are clearly stated in the RFP:

> *5.1.2.1 The acquisition documentation shall include any requirements for practicing reuse that the supplier will be required to meet. (This task defines reuse-related requirements in addition to those requirements specified in IEEE/EIA Std 12207.0-1996, task 5.1.2.1.)*[16]

Discussion

The 12207 Standard task 5.1.2.1 suggests that the documentation for the RFP include system requirements, scope statement, technical constraints, and so forth. However, it does not specifically mention the inclusion of reuse considerations. This IEEE Std. task 5.1.2.1 is another example of how attention is called to reuse at the beginning of the life cycle. In this case, the supplier of the requested software product is informed of reuse requirements that must be met before responding to the RFP.

4.2.3 Adding Consumer Reuse Requirements to the Acceptance and Completion Activity

The purpose of the 12207 Standard Acceptance and Completion Activity is to define and conduct acceptance review and testing of a software product or software service delivered by a supplier. Acceptance review and testing are performed by the acquirer, with the possible involvement of the supplier. IEEE Std. 1517 adds one reuse-related task to this activity to assure that acceptance review and testing address the reusability of the software product.

4.2.3.1 Include Reusability Tests in Acceptance Tests

If the acquirer expects the requested software product to be reusable, then reusability should be included in its acceptance criteria. IEEE Std. 1517 makes this requirement explicit with the addition of the following task to the Acceptance and Completion Activity in the Acquisition Process:

> *5.1.3.1 If the software product is to be reusable, then acceptance test cases should include reusability tests and domain architecture compatibility tests. (This task defines reuse-related requirements in addition to those requirements specified in the IEEE/EIA Std 12207.0-1996, task 5.1.5.1.)*[17]

Discussion

It is necessary to specifically include reusability in the acceptance tests simply because a software product that meets normal quality criteria, such as reliability, does not guarantee that it is reusable. For example, a reusable software product must be able to be used in multiple contexts. Additional acceptance tests are needed to demonstrate reusability.

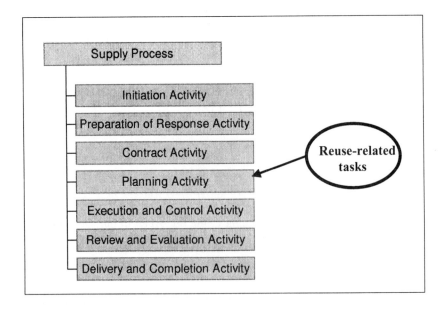

Figure 4-8. IEEE Std. 1517 Extensions to the IEEE/EIA Std. 12207
Supply Process to Support Consumer Reuse

4.3 Reuse Requirements for the Supply Process

The 12207 Standard Supply Process specifies the requirements for supplying a software product (system or software service). The main function of the Supply Process is to respond to a request-for-proposal (RFP) for a software product with a contract and a plan specifying how the requested product will be delivered. IEEE Std. 1517 extends the Supply Process to also apply to an asset. The party responsible for performing the Supply Process is the *supplier*.

The 12207 Standard defines the Supply Process as consisting of seven activities:

1. Initiation

2. Preparation of Response

3. Contract

4. Planning

5. Execution and Control

6. Review and Evaluation

7. Delivery and Completion

As Figure 4-8 shows, IEEE Std. 1517 adds reuse-related tasks to the Planning Activity of the Supply Process. All other activities and tasks of the 12207 Standard Supply Process are included without change in IEEE Std. 1517.

4.3.1 Adding Consumer Reuse Requirements to the Planning Activity

The primary deliverable produced by the Planning Activity is a software project plan for providing a software product. Two important elements of the plan are the software life cycle model and the development approach to be used to develop the software product.

IEEE Std. 1517 adds five new reuse-related tasks to assure that reuse is explicitly addressed in the project plan. These new tasks are discussed below.

4.3.1.1 Evaluate the Reuse Capabilities of the Software Life Cycle Model

Since reuse is a different software development paradigm, it forces a different way of thinking and working in a software project. If the software life cycle model does not integrate the specifics of reuse into its processes, it is unlikely that the project will be able to successfully employ a reuse approach:

> *5.2.1.1 When defining or selecting a software life cycle model for this supply project, the supplier shall evaluate and document the capabilities of this model to satisfy reuse process requirements. The supplier should explore with the acquirer the possibility of modifying software requirements to enable or increase the reuse of assets and, if proper, evaluate and document the costs and benefits thereof. (This task defines reuse-related requirements*

in addition to those requirements specified in IEEE/EIA Std 12207.0-1996, task 5.2.2.4.)[18]

Discussion

A reuse development approach requires leveraging work done in past software projects to the extent that reuse may be given precedence over the acquirer's software requirements. In other words, the tradeoffs between custom building software from scratch in order to exactly match the acquirer's requirements should be weighed against modifying the requirements to enable the reuse for assets in order to produce high-quality software in a faster, more cost-effective manner.

Implementation Considerations

To determine the reuse capability of the software life cycle model selected by the supplier, the processes, activities, and tasks specified in IEEE Std. 1517 should be mapped to the supplier's software life cycle model.

When a reuse approach is chosen for a project, the acquirer must be willing to adjust software requirements to take advantage of reusing assets unless sound business and/or technical reasons for not doing so can be demonstrated.

4.3.1.2 Analyze the Risks and Benefits of Using a Reuse Approach

Normally, a supplier is expected to justify the selection of a particular supply approach in terms of the benefits it can offer, as well as identify the risks it may present. This is also true when a reuse approach is chosen to supply the requested software product, system, or asset:

> *5.2.1.2 Once the planning requirements are established, the supplier shall consider and document the option of developing the system, software product, or asset with assets as part of the supplier's analysis of risks and benefits associated with this option. (This task defines reuse-related requirements in addition to those requirements specified in IEEE/EIA Std 12207.0-1996, task 5.2.4.4.)*[19]

Implementation Considerations

Reuse cost/benefit analysis entails estimating the costs and benefits of practicing reuse in a project. The cost of practicing reuse is estimated based on the cost of using assets to produce the system, software product, or asset requested. Both the direct and indirect costs of reuse, such as special training costs for the project team, should be taken into account. The estimated cost of developing the software product, system, or asset with assets is compared to the estimated cost of developing the software product (system or asset) from scratch. To cost justify a reuse approach, the cost of developing the software product (system or asset) with assets must be less than developing it from scratch.

Other reuse benefits, such as reducing the risk of project failure, improving software quality, and shortening the project schedule, should also be evaluated and may be used to justify using a reuse approach in a project.

Figure 4-9 illustrates how the Development Approach Deliverable description from the Project Definition Phase of INVESCO OO methodology is extended to implement IEEE Std. 1517 reuse requirements. The extensions are illustrated in italic type.

4.3.1.3 Select Reuse Strategy for a Software Project

When reuse is chosen as the software development approach, why and how reuse will be practiced in the project should be defined in the project plan:

> *5.2.1.3 Reuse strategies that the supplier shall consider and document in the project plan include the following:*
>
> > *a) Developing the software product with assets;*
> >
> > *b) Developing the software product, or some part of it, as an asset.*
>
> *(This task defines reuse-related requirements in addition to those requirements specified in IEEE/EIA Std 12207.0-1996, task 5.2.4.2.)*[20]

Discussion

Basically, two reuse strategies can be followed with a reuse development approach. One strategy is to strictly practice consumer reuse in the project (i.e., assets will be reused but not created within the project scope); the other strategy is to also practice producer reuse (i.e., assets will be reused and new assets created within the project scope) in the project. Clarifying the reuse strategy in the project plan is important because it affects the reuse project requirements, such as the reuse skills needed by the project team and the reuse tools needed in the project. If reuse requirements are not recognized and planned for at the outset of the project, they may increase the risks associated with employing a reuse development approach.

PROJECT RESOURCE REQUIREMENTS DELIVERABLE DESCRIPTION

Deliverable Description: The estimates for the resource requirements for the complete project are defined.

Required or Optional: Required

Supporting Techniques: Review previous project's resource planning documents.

Relationship to Other Deliverables:

Deliverables which contribute to this deliverable:
High Level Project Description; High Level Estimates And Estimate Assumptions; Development Approach; *Project Reuse Strategy*
Deliverables which this deliverable contributes to:
Project Definition Report

Life of Deliverable: Project duration

Review Audience: Reviewed as part of the Project Definition Report review

Producer of Deliverable: Project team

Custodian of Deliverable: Project team

Suggested Tools: Word Processor, Spreadsheet Tool

Tasks to Produce this Deliverable:

1. Determine/document the ideal project team. *If a reuse-driven approach is to be used, then a reuse consultant should be assigned to the project.*

2. Determine/document training needs, *including reuse training such as software developer reuse skills to search for and integrate reusable assets into project deliverables.*

3. Determine/document tools needed, *including reuse tools.*

4. Determine/document specific project needs.

Figure 4-9. Example of Adding IEEE Std. 1517 Reuse Requirements to the INVESCO Methodology Project Resource Requirements Deliverable

Defining the reuse strategy in the project plan ensures that:

- Reuse objectives for the project will be defined

- Reuse target levels for the project will be set

- The justification for practicing reuse in the project will be communicated to the acquirer and/or management

- The appropriate measures will be taken to provide the necessary project infrastructure for a reuse development approach

4.3.1.4 Gather Candidate Assets

When a reuse development approach is to be used, the software project plan should include a list of candidate assets to be considered for reuse in the development of the requested software product:

> *5.2.1.4 The supplier shall gather existing candidate software products and assets that may be used develop a software product that satisfies the requirements specifications from sources including the following:*
>
> a) *Domain engineering deliverables*
>
> b) *Internal and external suppliers*
>
> c) *Organization's reuse libraries*
>
> d) *Other ongoing projects in the organization*
>
> e) *Off-the-shelf software products and assets.*
>
> *The supplier shall document this information in the project plans and communicate it using the domain engineering feedback mechanism and the asset management communication mechanism.[21]*

Discussion

It is important to search for assets to use in the project during the project planning stage. Recognizing reuse opportunities early in the project maximizes the project's ability to take the fullest advantage of existing assets. Also, different types of assets should be considered. IEEE Std. 1517 mentions that an entire software product, as well as software parts should be considered for reuse in the project. Software parts can be assets, such as generic architectures, frameworks, or code for building a software application or for producing other types of project deliverables, such as test plans and user documentation. To ensure that all the appropriate sources are examined for candidate assets, IEEE Std. 1517 lists key sources where assets can be found.

Informing the domain engineers who are responsible for building the assets and the asset managers who are responsible for managing storage and retrieval of assets will help ensure that the assets needed by the project are properly prepared and actually available for reuse.

4.3.1.5 Identify New Assets to be Produced in the Project

If the reuse strategy for the project is to practice producer reuse, then the candidate assets to be created within the scope of the project should be identified in the project plan:

> *5.2.1.5 The supplier should identify and document in the project plans, candidate software products and assets that may be developed within the scope and context of this project. This information should be communicated using the domain engineering feedback mechanism and the asset communication mechanism.[22]*

Discussion

Notice that IEEE Std. 1517 advises contacting domain engineering and asset management about the project plans to create new assets. Domain engineers may already be developing similar assets or have valuable suggestions about how to create the asset. Asset managers may know of a source for obtaining these assets or of other projects that also need these assets. This information may help prevent a project team from needlessly creating assets that already exist or may help the project team develop a new asset in a more reusable form.

Implementation Considerations

Requirements that the software product to be produced in this project shares with other concurrent and future software products and projects should be identified. Based on these common requirements, a determination should be made whether the software product, its constituent parts, or associated deliverables should be created as assets within the scope of this project. A list of candidate assets that should be created for reuse within the context of this project should be included in the project plan.

4.4 Reuse Requirements for the Development Process

The 12207 Standard Development Process specifies the requirements for developing a software product. As Figure 4-10 shows, software product development generally entails analysis, design, coding, testing, integration, and installation. IEEE Std. 1517 extends the 12207 Standard Development Process by adding the requirements for developing a software product *with* the use of assets; that is, adding the consumer reuse requirements to software development. Also, IEEE Std. 1517 extends the 12207 Standard Development Process to apply to the development of an asset as well as a software product.

The party responsible for performing the Development Process in both the 12207 Standard and IEEE Std. 1517 is the *developer.*

The 12207 Standard defines the Development Process as consisting of:

- Process Implementation
- System Requirements Analysis
- System Architectural Design
- Software Requirements Analysis
- Software Architectural Design
- Software Detailed Design
- Software Coding and Testing
- Software Integration
- Software Qualification Testing

- System Integration
- System Qualification Testing
- Software Installation
- Software Acceptance Support

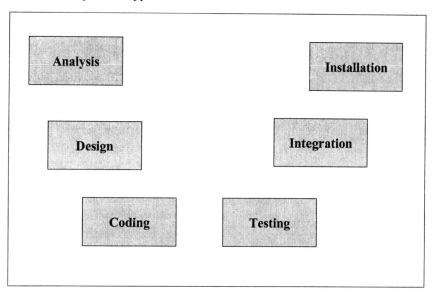

Figure 4-10. Phases of the Software Development Process

Although the Development Process mainly concerns the development of a software product, IEEE/EIA Std. 12207.0-1996 also includes activities related to system development to guide a developer who is required by a contact to perform system as well as software product development activities (e.g., System Requirements Analysis, System, Integration, etc.).

As Figure 4-11 shows, IEEE Std. 1517 adds the consumer reuse mini life cycle to the following Development Process activities:

- Process Implementation
- System Requirements Analysis
- System Architectural Design
- Software Requirements Analysis
- Software Architectural Design
- Software Detailed Design
- Software Coding and Testing
- Software Integration

- Software Qualification Testing
- System Integration
- System Qualification Testing
- Software Installation

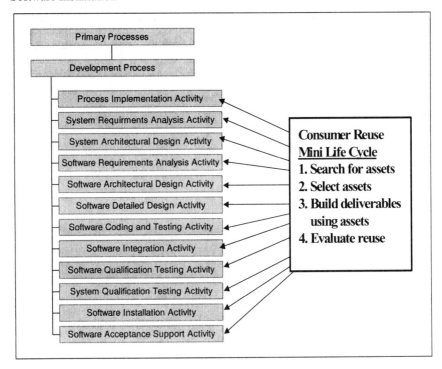

Figure 4-11. IEEE Std. 1517 Extensions to the IEEE/EIA Std. 12207
Development Process to Support Consumer Reuse

The same pattern is followed by IEEE Std. 1517 to introduce the consumer reuse mini life cycle into each Development Process activity. First, IEEE Std. 1517 adds a task(s) to specify the requirements for selecting and reusing asset(s) to develop the activity deliverable(s). This task implements consumer mini life cycle step 1: search for assets; step 2: select assets; and step 3: built with assets. Second, IEEE Std. 1517 adds a task(s) to evaluate and report the reusability of the deliverable(s) produced by the activity. This task implements consumer mini life cycle step 4: evaluate reusability and report reuse information.

4.4.1 Adding Consumer Reuse Requirements to the Process Implementation Activity

The Process Implementation Activity is performed to set up a software development project. This activity requires that the developer:

1. Select the software life cycle process model, standards, tools, methods and programming languages to be used in the project

2. Create the project plan

3. Set up project communication mechanisms

IEEE Std. 1517 adds four new tasks to the 12207 Process Implementation Activity to support consumer reuse. Table 4-4 summarizes how IEEE Std. 1517 extends the 12207 Process Implementation Activity.

Table 4-4. Extending the Process Implementation Activity to Include Consumer Reuse

12207 TASK	1517 TASK	MINI LIFE CYCLE	DELIVERABLES BUILT / EVALUATED	ASSETS REUSED / EVALUATED
5.3.1.1	5.3.1.1	Step 1: Search Step 2: Select Step 3: Build	Software life cycle process model	Software life cycle process model
5.3.1.3	5.3.1.2	Step 1: Search Step 2: Select	Software standards, methods, tools, and computer programming languages	—
5.3.1.4	5.3.1.3 5.3.1.4	Step 1: Search Step 2: Select Step 3: Build	Project plan	Project plan template

4.4.1.1 Evaluate the Reuse Capability of the Software Life Cycle Model

When a reuse development approach is to be used in the project, IEEE Std. 1517 requires the developer is to evaluate the reuse capabilities of the software life cycle model:

> *5.3.1.1 The developer shall evaluate and document the capabilities of the model to satisfy reuse requirements when selecting or defining a life cycle process model appropriate to the scope, magnitude, and complexity of this project. The reuse-related activities and tasks shall be selected and mapped onto the life cycle process model chosen. (This task defines reuse-related re-*

*quirements in addition to those requirements specified in IEEE/EIA 12207.0-
1996, task 5.3.1.1).[23]*

Discussion

Although not specifically stated, it is assumed that the reuse-related activities and tasks that the
developer will map onto the project's life cycle process model are those specified in IEEE Std.
1517. Also, it is implied that the developer may select an appropriate subset of the reuse-related
activities and tasks to fit the needs of the project and still comply with the standard. This is discussed further in Chapter 8, Section 8.3.

4.4.1.2 Select Standards, Methods, Tools, and Programming Languages that Support Reuse

An important element of project preparation is to define the resources that will be needed by
the project. IEEE Std. 1517 includes the following task in the Process Implementation Activity to
assure that the reuse resources needed for the project are defined at project planning time:

*5.3.1.2 The developer shall select and use standards, methods, tools, and
computer programming languages that enable, support, and enforce the
practice of reuse in the project. (This task defines reuse-related requirements
in addition to those requirements specified in the IEEE Std. 12207.0-1996.)[24]*

Discussion

Software reuse is made easier by standardization. When software features (such as menus,
GUIs, help functions, error handling and so on) are standardized, opportunities for reuse arise
through the creation of reusable components to implement these standardized features. If a component complies with standards in the areas of documentation, interface design, and testing its reusability is increased because it has better quality and general usefulness.

Implementation Considerations

Project standards, methods, and procedures should be specified in a manner that promotes reuse. For example, following an organization's software quality standards is key to making a software product and its parts reusable. A quality software product is modularized, well documented,
thoroughly tested, and complies with software standards. Table 4-5 lists some areas in which software should be standardized to ensure its overall quality and reusability.

The project plan should contain a list of the tools that will be used to support the practice of reuse in the project. Tools such as generators that automatically produce code or documentation and
GUI builders should be considered for use in the project. With the use of generator tools, the project team can practice *generative reuse*—a form of reuse where the assets are built into the tools.

Hypertext tools can be used to locate related assets, such as the code that implements a design
or the test suite used to test a requirement. Also, re-engineering tools such as code analyzers, flow-
graphing tools, data tracers, and complexity analyzers, can be used to aid in understanding and

modifying assets. Finally, software tool environments with repositories that are populated with "starter" reuse libraries can be useful in a software project that intends to practice consumer reuse.

The italic type in Figure 4-12 illustrates how the Development Approach Deliverable from the Project Definition Phase of the INVESCO OO methodology is extended to implement IEEE Std. 1517 requirements in this task.

Table 4-5. Areas in which to Standardize Software

- Invoking, controlling and terminating function
- Error handling
- Help
- User Interface (e.g., common user dialogue)
- Communication (e.g., common access to networks)
- Component documentation and format such as including standardized preamble fields to describe component in terms of name, author, date created, version number, parameter descriptions, data definitions, standardized template structure for different types of reusable components
- Conforming to modeling standards such as UML, or to interoperability standards such as COM or CORBA
- Naming conventions
- Query processing
- Storage structure
- Interface standards

4.4.1.3 Create the Project Plan Reusing a Project Plan Template

The primary deliverable produced by the Process Implementation Activity of the Development Process is the project plan. To produce a high quality project plan that meets the organization's standards, IEEE Std. 1517 requires the use of a project plan template:

> *5.3.1.3 The developer shall create and document a project plan, reusing an applicable project plan template, if any exists, to define the resources and procedures to develop the software. The plan should include specific standards, methods, tools, and programming languages that have been selected to enable the practice of reuse in the project. (This task defines reuse-related requirements in addition to those requirements specified in IEEE/EIA Std. 12207.0-1996, task 5.3.1.4.)[27]*

DEVELOPMENT APPROACH DELIVERABLE DEFINITION

Deliverable Description: The development approach for the project is described in terms of the following: 1) methodology to be followed; 2) platforms to be supported; 3) tools to be used; 4) data gathering techniques; 4) languages; 5) metrics; 6) *reuse-driven approach*

Required or Optional: Required

Supporting Techniques: Review previous project's development sections. Evaluate Competitive alternatives. *If a reuse-driven approach is to be used, refer to Project Reuse Strategy DefinitionTechnique.*[25]

Relationship to Other Deliverables:

Deliverables which contribute to this deliverable:
Risk Analysis; Resource Requirements for the Project
Deliverables which this deliverable contributes to:
Project Definition Report

Life of Deliverable: Project duration

Review Audience: Reviewed as part of the Project Definition Report review

Producer of Deliverable: Project team

Custodian of Deliverable: Project team

Suggested Tools: Word Processor

Tasks to Produce this Deliverable:

1. Determine/document the methodology path to be used.
2. Determine/document platforms to be supported.
3. Determine/document tools needed, *including reuse tools.*
4. Determine/document data gathering techniques, *including techniques that gather reuse-related measurement data.*
5. Determine/document languages to be used.
6. Determine/document metrics, *including reuse-related metrics.*
7. *Determine/document the project reuse strategy. Refer to Project Reuse Strategy Definition Technique.*[26]

Figure 4-12. Example of Adding IEEE Std. 1517 Reuse Requirements to the INVESCO Methodology Development Approach Deliverable

Implementation Considerations

Adequate reuse planning is essential to insuring that the project will have the necessary resources to succeed with reuse. Table 4-6 lists the reuse items commonly included in a project plan.

Table 4-6. Example of a Project Reuse Plan Template

Project Name

Project Contact

Project Reuse Goals and Objectives

Reuse Level to be practiced in the Project

- **Consumer Reuse**

- **Producer Reuse**

List of Tools needed to Support the Practice of Reuse in the Project

- **List of tools by type and specific tool name**

List of Assets to be used in the Project

List of Assets to be created within the Scope of the Project

Proposed Software Reuse Target Level to be achieved in the Project

Metrics and Measurements used to Measure the Impact of Reuse on the Project

- **Data to be collected**

- **Collection method**

- **Evaluation method**

- **Reporting method**

Software Life Cycle Model to be used in the Project

Reuse Standards and Procedures to be followed in the Project

List of Reuse Asset and Tool Vendors

Actions to overcome Reuse Inhibitors in the Project

Reuse Training Needs for the Project Team

Ways to Motivate the Practice of Reuse in the Project

Figure 4-13 illustrates how the Project Definition report deliverable from the Project definition Phase of the INVESCO OO methodology is extended to implement the IEEE Std 1517 reuse requirements specified in this task. Figure 4-14 shows a new deliverable that is added to the INVESCO OO methodology to implement the reuse requirements in this task.

PROJECT DEFINITION REPORT DELIVERABLE

Deliverable Description: The Project Definition Report defines the high-level project description, assumptions, success criteria, planning estimates, risk analysis, cost/benefit analysis, *and reuse strategy.*

Required or Optional: Required

Supporting Techniques: *Project Reuse Strategy Definition Technique*[28]

Relationship to Other Deliverables:

Deliverables which contribute to this deliverable:
High Level Project Description; High Level Estimates and Estimate Assumptions; Cost/Benefit Analysis; Risk Analysis; Project Resource Requirements; Context Diagram; Development Approach; Project Administration Plan; *Project Reuse Strategy*
Deliverables which this deliverable contributes to:
Analysis Report

Life of Deliverable: Project duration

Review Audience: INVESCO management

Producer of Deliverable: Project team

Custodian of Deliverable: Project team

Suggested Tools: Word Processor

Tasks to Produce this Deliverable:

1. Assemble applicable Project Definition Phase deliverables.
2. *If a reuse strategy is to be used, include Project Reuse Strategy in the document. Refer to Project Reuse Strategy Definition Technique.*[29]
3. Ensure consistency across deliverables.
4. Review and revise draft.
5. Distribute to management for review.
6. Determine/document languages to be used.
7. Revise document based on management review.
8. *Determine/document the project reuse strategy.*

Figure 4-13. Example of Adding IEEE Std. 1517 Reuse Requirements to the Project Definition Report of the INVESCO Methodology

PROJECT REUSE STRATEGY DELIVERABLE DEFINITION

Deliverable Description: The Reuse Strategy Report defines the reuse strategy to be followed in the project. The report contains a list of the assets targeted for reuse in the project, a list of assets to be developed by the project, target reuse level, tools and methodology needed to support the practice of reuse in the project, and project reuse requirements, such as reuse training.

Required or Optional: Optional

Supporting Techniques: Project Reuse Strategy Definition Technique[30]

Relationship to Other Deliverables:

Deliverables which contribute to this deliverable:
High Level Project Definition; Project Resource Requirements; Development Approach; Project Administration Plan
Deliverables which this deliverable contributes to:
Project Definition Report

Life of Deliverable: Project duration

Review Audience: Reviewed as part of the Project Definition Report review Reviewed by INVESCO Reuse Support Group

Producer of Deliverable: Project team

Custodian of Deliverable: Project team

Suggested Tools: Word Processor, INVESCO Reuse Libraries & Catalogs

Tasks to Produce this Deliverable: Project Reuse Strategy Definition Technique[31]

1. Define project reuse strategy and level or reuse to be practiced (consumer reuse, producer reuse, reuse pilot).
2. Make a list of assets to be reused by the project.
3. Make a list of assets to be produced by the project.
4. List the tools needed to support reuse in the project.
5. Set the reuse target level for the project (percentage of application expected to be developed from assets.
6. Specify reuse standards to be followed by the project.
7. Determine project team reuse training needs and ways to promote their acceptance of reuse in the project.

Figure 4-14. Example of Adding a New Deliverable to the INVESCO Methodology to Implement IEEE Std. 1517 Reuse Requirements

4.4.1.4 Establish Project Communication Mechanisms

One of the ways in which a reuse development approach differs from traditional development approaches is that the developer must communicate with outside groups to a much greater degree. To assure that all the necessary communication channels are set up between the project team and the necessary outside groups, IEEE Std. 1517 requires the establishment of communication mechanisms during project initiation:

> *The developer shall utilize the following project mechanisms:*
>
> - *Feedback mechanism to the domain engineer to communicate the use and impact of software products and assets on this project;*
>
> - *Communication mechanism with the asset manager to resolve problems, answer questions, and make recommendations concerning software products and assets that the project encounters;*
>
> - *Notification mechanism that makes the developer aware of the prevailing trade laws, the licensing properties of software products and assets, the organization's restrictions that protect its proprietary interests, and the contract that may restrict or exclude the use of specific software products or assets by this project;*
>
> - *Notification mechanism that informs the developer about changes or problems or other useful information concerning relevant assets.*[32]

Discussion

Notice that there is a two-way flow of information about assets to and from the project. Asset information flowing into the project concerns the availability of the most current versions of assets and how to properly use the assets. Asset information is provided by the asset manager responsible for asset access, management, version control and change control, and by the domain engineer that created/acquired and maintains the asset. Asset information flowing from the project concerns how the asset was used and how valuable it was.

Establishment of the communication channels needed to support and enable the practice or reuse in an organization is a task belonging to the Initiation Activity in the Reuse Program Administration Process discussed in Chapter 6. Figure 6-2 in Chapter 6 shows the various communication channels that should be established between the parties that practice reuse.

4.4.2 Adding Consumer Reuse to the System Requirements Analysis Activity

Practicing consumer reuse in this activity requires that the system requirements specifications are produced from existing specifications and are evaluated in terms of their reuse potential. IEEE Std. 1517 adds five new tasks to the 12207 Systems Requirements Analysis Activity to support consumer reuse. Table 4-7 summarizes how IEEE Std. 1517 extends the 12207 System Requirements Analysis Activity.

Table 4-7. Extending the System Requirements Analysis Activity to Include Consumer Reuse

12207 TASK	1517 TASK	CONSUMER RE- USE MINI LIFE CYCLE	DELIVER- ABLE BUILT / EVALUATED	ASSET REUSED / EVALUATED
—	5.3.2.1	Step 1: Search Step 2: Select	Domains	Domain models
5.3.4.1	5.3.4.2 5.3.4.3	Step 1: Search Step 2: Select Step 3: Build	System requirements specifications	System requirements specifications; Domain models; Domain architectures
5.3.2.2	5.3.2.4 5.3.2.5	Step 4: Evaluate and report	System requirements specifications	Assets used or attempted to be used to create activity deliverables

4.4.2.1 Identify the System Domain

Identifying the domain(s) to which the system belongs will help the developer identify appropriate assets for use in this project. The first task that IEEE Std. 1517 adds to the System Requirements Analysis Activity is a requirement to identify the system domains:

> *5.3.2.1 The developer shall identify applicable domains and select their corresponding domain models, if they exist.*[32]

Discussion

The domain models are produced by the Domain Analysis Activity of the Domain Engineering Process (see Chapter 7). As defined in this standard, the domain model "provides a representation of the requirements of the domain [and] describes the commonalities and variabilities among requirements for software systems in the domain."[33]

Implementation Considerations

The domain model generally applies to all systems that belong to the domain. It can be used to identify which, if any, of this system's requirements are common. Common requirements that have been previously defined can be reused in this project to define this system's requirements specifications. In addition, common requirements can be used to identify other reuse opportunities in the project, since assets that implement those common requirements should be considered candidates for reuse in the project. Finally, the domain model can be used to check the completeness and consistency of the system requirements specifications defined in this project.

4.4.2.2 Select and Reuse System Requirements Specifications

The second task that IEEE Std. 1517 adds to the System Requirements Analysis Activity is an application of the first, second, and third steps of the consumer reuse mini life cycle to system requirements analysis:

> *5.3.2.2 The developer shall select and reuse applicable system requirements specifications, if any exist, before writing new requirements specifications. When writing new requirements specifications, the developer shall use the language and concepts of the domain models for the domain to which this software system belongs.*[34]

Discussion

When early-life-cycle software deliverables are defined according to reuse standards, it is more likely that later-life-cycle deliverables may be produced from assets. To ensure that the system requirements specifications are defined in a manner that is conducive to reuse of assets later in the life cycle, IEEE Std. 1517 requires the system requirements specifications to comply with the domain model language and concepts. For example, if the domain model is expressed in UML notation, then the system requirements specifications should also be expressed in UML notation.

4.4.2.3 Describe System Reusability Requirements

The 12207 Standard (IEEE/EIA 12207.0-1996, task 5.3.2.1) requires the contents of the system requirements specifications to describe:[35]

- system functions
- business requirements
- user requirements
- safety and security requirements
- interface requirements
- operations requirements

- maintenance requirements

- constraints.

IEEE Std. 1517 adds reusability as another requirement to be included in the system requirements specification:

> *5.3.2.3 The system requirements specification shall describe system reusability requirements, including the domain architecture interface requirements. (This task defines reuse-related requirements in addition to those requirements specified in IEEE/EIA Std. 12207.0-1996, task 5.3.2.1.)*[36]

Discussion

The domain architecture is essential to ensuring and increasing the reusability of a software product. The domain architecture defines interface standards for components that comprise the software product. By complying with the domain interface standards, existing assets and new components developed by the project will fit together and work together.

4.4.2.4 Evaluate the Reusability of System Requirements Specifications

Although developing new assets is not strictly within the scope of practicing consumer reuse, all project deliverables should be developed with reuse in mind; that is, with the assumption that all project deliverables may eventually be considered for reuse within or outside the scope of the project. For this reason, IEEE Std. 1517 expands the 12207 system requirements specification evaluation criteria to include reusability:

> *5.3.2.4 The system requirements specification shall be evaluated according to reusability criteria. The results of the evaluation shall be documented. (This task defines reuse-related requirements in addition to those requirements specified in IEEE/EIA Std 13307.0-1996, task 5.3.2.2.)*[37]

Discussion

In task 5.2.2.2, the 12207 Standard lists traceability to and consistency with the system requirements to system acquisition needs, testability, and feasibility of the system design, operations, and maintenance as the evaluation criteria. In the following note attached to task 5.3.2.4, IEEE Std. 1517 expands upon what is meant by reusability criteria:

> *NOTE—Reusability criteria include, but are not limited to:*
>
> a) *Usability and reusability of the system requirements*
>
> b) *Identification of customized requirements that can be replaced by reused requirements if the acquisition needs are adjusted*
>
> c) *Reuse potential of the requirements to be used in multiple contexts*[38]

Implementation Suggestions

Reusability of the system requirements specifications should be examined from two perspectives. First, the reuse potential of the specifications is examined. How easy will it be to reuse the specifications? How broadly can the specifications be used? Second, the possibility of changing the requirements of this system to increase the reuse of common requirements specifications is examined.

4.4.2.5 Report System Requirements Specifications Reuse Information

Information about the reuse potential of the system requirements specifications and how to increase reuse in the project should be captured and passed to other concerned parties. IEEE Std. 1517 adds the following task to the System Requirements Analysis Activity to assure that relevant reuse information is passed on to other interested parties:

> *5.3.2.5 The developer shall use the domain engineering feedback mechanism and the asset management communication mechanism to report reuse information about the requirements specifications.*[39]

Discussion

IEEE Std. 1517 attaches the following note to this task to further explain the contents of reuse information:

> *NOTE - Reuse information includes, but is not limited to*
> a) *Missing assets for the domain*
>
> b) *Nominally reusable assets for the domain rejected for this project and the rejection reasons*
>
> c) *Suggested modifications to assets*
>
> d) *List of assets reused by this project*
>
> e) *List of new candidate assets suggested by this project*[40]

Both the domain engineer and the asset manager should be interested in learning about how existing system requirements specifications were used in the project, as well as any suggestions from the developer about how to improve the reusability of existing specifications and the availability of new specifications that may have potential for reuse.

4.4.3 Adding Consumer Reuse to the System Architectural Design Activity

The system architecture is the principal deliverable produced by the 12207 System Architectural Design Activity. IEEE Std. 1517 adds four new tasks to this activity to enable the development of system architecture from assets and to evaluate the reusability of the system architecture.

Table 4-8 summarizes how the 12207 System Architectural Design Activity is extended by IEEE Std. 1517 to support consumer reuse.

Table 4-8. Extending the System Architectural Design Activity to Include Consumer Reuse

12207 TASK	1517 TASK	MINI LIFE CYCLE	DELIVERABLES BUILT / EVALUATED	ASSETS REUSED / EVALUATED
5.3.3.1	5.3.3.1 5.3.3.2	Step 1: Search Step 2: Select Step 3: Build	System architecture	Domain architectures; Domain models
5.3.3.2	5.3.3.3 5.3.3.4	Step 4: Evaluate and report	System architecture	Domain architectures and Domain models

4.4.3.1 Select Domain Architecture

IEEE Std. 1517 adds the following task to implement the first two steps of the consumer reuse mini life cycle in the System Architectural Design Activity:

> *5.3.3.1 The developer shall select applicable domain architectures consistent with the domain models, if they exist.*[41]

Discussion

According to IEEE Std. 1517, the domain architecture is "a generic design that is intended to satisfy requirements specified in the domain model."[42] If a domain model has been selected for reuse in this project, then the best way to ensure that the maximum level of reuse will be achieved is to use its companion domain architecture to implement the system design. Also, according to IEEE Std. 1517, the domain architecture "provides a framework for configuring assets within individual software systems."[4]

4.4.3.2 Derive the System Architecture from the Domain Architecture

Practicing consumer reuse in this activity means that the system architecture should not be developed from scratch unless no appropriate domain architecture exists. In the following task, IEEE Std. 1517 implements the third step of the consumer reuse mini life cycle as it applies to the development of the system architecture:

5.3.3.2 The system architecture shall be derived from the selected domain architectures. The allocation of the system requirements shall follow the domain models that correspond to the domain architectures.[44]

Implementation Considerations

The domain model that corresponds to the domain architecture is used to assure that all system requirements are mapped to the system architecture.

4.4.3.3 Evaluate the Reusability of the System Architecture

In the following task, IEEE Std. 1517 implements the fourth step of the consumer reuse mini life cycle as it applies to the development of the system architecture:

5.3.3.3 The system architecture shall be evaluated according to reusability criteria. The results of the evaluation shall be documented. (This task defines reuse-related requirements in addition to those requirements specified in IEEE/EIA Std. 12207.0-1996, task 5.3.3.2.)[45]

Discussion

Since all project deliverables may be considered candidates for reuse by other concurrent and future projects, IEEE Std. 1517 extends the 12207 Standard evaluation criteria for each type of deliverable to also include reusability criteria. As discussed above in Section 4.4.2.4 of this book, IEEE Std. 1517 provides a note to explain what should be included in the reusability criteria.

4.4.3.4 Report System Architectural Design Reuse Information

Information about the value of practicing consumer reuse to produce the system architectural design should be captured and passed onto other concerned parties. IEEE Std. 1517 adds the following task to the System Architectural Design Activity to assure that relevant reuse information is passed on to other interested parties:

5.3.3.4 The developer shall use the domain engineering feedback mechanism and the asset management communication mechanism to report reusability problems and recommendations for the system architectural design.[46]

Discussion

Feedback information about the usability and reusability of an existing domain architecture is extremely important since the domain architecture is a key asset. The domain architecture is expected to be the foundation design for all software systems belonging to the domain. Problems with or suggestions for improvements to the domain architecture should be reported to the asset manager and to the domain engineer since other current or future projects also may be affected.

On the other hand, if there is no appropriate domain architecture, then the system architectural design may be a candidate for the domain architecture. The developer should submit any recommendations for new candidate assets to the asset manager.

4.4.4 Adding Consumer Reuse to the Software Requirements Analysis Activity

The objective of this activity is to produce the software product requirements. The IEEE Std.1517 adds five new tasks to this activity to support the practice of consumer reuse. The requirements specified in these tasks address the development of software requirements with the use of assets and the evaluation of the reusability of these software requirements. Table 4-9 summarizes how the 12207 Software Requirements Activity is extended to support consumer reuse.

4.4.4.1 Add Reusability Requirements to Quality Characteristic Specifications

The 12207 Standard requires that the developer define the software requirements in the Software Requirements Analysis Activity. According to the IEEE/EIA Std. 12207.0-1996 task 5.3.4.1, software requirements include software quality characteristics such as functional specifications, safety specifications, security specifications, human-factors engineering specifications, and so forth.[47] IEEE Std. 1517 adds software quality characteristics to be applied to assets.

Table 4-9. Extending the Software Requirements Analysis Activity to Include Consumer Reuse

12207 TASK	1517 TASK	CONSUMER REUSE MINI LIFE CYCLE	DELIVERABLE BUILT / EVALUATED	ASSET REUSED / EVALUATED
5.3.4.1	5.3.4.1 5.3.4.2 5.3.4.3	Step 1: Search Step 2: Select Step 3: Build	Software requirements	Software requirements; Requirements template
5.3.4.2	5.3.4.4 5.4.4.5	Step 4: Evaluate and report	Software requirements	Assets used or attempted to be used to create activity deliverables

In the following task, IEEE Std. 1517 specifies that assets selected for reuse in the project must meet certain reusability criteria:

> *5.4.3.1 The developer shall include software reusability requirements for assets in the quality characteristics specifications to assure the quality of the assets selected for reuse in the development of the software product. The following criteria may be used to evaluate the quality of reusability:*

a)   *The reliability experience of assets reused in similar projects*

b)   *The results of inspecting the assets for defects*

c)   *The results of testing the assets against the system and software re-quirements.*[48]

Discussion

The purpose of this requirement is to provide the developer with a means for evaluating the quality of candidate assets for use in the project. If assets are defective in that they are not reliable or do not comply with the organization's software standards, they can compromise the quality of the software product in which they are reused.

Implementation Considerations

Table 4-10 lists some suggested reusability criteria for assets.

Table 4-10. Reusability Criteria for Assets

Previous reuse of asset	The asset should have been successfully reused at least two times to demonstrate its reusability and usability.
Reliability of the asset	For acquired software, such as application packages or class libraries, warranties that describe the policy for determining the responsibility for error corrections should be examined.
	For code-level assets, the asset's defect density or mean-time-to-correct, history-of-usage, and usage data should be reviewed.
	Code should have been tested with 100 percent statement coverage and at least 80 percent branch coverage.
	For design and code level assets, their complexity level should be analyzed using McCabe or Lorenz complexity metrics. The McCabe complexity of a module should be less than 10.
Matching the asset to the software requirements	To consider the requirements that the asset meets a "good fit" with the requirements of the software, generally less than 15 percent of the asset should require modification.

4.4.4.2 Select and Reuse Existing Software Requirements

IEEE Std. 1517 makes explicit the fundamental consumer reuse requirement to develop software project deliverables, including software requirements, from existing assets in the following task:

> *5.3.4.2 The developer shall select and reuse applicable software require-ments, if they exist and remain current, before establishing new ones. The developer shall define and document new software requirements to include, but not be limited to, reusability characteristics. (This task defines reuse-*

*related requirements in addition to those requirements specified in
IEEE/EIA Std. 12207.0-1996, task 5.3.4.1.)*[49]

Discussion

With this task, the developer is required to search for existing software requirements for use in this project. Also, the developer is required to include reusability characteristics in the requirements for the software product. The 12207 Standard specifies that software requirements define functional and capability specifications, interface specifications, safety specifications, security specifications, human-factors engineering requirements, data requirements, installation and acceptance requirements, documentation requirements, operation requirements, and maintenance requirements, but does not specifically mention reusability requirements. Reusability requirements define capability of the software product and/or its constituent parts to be used in multiple contexts.

Implementation Considerations

Figure 4-15 illustrates how the Use Case Model Deliverable from the Analysis Phase of the INVESCO OO methodology is extended to implement reuse requirements to develop software requirements using applicable assets. Reuse extensions to the deliverable are shown in italic type.

4.4.4.3 Use a Requirements Template to Write New Software Requirements

To assure overall software quality and compliance to the organization's software standards, IEEE Std. 1517 requires that new software requirements are developed with the use of a requirements template:

5.3.4.3 The developer shall write new requirements using an applicable requirements template, if any exists, and using the language and concepts from the domain models of the domains to which this software product belongs. The developer shall document software requirements. (This task defines reuse-related requirements in addition to those requirements specified in IEEE/EIA Std. 12207.0-1996, task 5.3.41.)[51]

Discussion

Typically, a requirements template is an outline of a specification document expressed in the organization's standard format. Using a template offers several advantages. It reduces the time needed to produce requirements specifications, ensures that the requirements specifications meet organization's standards, and improves the overall quality and completeness of the software requirements specifications as well as the software product itself.

The purpose of the domain model is to provide a common understanding of the domain's essential common components and the relationships that exist between them. The domain model serves as the foundation specification for requirements of software products belonging to the domain. It specifies the essential common and different features, functions, capabilities, and concepts that define the domain. It also specifies the terminology (language) that is to be used to describe the domain. In this task, IEEE Std. 1517 directs the developer to express software requirements using the domain model concepts and terminology. This will assist the developer in identifying candidate assets that can be used to develop this software product, as well as in identifying the reuse potential of this software product and its parts.

4.4.4.4 Evaluate Software Requirements

The 12207 Standard specifies a task to evaluate the general quality of each software project deliverable. However, it does not specifically mention that the evaluation should address the reusability of the deliverable. The IEEE Std. 1715 adds the following task to evaluate the reusability of the software requirements:

> *5.3.4.4 The developer shall evaluate software requirements according to reusability criteria. The results of the evaluation shall be documented. (This task defines reuse-related requirements in addition to those requirements specified in IEEE/EIA Std.12207.0-1996, task 5.3.4.2.)*[52]

Discussion

According to a note attached to the above task in IEEE Std. 1517, reusability of software requirements can be determined by checking:

- the compatibility of the software requirements to the domain models and domain architectures
- the compliance of the software requirements to the organization's reuse standards
- the usability of the software requirements

IEEE Std. 1517 defines usability as a measure of a software deliverable's functionality, ease of use, and efficiency.

USE CASE MODEL DELIVERABLE DESCRIPTION

Deliverable Description: The use case model provides a means of documenting the user's business needs in non-abstract business terms. It specifies the requirements for some area of software system functionality.

Required or Optional: Required

Supporting Techniques: *Selecting Reusable Assets Technique; Identifying New Reusable Assets Technique; Guidelines for Preparing an Asset for Reuse Technique; Redundancy Checking Technique*[50]

Relationship to Other Deliverables:

Deliverables which contribute to this deliverable:

Project Reuse Strategy; Context Diagram; Use Cases

Deliverables which this deliverable contributes to:

Analysis Report; All other analysis phase deliverables

And user interface design deliverables

Life of Deliverable: Living

Review Audience: Business Analyst, Project Leader, User Committee

Producer of Deliverable: Business Analyst

Custodian of Deliverable: Data Management

Suggested Tools: Select OMT

Tasks to Produce this Deliverable:

1. Obtain relevant actors from the context diagram.

2. *Look at the list of assets targeted for reuse in this project to identify any available use case models for possible reuse. Determine if the same or similar business area (domain) has been analyzed previously and if so, look for associated use cases and use case models. For each event that was defined by reusing an available event, look for its associated use case. To ensure optimal reuse occurs examine: use case models from within the project, use case models from previous projects, use case models from concurrent projects, use case templates, and search the reuse libraries and catalogs.*

3. For each stimulus on the context diagram, model an interaction from the actor to the appropriate use case.

4. For each response on the context diagram, model an interaction from the appropriate use case to the actor.

5. Model the interactions between use cases.

6. *Check and eliminate redundant use cases. Refer to Redundancy Checking Technique.*

7. *Determine if the use case model has future reuse potential. Refer to the Identifying New Reusable Assets Technique. If the project team believes that the use case model has reuse potential, follow the criteria of asset acceptance into the reuse library/catalog. Follow naming conventions, documentation standards, and enforce consistency of style. Refer to Guidelines for Preparing an Asset for Reuse Technique. Submit the candidate reusable use case model to the Reuse Support Group for possible inclusion in the reuse library/catalog.*

Figure 4-15. Example of Adding IEEE Std. 1517 Reuse Requirements to the Use Case Deliverable from the INVESCO OO Methodology

Implementation Considerations

Figure 4-16 illustrates how the Use Case to Requirements Cross Reference Deliverable description from the Analysis Phase of the INVESCO OO methodology is extended to implement the reuse requirement to include reusability criteria when evaluating software requirements. Reuse extensions are shown in italic type.

4.4.4.5 Report Software Requirements Reuse Information

Information about the value of practicing consumer reuse to produce the software requirements in this project should be captured and passed to the asset developers and asset managers. IEEE Std. 1517 adds the following task to the 12207 Standard Software Requirements Analysis Activity to assure that relevant reuse information is passed on to other interested parties:

> *5.3.4.5 The developer shall use the domain engineering feedback mechanism and the asset management communication mechanism to report reuse information about the software requirements.*[54]

Discussion

Capturing asset evaluation information from software projects is an excellent way to continually improve the future reusability and usability of an organization's asset inventory.

4.4.5 Adding Consumer Reuse to the Software Architectural Design Activity

In the 12207 Standard, the purpose of the Software Architectural Design Activity is to develop the software architectural design, along with associated deliverables, such as database designs, user documentation, and test requirements. The purpose remains the same in IEEE Std. 1517 with the added requirement that these deliverables shall be produced from existing assets whenever feasible to support and enable the practice of consumer reuse.

IEEE Std. 1517 adds seven new tasks to the Software Architectural Design Activity to support the practice of consumer reuse in this activity. Table 4-11 summarizes how the consumer reuse requirements are added to the 12207 Software Architectural Design Activity.

USE CASE TO REQUIREMENTS CROSS REFERENCE DELIVERABLE DESCRIPTION

Deliverable Description: Ensures completeness by mapping use cases to
                                 the business requirements in order to ensure that all
                                 requirements have been addressed by a use case.

Required or Optional: Required

Supporting Techniques: *Identifying New Reusable Assets; Guidelines for
                                 Preparing an Asset for Reuse*[53]

Relationship to Other Deliverables:

                                 Deliverables which contribute to this deliverable:
                                 Business Requirements; Architectural and Technical
                                 Requirements; Use Cases
                                 Deliverables which this deliverable contributes to:
                                 Analysis Report; Technical design Document

Life of Deliverable: Project duration

Review Audience: Business Analyst, Project Leader, Client Partner (optional)

Producer of Deliverable: Business Analyst

Custodian of Deliverable: Project team

Suggested Tools: Word Processor, Spreadsheet, KEY Planning Workstation
                                 Tool

Tasks to Produce this Deliverable:

1. Create a matrix of business requirements from Business Requirements to Uses Cases deliverables
2. Complete the matrix by marking the use cases that fulfill the requirement.
3. Review the matrix for any requirements not fulfilled by use cases and create new use cases or modify existing use cases to fulfill the requirements.
4. Review the matrix for any use cases which do not fulfill requirements and any new requirements or delete any unneeded use cases.
5. *Common business requirements were identified in Business Requirements deliverable. Review the matrix of common business requirements and mark the uses cases that fulfill these common requirements.*
6. *Make certain that these use cases have been developed with reuse in mind by following naming conventions, using the use case template to ensure consistency and following documentation standards. Refer to the Guidelines for Preparing an Asset for Reuse Technique.*

Figure 4-16. Example of Adding IEEE Std. 1517 Reuse Requirements to the Use Case to Requirements Cross reference Deliverable from the INVESCO OO Methodology

Table 4-11. Extending the Software Architectural Design Activity to Include Consumer Reuse

12207 TASK	1517 TASK	CONSUMER REUSE MINI LIFE CYCLE	DELIVERABLE BUILT / EVALUATED	ASSET REUSED / EVALUATED
5.3.5.1	5.3.5.1	Step 1: Search Step 2: Select Step 3: Build	Software architecture	Domain architecture; Domain models; Documentation assets
5.3.5.2	5.3.5.2	Step 1: Search Step 2: Select Step 3: Build	Software interfaces	Domain architecture; Interface assets
5.3.5.3	5.3.5.3	Step 1: Search Step 2: Select Step 3: Build	Database designs	Domain models; Database designs
5.3.5.4	5.3.5.4	Step 1: Search Step 2: Select Step 3: Build	User documentation	Documentation assets
5.3.5.5	5.3.5.5	Step 1: Search Step 2: Select Step 3: Build	Preliminary test requirements	Test requirements assets
5.3.5.6	5.3.5.6 5.3.5.7	Step 4: Evaluate and report	Activity deliverables	Assets used or attempted to be used to create activity deliverables

4.4.5.1 Derive the Software Architecture from the Domain Architecture

According to the 12207 Standard, a software architecture is a high-level design structure which identifies the software product's components. The software architecture is derived from a transformation of the software requirements into the design structure. In the following task, the IEEE Std. adds the requirement that the software architecture must also be derived from the domain architecture:

> *5.3.5.1 The developer shall derive a software architecture that is based on selected, applicable domain architectures. If no such domain architectures exist, the developer may define an architecture for this software product that is consistent with the domain models and that describes the structure of the software product and the software components that comprise this structure. The developer shall allocate software requirements to this architecture fol-*

lowing the domain models that correspond to the selected domain architecture, if it exists. The software architecture shall be documented reusing applicable documentation assets, if any exist. (This task defines reuse-related requirements in addition to those requirements specified in IEEE/EIA Std 12207.0-1996, task 5.3.5.1.)[55]

Discussion

The domain architecture is a high-level design structure serving as the "starter" design structure for all software products that belong to the domain. Many of the common design decisions are made when the domain architecture is created. This means that when the domain architecture is used by the developer, these decisions need not be remade. When all software products in the domain are based upon the same architecture, their ability to share and reuse assets is greatly enhanced. This speeds up the software product development process and eliminates rebuilding common components. Using a common architecture also improves the ability of the developer to identify appropriate assets that can be used to build software components and to recognize the reuse potential of software components built in this project.

Although ideal, IEEE Std. 1517 does not assume that an applicable domain architecture exists. The Standard provides for this situation by requiring the developer to search for domain models that may exist even though there is no applicable domain architecture. The domain models specify the common requirements shared by software products belonging to the domain. When applicable domain models exist, the developer will find them a useful guide to determine the software components that must be included in the design structure to implement the requirements for the software product.

A software architecture is not complete unless each software requirement is allocated to a software component in the architecture.

4.4.5.2 Derive Software Interface Designs that Comply with the Domain Architecture

To assure that the components in the software architecture will fit together and be able to work together, IEEE Std. 1517 adds the following task to the Software Architectural Design Activity:

5.3.5.2 Interfaces external to the software item and between the software components within the software item shall comply with the domain architectures interfaces and shall be derived from applicable assets, such as interface assets, if any exist. (This task defines reuse-related requirements in addition to those requirements specified in IEEE/EIA Std 12207.0-1996, task 5.3.5.2.)[56]

Discussion

An explanation of the terminology used in the above task will help explain its meaning. IEEE Std. 1517 defines the terms *software item* and *software component* in the same way as does the 12207 Standard. In the 12207 Standard, a system architecture may be composed of one or more software parts called *software configuration items,* or simply *software items.* A *configuration item* is described as "an entity within a configuration that satisfies an end use function and that can be uniquely identified at a given reference point."[57] The 12207 Standard requires that a software architecture, which is decomposed into software components, is developed for each software item.

In task 5.3.5.2 of the 12207 Standard, the developer is required to develop and document interface designs.[58] The interface provides information about what the component does (i.e., its function or behaviors) and how to use the component (i.e., its interaction mechanisms). In the companion task 5.3.5.2 of IEEE Std. 1517, the interface design requirement is extended to include compliance with the domain architecture. The domain architecture provides a "domain standard" for interface design that simplifies the interface design task and assures the design quality.

Implementation Considerations

Figure 4-17 illustrates how the Product/Machine Interface Deliverable from the Design Phase of the INVESCO OO methodology is extended to implement IEEE Std. 1517 requirements to derive software interfaces from applicable assets. Reuse-related extensions are shown in italic type.

4.4.5.3 Derive Database Designs from the Domain Models

In task 5.3.5.3 of the 12207 Standard, the developer is required to develop high-level database designs for the software product. In the companion task 5.3.5.3 of IEEE Std. 1517, the requirement is extended to support the practice of consumer reuse as follows:

> *5.3.5.3 Database designs shall be derived from selected domain models and database designs, if any exist. (This task defines reuse-related requirements in addition to those requirements specified in IEEE/EIA Std 12207.0-1996, task 5.3.5.3.)[60]*

Discussion

It is useful to develop the database designs from the domain models because the domain models define the fundamental concepts and the relationships between the concepts that are commonly shared by software products belonging to the domain.

Implementation Considerations

Domain models may be represented by commonly used analysis models such as entity relationship models, data flow diagram, or state transition diagrams. Basing database designs on the domain model can lead to further reuse in detailed design and implementation activities later on in the software life cycle.

4.4.5.4 Create User Documentation with Assets

Practicing consumer reuse requires that all software project deliverables including documentation deliverables are created from existing assets, if possible. IEEE Std. 1517 applies consumer reuse requirements to the creation of user documentation in the following task:

> *5.3.5.4 User documentation shall be created reusing applicable documentation assets, if any exist. (This task defines reuse-related requirements in addition to those requirements specified in IEEE/EIA 12207.0-1996, task 5.3.5.4.)*[61]

Implementation Considerations

Documentation assets should be high on the list of types of assets that provide reuse benefits to every software project. Documentation templates that aid in creation of any kind of software documentation, project report, and project plan can be provided in the form of word processing files. Documentation templates are fast and easy to create and make available in the organization's reuse catalog or reuse library. The reuse benefits of documentation templates are not only saving project time, but also ensuring that organization standards are followed and consistency is enforced across software project deliverables. This leads to higher quality software products that are easier to understand and hence, to maintain and reuse. Finally, documentation templates are not likely to offend the creative side of software developers because documentation is not something they enjoy doing. Many documentation templates are probably already in existence in some parts of the organization, just waiting to be harvested for reuse and added to the reuse catalog.

4.4.5.5 Create Preliminary Test Requirements with Assets

IEEE Std. 1517 supports the practice of consumer reuse by requiring that test requirements be developed from assets:

> *5.3.5.5 Preliminary test requirements shall be created reusing applicable test requirements, if any exist. (This task defines reuse-related requirements in addition to those requirements specified in IEEE/EIA Std 12207.0-1996, task 5.3.5.5.)*[62]

PRODUCT/MACHINE INTERFACES DELIVERABLE DESCRIPTION

Deliverable Description: Interfaces being developed to other products including data flowing in or out of the product from outside sources are described in terms of the API's or interface's functionality, parameters passed, and test cases.

Required or Optional: Required

Supporting Techniques: *Selecting Reusable Assets Technique; Identifying New Reusable Assets Technique; Guidelines for Preparing an Asset for Reuse Technique*[59]

Relationship to Other Deliverables:

Deliverables which contribute to this deliverable:
Business Requirements; Architectural and Technical Requirements; Design Object Interaction Diagram; Hardware Architecture Diagram
Deliverables which this deliverable contributes to:
Risk Analysis; Technical Design

Life of Deliverable: Project duration

Review Audience: Reviewed as part of the Technical Design review

Producer of Deliverable: Project team

Custodian of Deliverable: Project team

Suggested Tools: Word Processor

Tasks to Produce this Deliverable:

1. Develop a list of company and external products that interface with this product.
2. Obtain the interface information from the applicable INVESCO product area or external product vendors.
3. Document the formats of the API or interface. *Reuse available INVESCO standard GUI assets and other interface assets from the Reuse Library/Catalog. Look at the Project Reuse Strategy List of Assets Targeted for Reuse and the list of Assets Targeted to be Developed in this Project.*
4. Document test cases for the API or interface.
5. *Identify any newly created interface assets that have potential for reuse. Refer to the Identifying New Reusable Assets Technique. If an interface component has sufficient potential for future reuse, create it as an asset following the Guidelines for Preparing an Asset for Reuse Technique, and submit it to the Reuse Support Group for possible inclusion in the Reuse Library/Catalog.*

Figure 4-17. Example of Adding IEEE Std. 1517 Reuse Requirements to the INVESCO Methodology Product/Machine Interfaces Deliverable Description

Discussion

Test assets (such as test data, test scripts, test cases, and test plans) can provide the same reuse benefits to a project, as documentation assets. Reusing test assets helps to ensure that a software product is thoroughly tested and, hence, more reliable and maintainable. Since software testing is a very expensive component of the budget, reusing test assets can greatly reduce the overall cost of a software project.

Implementation Considerations

Figure 4-18 illustrates how the Business Requirements Test Plan Deliverable from the Analysis Phase of the INVESCO OO methodology is extended to implement IEEE Std. 1517 to create test requirements reusing test requirement assets. Extensions are shown in italic type.

4.4.5.6 Evaluate the Reusability of the Software Designs

The 12207 Standard requires an evaluation of the software architecture interface and database designs produced in the Software Architectural Design Activity based on the following evaluation criteria:

- Traceability of the software requirements to the software architecture

- Consistency between the components of the software architecture

- Appropriateness of design methods and standards used

- Feasibility of developing a detailed design based on this high-level design

- Feasibility of the operation and maintenance of a software product based on this software architecture, interface design, and database design

Since reuse is not explicitly mentioned in the 12207 Standard evaluation criteria, IEEE Std. 1517 adds reusability as an additional software design evaluation criterion in the following task:

> *5.3.5.6 The developer shall evaluate the software architecture, the interface, and database designs according to reusability criteria. The results of the evaluation shall be documented. (This task defines reuse-related requirements in addition to those requirements specified in IEEE/EIA Std. 12207.0-1996, task 5.3.5.6.)*[63]

Discussion

A note attached to IEEE Std. 1517 task 5.3.5.6 suggests reusability criteria to use to evaluate a high-level software design. Criteria include compliance with the organization's reuse standards, and the usability and reusability of the software architecture, the software component designs, and the database designs.

BUSINESS REQUIREMENTS TEST PLAN DELIVERABLE DESCRIPTION

Deliverable Description: Identify the business requirements that will need to be tested. The test plan should include schedules, quantitative and qualitative measures, test criteria, *reuse opportunities,* and reporting procedures.

Required or Optional: Required

Supporting Techniques:

Relationship to Other Deliverables:

    Deliverables which contribute to this deliverable: Business Requirements; Proposed High Level User Interface; Prototypes and Mockups; *Project Reuse Strategy*

    Deliverables which this deliverable contributes to: Analysis Report

Life of Deliverable: Project duration

Review Audience: Reviewed as part of the Analysis Report review

Producer of Deliverable: Business/Testing Analyst

Custodian of Deliverable: Business/Testing Analyst

Suggested Tools: Word Processor

Tasks to Produce this Deliverable:

1. *Determine whether any of the business requirements are common; i.e., occur in another software project.*

2. *For each common requirement, determine if it has been previously implemented and if a previously used test plan exists that can be reused in this project. Review the INVESCO Product Architecture Plan and the INVESCO Cross Product Matrix to determine where reuse of test plans is feasible.*

3. *If it does not exist but the requirement is common and therefore will need to be tested in multiple projects, then create the Business Requirements Test Plan in a manner that enables its reuse. Refer to the List of Assets Targeted for Reuse from the Project Reuse Strategy.*

Figure 4-18. Example of Adding IEEE Std. 1517 Reuse Requirements to the INVESCO Methodology Business Requirements Test Plan Deliverable

4.4.5.7 Report Software Architecture Reuse Information

Information about the value of practicing consumer reuse to produce the software architectural design in this project should be documented and made available throughout the organization. IEEE Std. 1517 adds the following task to the 12207 Standard Software Requirements Analysis Activity to assure that feedback about a project's reuse of existing assets and a project's development of new candidate assets is passed onto other reuse consumers and reuse producers:

> *5.3.5.7 The developer shall use the domain engineering feedback mechanism and the asset management communication mechanism to report reuse infor-mation about the software architectural design.*[64]

Discussion

Capturing design evaluation information from software projects is an excellent way to improve the reusability and usability of software designs that are developed by the organization's software project teams and to improve the organization's current design assets.

In a note attached to this task, IEEE Std. 1517 suggests that the following types of reuse design information should be captured by the project team at this stage of software development:

- Problems with domain architectures or domain models that the project team attempted to reuse to produce the software architectural design

- The project team's suggestions for improving the domain architectures and domain models they attempted to reuse or actually reused in this project

- List of the domain architectures and domain models that were reused in this project to produce the software architectural design

- Suggestions for using the software architectural design or its parts as the basis for creating new assets

4.4.6 Adding Consumer Reuse to Software Detailed Design Activity

The purpose of the Software Detailed Design Activity is to expand the high-level software product design produced by the Software Architectural Design Activity into a detailed design. Detailed designs are developed for each component of the software architecture, for the interface designs, for the database designs, and for the test requirements.

IEEE Std. 1517 adds six new tasks to the 12207 Standard Software Detailed Design Activity to require that the detailed designs are developed from existing assets whenever possible. Table 4-12 summarizes how IEEE Std. 1517 extends the tasks in 12207 Software Detailed Design Activity to introduce consumer reuse. The steps of the consumer mini life cycle are implemented by adding reuse tasks that correspond to existing 12207 tasks.

Table 4-12. Extending the Software Detailed Design Activity to
Include Consumer Reuse

12207 TASK	1517 TASK	CONSUMER REUSE MINI LIFE CYCLE	DELIVERABLE BUILT / EVALUATED	ASSET REUSED / EVALUATED
5.3.6.1	5.3.6.1	Step1: Search Step 2: Select Step 3: Build	Software component detailed design	Existing detailed design; Domain model
5.3.6.2	5.3.6.2	Step 1: Search Step 2: Select Step 3: Build	Interfaces; Interface documentation	Interface assets; Documentation assets
5.3.6.3	5.3.6.3	Step 1: Search Step 2: Select Step 3: Build	Database designs; Database documentation	Database design assets; Documentation assets
5.3.6.5	5.3.6.4	Step 1: Search Step 2: Select Step 3: Build	Test requirements	Test assets
5.3.6.7	5.3.6.5 5.3.6.6	Step 4: Evaluate and report	Deliverables built	Assets reused or attempted to be reused

Table 4-12. Extending the Software Detailed Design Activity to Include
Consumer Reuse

4.4.6.1 Select Software Component Detailed Design Assets

IEEE Std. 1517 adds the following task to require the developer to search for applicable design assets to use to create the detailed design for each software component in the software architecture:

> *5.3.6.1 The developer shall select and reuse an applicable detailed design for each software component, if any exists. If none exists, the developer shall develop a new detailed design for the software component. When writing new detailed designs, the developer shall use the language and concepts from the selected domain models. The developer shall use data structures and naming conventions from the domain models when describing detailed designs. (This task defines reuse-related requirements in addition to those requirements specified in IEEE/EIA Std. 12207.0-1996, task 5.3.6.1.)[65]*

Discussion

Practicing consumer reuse at the design stage of the software life cycle means that the development of every design deliverable ideally should be guided by the domain architecture and the domain models. This applies to both high-level and detailed software designs. Using the language and concepts from the domain models to develop the detailed design of a software component ensures that the developers in this project and in other projects (development and maintenance) will share a common understanding of the component.

Implementation Considerations

Figure 4-19 illustrates how the Design Class Model Deliverable Description from the Design Phase of the INVESCO OO methodology is extended to implement IEEE Std. 1517 reuse requirement to create software designs from available, applicable assets. Extensions are in italic type.

4.4.6.2 Develop Interface Designs with Assets

Software interface designs are another major deliverable of the design stage of the software life cycle. The 12207 Standard requires the development of a detailed design for each software interface. In the following task, IEEE Std. 1517 expands this requirement by adding the use of assets and compliance to the domain standards to support the practice of consumer reuse in the detailed design stage:

> *5.3.6.2 The developer shall develop and document interfaces external to the software item, between software components, and between software units that are compliant domain interface standards. The developer shall reuse applicable assets, if any exist. (This task defines reuse-related requirements in addition to those requirements specified in IEEE/EIA Std. 12207.0-1996, task 5.3.6.2.)[67]*

Discussion

IEEE Std. 1517 uses the term *software unit* in the same way as the 12207 Standard. The 12207 Standard defines *software unit* as "a separately compilable piece of code."[68]

4.4.6.3 Develop Detailed Database Designs with Assets

The 12207 Standard specifies task 5.3.6.3 to require the development of detailed database designs in the Software Detailed Design Activity. With the following task, IEEE Std. 1517 expands the 12207 Standard task to support the practice of consumer reuse:

> *5.3.6.3 The developer shall select and reuse applicable detailed designs and documentation for the database, if they exist. (This task defines reuse-related requirements in addition to those requirements specified in IEEE/EIA Std. 12207.0-1996, task 5.3.6.3.)[69]*

DESIGN CLASS MODEL DELIVERABLE DESCRIPTION

Deliverable Description: The design class model defines the business classes, their attributes, operations and relationships with one another as they are intended to be implemented.

Required or Optional: Required

Supporting Techniques: *If reuse is to be practiced in the project, refer to these reuse techniques: Selecting Reusable Assets Technique; Identifying New Reusable Assets Technique; Guidelines for Preparing an Asset for Reuse Technique; Redundancy Checking Technique[66]*

Relationship to Other Deliverables:

Deliverables which contribute to this deliverable:

Project Reuse Strategy; Analysis Class Model

Deliverables which this deliverable contributes to:

Design Interaction Diagram; Design State Transition Diagram; Technical Design Document

Applicable Standards: Fairway Object Modeling Standards until general standards are approved.

Life of Deliverable: Living

Review Audience: Reviewed as part of the Design Document review

Producer of Deliverable: Object Analyst and Systems Analyst

Custodian of Deliverable: Information Resource Management Group

Suggested Tools: Select OMT Tool

Tasks to Produce this Deliverable:

1. *Look for any classes or class parts than can be reused to create this class model. Refer to the Selecting Asset for Reuse Technique and the Project Reuse Strategy.*

2. Business classes and their associations are used intact from the analysis class model by including them from a corporate view in the Select OMT tool.

3. Business control classes are transformed intact into the design model.

4. Additional control classes are added as required.

5. Design patterns (e.g., Gamma) may be applied.

6. Design container classes are created for each 1:M association.

7. Data manipulation classes may be added.

8. Wrapper classes may be added.

9. Any additional associations between design classes are modeled.

10. *Redundancies in the model are eliminated. Refer to Redundancy Checking Technique.*

11. *Future reuse potential of the class model is determined. Refer to the Identifying New Reusable Assets Technique. If it is deemed sufficient, then the class model is prepared for reuse by following the Guidelines to Prepare an Asset for Reuse Technique. The class model is then submitted to the Reuse Support Group for possible inclusion in the Reuse Library/Catalog.*

Figure 4-19. Example of Adding IEEE Std. 1517 Reuse Requirements to the INVESCO Methodology Design Class Model Deliverable

Implementation Considerations

When searching for any type of design asset, and finding that only the associated code asset exists, attempt to reverse engineer the design from the code using reverse engineering and program code analyzer tools.

4.4.6.4 Develop Test Requirements with Assets

The 12207 Standard includes a task in the Software Detailed Design Activity to expand the preliminary test requirements created in the Software Architectural Design Activity. IEEE Std. 1517 adds the consumer reuse requirements for this task by adding the following task:

> *5.3.6.4 The developer shall reuse applicable test assets to create test requirements, if any exist. (This task defines reuse-related requirements in addition to those requirements specified in IEE/EIA Std. 12207.0-1996, task 5.3.5.5.)*[70]

Implementation Considerations

To identify reusable test requirements for this software product, match the product's software requirements to any common requirements included in the domain model. Then, search for existing test requirements that match the domain model requirements shared by this product. Figure 4-20 illustrates how the INVESCO Methodology adds reuse considerations to test requirements development.

4.4.6.5 Evaluate and Report the Reusability of the Detailed Software Designs

The 12207 Standard requires an evaluation of the detailed software designs and test requirements using the following evaluation criteria:

- Traceability of the software requirements
- Consistency with the software architectural design
- Appropriateness of design methods and standards used
- Feasibility of testing a software product developed from these designs
- Feasibility of the operation and maintenance of a software product developed from these designs

Since reuse is not explicitly mentioned in the 12207 Standard evaluation criteria, IEEE Std. 1517 adds the following tasks to evaluate and report the reusability of the software designs:

> *5.3.6.5 The developer shall evaluate the software detailed design and test requirements according to reusability criteria. The results of the evaluation shall be documented. (This task defines reuse-related requirements in addition to those requirements specified in IEEE/EIA Std. 12207.0-1996, task 5.3.6.7.)*[71]

5.3.6.6 The developer shall use the domain engineering feedback mechanism and the asset management mechanism to report the reuse information about the software design.[72]

Discussion

In a note attached to IEEE Std. 1517 task 5.3.6.5, it is suggested that reusability criteria to use to evaluate a detailed software design include:

- Compliance with the domain models, domain architectures and the organization's reuse standards
- Usability and reusability of the software designs and test requirements
- Suggestions for modifying the software product requirements to enable a higher level of reuse in developing the software product deliverables
- Future potential for reusing the software designs and test requirements

4.4.7 Adding Consumer Reuse to the Coding and Testing Activity

The principal deliverable of the 12207 Standard Coding and Testing Activity is tested and documented software code. IEEE Std. 1517 adds the requirement that the software code must be produced reusing code and test assets, if applicable assets exist. Table 4-13 summarizes the tasks that IEEE Std. 1517 adds to the 12207 Coding and Testing Activity to introduce consumer reuse requirements.

Table 4-13. Extending the Software Coding and Testing Activity to Include Consumer Reuse

12207 TASK	1517 TASK	CONSUMER REUSE MINI LIFE CYCLE	DELIVERABLE BUILT / EVALUATED	ASSET REUSED / EVALUATED
5.3.7.1	5.3.7.1	Step 1: Search Step 2: Select Step 3: Evaluate and report	Tested and documented code for a software unit	Code; Databases; Test procedures; Test data; Domain models; Domain architectures
5.3.7.5	5.3.7.2 5.3.7.3	Step 4: Evaluate and report	Deliverables built	Assets reused or attempted to be reused in this activity

TESTING REQUIREMENTS DELIVERABLE DESCRIPTION

Deliverable Description: A description of the testing needed to test the functional business requirements of the software system

Required or Optional: Required

Supporting Techniques: *Selecting Reusable Assets Technique; Identifying New Reusable Assets Technique; Guidelines for Preparing an Asset for Reuse Technique*

Relationship to Other Deliverables:

Deliverables which contribute to this deliverable:

Business Requirements; Expected Volumes and

Frequencies; Use Cases; *Project Reuse Strategy;*

Usability Test Plan; Design Class Model; Use Case/

Class CRUD Matrix; Systems Controls; Database Design

Deliverables which this deliverable contributes to:

Analysis Report; Business Design Document; Technical

Design Document; Detailed Test Scripts

Life of Deliverable: Project duration

Review Audience: Reviewed as part of the Business Requirements Document and the Business/Technical Design Document review

Producer of Deliverable: Testing Analyst

Custodian of Deliverable: Testing Analyst

Suggested Tools: Word Processor

Tasks to Produce this Deliverable:

1. Create a high-level description of the testing needed. *For each functional business requirement, determine if the requirement is common; i.e., occurs in multiple software systems. If yes, determine if it has been previously tested and if its test plan can be reused in this project. If it is common, but has not been previously tested, consider how to create its test plan so it will be reusable. Refer to the Selecting Reusable Assets Technique, and Identifying New Reusable Assets Technique.*

2. Determine if any set up is needed before testing (file conversions, option settings, etc.).

3. Include special types of data that may be needed: fund types, accounts, year end matrices, etc.

4. Note any expected volumes and frequencies.

5. Incorporate all expected outcomes from your test cases.

6. Identify regression testing needed for modified classes, frameworks, or other subsystems.

7. Build on the plan developed in the analysis phase by adding detail for all the above items.

8. Identify any network configurations for both hardware and software.

9. Incorporate any technical implementation items that need to be covered by testing; e.g., referential integrity between database tables, foreign keys on databases, object inheritance, etc.

10. *Determine if this test plan could be reused. If yes, define the test plan for reuse by taking into consideration where and how it would be reused. Refer to Identifying New Reusable Assets Technique and Guidelines for Preparing an Asset for Reuse Technique.*

Figure 4-20. Example of Adding IEEE Std. 1517 Reuse Requirements to the INVESCO Methodology Testing Requirements Deliverable

4.4.7.1 Produce and Test Software Units with the Use of Assets

To encourage consumer reuse, IEEE Std. 1517 adds a task to remind the developer to produce software life cycle deliverables (such as code, test procedures and test data) using assets:

> *5.3.7.1 The developer shall select and reuse applicable software units, databases, test procedures, and test data, if any exist, in order to produce and test each software unit. When producing new code for software units or a new database, the developer shall use the language and concepts from the domain models and domain architectures. Each software unit and database developed shall be documented reusing applicable documentation assets, if any exist. (This task defines reuse-related requirements in addition to those requirements specified in IEEE/EIA Std. 12207.0-1996, task 5.3.7.1.)*[73]

Discussion

Using the language and concepts from the domain models and the domain architectures to develop software code increases the reusability of the code and the possibility of finding applicable existing documentation and test assets for the software units.

Implementation Considerations

Since reusing test assets can save a great deal of time, the developer should perform a thorough search for candidate test assets. When searching for reusable test data, test scripts, and test cases, the developer should remember that although the existing software code may not be reusable, its associated test plan and test data may be reusable.

Figure 4-21 illustrates how the Code/Executable Component Deliverable description from the Construction Phase of the INVESCO OO methodology is extended to implement IEEE Std. 1517 reuse requirement to reuse applicable code assets. Figure 4-22 illustrates how the Detailed Test Scripts Deliverable from the Construction Phase of the INVESCO OO methodology is extended to implement IEEE Std. 1517 requirement to reuse applicable test assets. Extensions are indicated in italic type.

4.4.7.2 Evaluate the Reusability of the Software Code

The 12207 Standard requires an evaluation of the software code and tests using the following evaluation criteria in the 12207 task 5.3.7.5:[76]

- Traceability of code and tests to software requirements and software design
- Consistency with the design of the software item
- Appropriateness of coding methods and standards used
- Feasibility of software integration and testing of the code
- Test coverage of the code
- Feasibility of the operation and maintenance of the code

CODE/EXECUTABLE COMPONENT DELIVERABLE DESCRIPTION

Deliverable Description:	Executable components or code is the final deliverable of the construction phase.
Required or Optional:	Required
Supporting Techniques:	*Redundancy Checking Technique; Selecting Reusable Assets technique; Identifying New reusable Assets Technique; Guidelines for Preparing an Asset for ReuseTechnique[74]*

Relationship to Other Deliverables:

Deliverables which contribute to this deliverable:

Project Reuse Strategy; Prototypes and Mockups;

Design Class Model; Design Object Interaction Diagram;

Design State Transition Diagram; System Controls;

Testing Requirements

Deliverables which this deliverable contributes to:

Installation Plan; Back-out Plan; Support Plan; Usability

Test reports; Installation; Technical Reviews

Life of Deliverable:	Living
Review Audience:	Programmers, Project Leaders, System Analysts
Producer of Deliverable:	Programmer
Custodian of Deliverable:	Library Management
Suggested Tools:	Visual Age, Smalltalk, C++, COBOL

Tasks to Produce this Deliverable:

1. Obtain appropriate coding standards.

2. Review the Technical Design Document.

3. Review the Business Design Document.

4. Develop a unit test script

5. *To ensure that code reuse occurs, search for code that can be reused to create this code component. Refer to Selecting Reusable Assets Technique and the Project Reuse Strategy.*

6. Develop the code

7. Unit test the code

8. Perform the code review

9. *Determine if the code and its associated test script have potential for future reuse. Refer to the Identifying New Reusable Assets Technique. If yes, develop the code component as a reusable asset following the Guidelines for Preparing an Asset for Reuse Technique. In all circumstances, develop the code to satisfy the INVESCO naming conventions, documentation standards, and testing standards. Use the code skeleton from the Reuse Catalog to ensure the format is consistent.*

Figure 4-21. Example of Adding IEEE Std. 1517 Reuse Requirements to the INVESCO Methodology Code/Executable Component Deliverable

---

DETAILED TEST SCRIPTS DELIVERABLE DESCRIPTION

Deliverable Description: A written, dated document that defines the required testing for each facility affected by the project, as well as the usability objectives or requirements.

Required or Optional: Required

Supporting Techniques: TA2000 scripts; *Selecting Reusable Assets Technique; Identifying New Reusable Assets Technique; Guidelines for Preparing an Asset for Reuse*[75]

Relationship to Other Deliverables:

Deliverables which contribute to this deliverable: *Reuse Project Strategy;* Construction: Use Cases; Testing Requirements

Life of Deliverable: Living

Review Audience: Reviewed as part of the Project testing review.

Producer of Deliverable: Testing Analyst

Custodian of Deliverable: Testing Analyst

Suggested Tools: Word Processor

Tasks to Produce this Deliverable:

1. Review the pertinent analysis phase deliverables.

2. Review the relevant portions of the Business Design.

3. Review other design phase deliverables.

4. Create a test script for each detailed use case that addresses specific business requirements. *For each use case created by reusing an available use case, obtain and examine the associated test script to determine if it can be reused to create this test script. Refer to Selecting Reusable Assets Technique and the Project Reuse Strategy.*

5. *For each newly created test script, determine if it along with its associated use case has sufficient future reuse potential to merit creating it as a reusable asset. Refer to Identifying New Reusable Assets Technique. If yes, refer to the Guidelines for Preparing an Asset for Reuse Technique.*

Figure 4-22. Example of Adding IEEE Std. 1517 Reuse Requirements to the INVESCO Methodology Detailed Test Scripts Deliverable

Since reuse is not explicitly mentioned in the 12207 Standard evaluation criteria, IEEE Std. 1517 adds the following task to evaluate the reusability of the software designs:

> *5.3.7.2 The developer shall evaluate the software code and tests according to reusability criteria. The results of the evaluation shall be documented. (This task defines reuse-related requirements in addition to those requirements specified in IEEE/EIA Std. 12207.0-1996, task 5.3.7.5.)*[76]

Discussion

A note attached to IEEE Std. 1517 task 5.3.7.2 suggests reusability criteria to use to evaluate a detailed software design include:

- Compliance with the domain models, domain architectures and the organization's reuse standards
- Usability and reusability of the code and tests assets to produce tested code
- Future potential for reusing the software code and tests

Implementation Considerations

Figure 4-21 is also an example of how the INVESCO OO methodology is extended to implement IEEE Std. 1517 reuse requirement for creating code to meet a company's reusability criteria.

4.4.7.3 Report Reuse Information about the Software Code and Tests

Any new code or tests that were developed in this project and are deemed by the project team to have potential for future reuse are to be reported to the groups who manage and develop assets for the domain:

> *5.3.7.3 The developer shall use the domain engineering feedback mechanism and the asset Management communication mechanism to report reuse information about new software code, test procedures, and test data.*[78]

4.4.8 Adding Consumer Reuse to the Software Integration Activity

The primary function of the 12207 Software Integration Activity is to integrate software units and software components into a documented, tested, software item based on a software integration plan. IEEE Std. 1517 extends the activity by adding the consumer reuse requirements for producing the software integration plan and the documented, tested software item from assets. Table 4-14 shows the IEEE Std. 1517 reuse-related tasks added to this activity.

Table 4-14. Extending the Software Integration Activity to Include Consumer Reuse

12207 TASK	1517 TASK	CONSUMER REUSE MINI LIFE CYCLE	DELIVERABLE BUILT / EVALUATED	ASSET REUSED / EVALUATED
5.3.8.1	5.3.8.1	Step 1: Search Step 2: Select Step 3: Build	Integration Plan	Integration plan template
5.3.8.2	5.8.8.2	Step 1: Search Step 2: Select Step 3: Build	Documented software item	Documentation assets
5.3.8.4	5.3.8.3	Step 1: Search Step 2: Select Step 3: Build	Qualification tests	Test assets
5.8.8.5	5.3.8.4 5.3.8.5	Step: 4 Evaluate and report	Integration plan; Software design; Software code; Tests: User documentation	Assets reused or attempted to be reused

4.4.8.1 Create and Document an Integration Plan Reusing an Integration Plan Template

Because an integration plan is a common requirement for all software projects, an organization should consider providing a template to produce a software integration plan. IEEE Std. 1517 requires the use of a template to build and document the software integration plan:

> *5.3.8.1 The developer shall create and document an integration plan, reusing an applicable integration plan template, if any exists, to define the resources and procedures for integrating software units and components into the software item. (This task defines reuse-related requirements in addition to those requirements specified in IEEE/EIA Std. 12207.0-1996, task 5.3.8.1.)*[79]

Discussion

Building the integration plan from a reusable template ensures that the plan will be complete and capable of meeting the organization's software integration and testing standards.

4.4.8.2 Create User Documentation with Assets

Practicing consumer reuse requires that all software life cycle documentation deliverables are created from existing documentation assets, if possible. IEEE Std. 1517 applies consumer reuse requirements to the creation of the software item documentation in the following task:

> *5.3.8.2 The developer shall document the software item and the test results reusing applicable documentation assets, if any exist. (This task defines re-use-related requirements in addition to those requirements specified in IEEE/EIA 12207.0-1996, task 5.3.5.4.)*[80]

Implementation Considerations

Figure 4-23 illustrates how the Technical Documentation Deliverable from the Construction Phase of the INVESCO OO methodology is extended to implement IEEE Std. 1517 reuse requirement to develop documentation reusing applicable assets. Extensions are shown in italic type.

4.4.8.3 Develop Qualification Tests Reusing Test Assets

The 12207 Standard requires the creation and execution of software qualification tests for each software item in a software product. The purpose of qualification testing is to demonstrate that the software product complies with its software requirements. As explained in the 12207 Standard, qualification is "the process of demonstrating whether an entity is capable of fulfilling specified requirements."[82] IEEE Std. 1517 extends this requirement with the addition of requiring the reuse of assets to create and document the software qualification tests:

> *5.3.8.3 The developer shall develop a set of qualification tests, test cases, and test procedures using applicable test assets, if any exist, to test each qualification requirement of the software item. (This task defines the reuse-related requirements in addition to those requirements specified in IEEE/EIA 12207.0-1996, task 5.3.8.4.)*[83]

Implementation Considerations

For example, if use cases expressed in UML notation have been used to describe the software requirements, then the existing test cases and test data associated with the use cases may be reused to create the software qualification tests.

TECHNICAL DOCUMENTATION DELIVERABLE DESCRIPTION

Deliverable Description: Technical documentation for object technology
                                   should include a discussion of the following components:
                                   objects, methods, libraries, classes, error messages,
                                   compiler versions, calling conventions, and
                                   inter-relatedness.

Required or Optional: Required

Supporting Techniques: *Guidelines for Preparing an Asset for Reuse Technique*[81]

Relationship to Other Deliverables:

                                   Deliverables which contribute to this deliverable:

                                   Business Design Document; Technical Design Document;
                                   Deferred Event Procedure

Life of Deliverable: Living

Review Audience: Project Leader; Corporate Marketing and Technical
                                   Communications

Producer of Deliverable: Project team

Custodian of Deliverable: Information Resource Management

Suggested Tools: Word Processor, Desktop publishing

Tasks to Produce this Deliverable:

1. Meet with the project team to develop an outline, to discuss the writing responsibilities for the various components for which documentation is required, and to determine the timeframes for completing each component.

2. Draft the document. *For each reusable component created in the project, document the component according to the Guidelines for Preparing an Asset for Reuse Technique.*

3. Conduct reviews of the document. *Include reusability in the review criteria.*

4. Conduct reviews of the document *including a reuse consultant among the reviewers.*

5. Update the document based on the reviews.

6. Finalize the document and make it available to all interested parties.

Figure 4-23. Example of Adding IEEE Std. 1517 Reuse Requirements to the INVESCO Methodology Technical Documentation Deliverable

4.4.8.4 Evaluate and Report the Reusability of the Software Integration Activity Deliverables

The 12207 Standard requires an evaluation of the software code and tests using the following evaluation criteria in the 12207 task 5.3.8.5:[84]

- Traceability of the software to the system requirements
- Consistency with the system requirements
- Appropriateness of testing methods and standards used

- Feasibility of software qualification testing
- Test coverage of the requirements of the software item
- Feasibility of the operation and maintenance of the software

Since reuse is not explicitly mentioned in the 12207 Standard evaluation criteria, IEEE Std. 1517 adds the following tasks to evaluate and report the reusability of the Software Integration Activity deliverables:

> *5.3.8.4 The developer shall evaluate the integration plan, software design, code, tests, and user documentation according to reusability criteria. The results of the evaluation shall be documented. (This task defines reuse-related requirements in addition to those requirements specified in IEEE/EIA Std 12207.0-1996, task 5.3.8.5.)*[65]

> *5.3.8.5 The developer shall use the domain engineering feedback mechanism and the asset management communication mechanism to report reuse information about software integration.*[66]

Discussion

A note attached to IEEE Std. 1517 task 5.3.8.4 suggests reusability criteria to use to evaluate the software integration plan, software design, code, test and user documentation include:

- Compliance with the organization's reuse standards
- Usability and reusability of the software item, test cases and test data
- Future potential for reusing the software design, code, user documentation, test cases, and test data

4.4.9 Adding Consumer Reuse to Software Qualification Testing Activity

The 12207 Standard includes an activity to demonstrate through software qualification testing that a software item complies with all of its requirements. The intention of the 12207 Standard is that this activity will be performed for each software item of the software product.

IEEE Std. 1517 adds consumer reuse requirements to qualification testing by adding tasks that require the qualification tests results to be created by reusing applicable assets. Table 4-15 summarizes how IEEE Std. 1517 adds consumer mini life cycle to the Software Qualification Testing Activity.

Table 4-15. Extending the Software Qualification Testing Activity to Include Consumer Reuse

12207 TASK	1517 TASK	CONSUMER REUSE MINI LIFE CYCLE	DELIVERABLE BUILT / EVALUATED	ASSET REUSED / EVALUATED
5.3.9.1	5.3.9.1	Step 1: Search Step 2: Select Step 3: Build	Software qualification testing documentation	Documentation assets
5.3.9.3	5.3.9.2 5.3.9.3	Step 4: Evaluate and report	Software design; Code; Test cases; User documentation	Documentation assets

4.4.9.1 Document Software Qualification Testing Results Using Assets

IEEE Std. 1517 requires that test documentation be produced using applicable documentation assets in the following task:

> *5.3.9.1 The developer shall document the results of the software qualification testing reusing applicable documentation assets, if any exist. (This task defines reuse-related requirements in addition to those requirements specified in IEEE/EIA Std 12207.0 - 1996, task 5.3.9.3.)*[87]

Discussion

Reusing documentation assets not only saves project time but also ensures that organization standards are followed and consistency is enforced across software project deliverables. This leads to higher quality software products that are easier to understand, maintain, and reuse. Figure 4-24 illustrates how the Code Review Issues Deliverable from the Construction Phase of the INVESCO OO methodology is extended to implement IEEE Std. 1517 reuse requirements for including reusability criteria in code reviews. Extensions are shown in italic type.

CODE REVIEW ISSUES DELIVERABLE DESCRIPTION

Deliverable Description: This deliverable lists all the issues, such as coding errors and non-conformance to standards *and to reuse requirements,* and associated resolutions as a result of a technical review of the code.

Required or Optional: Required

Supporting Techniques: *Guidelines for Preparing an Asset for Reuse Technique*[88]

Relationship to Other Deliverables:

Deliverables which contribute to this deliverable:
Code; Deferred Event Procedure; Design Class Model
Deliverables which this deliverable contributes to:
Code; Deferred Event Procedure

Life of Deliverable: Project phase

Review Audience: Project team, Systems Analyst; *Reuse Consultant*

Producer of Deliverable: Project team

Custodian of Deliverable: Project team

Suggested Tools: Word Processor

Tasks to Produce this Deliverable:

1.   Review the code review/inspection procedure.

2.   Schedule a review meeting.

3.   Review the appropriate language/design standards. *Review the Guidelines for Preparing an Asset for Reuse Technique. If the code is to be reused, evaluate its reusability in terms of the reuse guidelines.*

4.   Review the material before the meeting. Mark all the issues in the code. The meeting is the place to discuss issues, not review the code.

5.   Using the design Class Model, verify that the methods and programs have incorporated all the requested changes.

6.   Raise issues relating to standards, maintenance, logic, documentation *and reusability.*

7.   Logically walk-through the program to ensure that it will run as expected.

Figure 4-24. Example of Adding IEEE Std. 1517 Reuse Requirements to the INVESCO Methodology Code Review Issues Deliverable

4.4.9.2 Evaluate the Reusability of the Software, Design, Code, Test Assets and User Documentation

IEEE Std. 1517 adds tasks to evaluate and report the reusability of the major software projects deliverables as part of the Software Qualification Testing Activity:

5.3.9.2 The developer shall evaluate the software design, code, test assets, and user documentation according to reusability criteria. The results of the evaluation shall be documented. (This task defines reuse-related requirements in addition to those requirements specified in IEEE/EIA Std 12207.0-1996, task 5.3.93.)[89]

5.3.9.3 The developer shall use the domain engineering feedback mechanism and the asset management communication mechanism to report the reuse information about the software qualification testing.[90]

Discussion

A note attached to IEEE Std. 1517 task 5.3.9.2 suggests reusability criteria to use to evaluate the software integration plan, software design, code, test and user documentation include:

- Compliance with the organization's reuse standards
- Usability and reusability of the software design, code, test assets, and user documentation
- Future potential for reusing the software design, code, user documentation, and test assets

4.4.10 Adding Consumer Reuse to the System Integration Activity

According to the 12207 Standard, system integration is the responsibility of the software product developer only if it is required by the contract. System integration entails:

- integrating the software items with hardware items and manual items to form the complete system
- creating a set of system qualification tests
- evaluating the system.

Table 4-16 shows the consumer reuse requirements that IEEE Std. 1517 adds to System Integration Activity.

Table 4-16. Extending the System Integration Activity to Include Consumer Reuse

12207 TASK	1517 TASK	CONSUMER REUSE MINI LIFE CYCLE	DELIVERABLE BUILT / EVALUATED	ASSET REUSED / EVALUATED
5.3.10.2	5.3.10.1	Step 1: Search Step 2: Select Step 3: Build	System qualification test cases, test data, and test procedures	Test assets
5.3.10.3	5.3.10.2 5.3.10.3	Step 4: Evaluate and report	System	Test assets

4.4.10.1 Create System Qualification Tests with Test Assets

IEEE Std. 1517 adds the consumer reuse requirement that system qualification tests are created with the use of appropriate test assets rather than from scratch:

> *5.3.10.1 For each qualification requirement of the system, a set of tests, test cases, and test procedures shall be developed, reusing applicable test assets. (This task defines reuse-related requirements in addition to those requirements specified in IEEE/EIA Std. 12207.0-1996, task 5.3.10.1)[91]*

4.4.10.2. Evaluate and Report the Reusability of the System

In addition to adding the requirements that system qualification tests shall be created from test assets when possible, IEEE Std. 1517 adds the requirement that reusability is included in the system evaluation criteria and is formally reported:

> *5.3.10.2 The integrated system shall be evaluated according to reusability criteria. The results of the evaluation shall be documented. (This task defines reuse-related requirements in addition to those requirements specified in IEEE/EIA Std. 12207.0-1996, task 5.3.10.3.)[92]*

> *5.3.10.3 The developer shall use the domain engineering feedback mechanism and the asset management communication mechanism to report reuse information about the integrated system, set of tests, test cases and test procedures.[93]*

Discussion

With the addition of reusability criteria, the usefulness of the test assets, as well as the reuse potential of the system, its parts and its qualification tests are examined during the system evaluation.

By reporting the results of the reuse examination, software developers can provide information about the practical value of assets and about their suggestions for new assets that can be useful in future projects.

4.4.11 Adding Consumer Reuse to the System Qualification Testing Activity

According to the 12207 Standard, system qualification testing is performed to demonstrate that the system meets each and every one of its requirements and to evaluate the feasibility of operating and maintaining the system. As shown in table 4-17, the IEEE Std.1517 adds the requirement to include reusability in the system evaluation.

Table 4-17. Extending the System Qualification Testing Activity to Include Consumer Reuse

12207 TASK	1517 TASK	CONSUMER REUSE MINI LIFE CYCLE	DELIVERABLE BUILT / EVALUATED	ASSET REUSED / EVALUATED
5.3.11.2	5.3.11.1 5.3.11.2	Step 4: Evaluate and report	System	—

4.4.11.1 Evaluate and Report the Reusability of the System

Since the 12207 Standard does not explicitly mention reusability in its list of system evaluation criteria, IEEE Std. 1517 adds the criterion of reusability in the following task:

> 5.3.11.1 The system shall be evaluated according to reusability criteria. The results of the evaluation shall be documented. (This task defines the reuse-related requirements in addition to those requirements specified in IEEE/EIA Std. 12207.0-1996, task 5.3.11.2.)[94]

The consumer reuse requirement for reporting software reusability evaluation results is covered in the following IEEE Std.1517 task:

> 5.3.11.2 The developer shall use the domain engineering feedback mechanism and the asset management mechanism to report reuse information about system qualification testing.[95]

Discussion

Consumer reuse requires that reusability of every software life cycle deliverable, including the software parts of a system, should be examined and that reusability feedback should be given to those responsible for managing and/or creating software assets for the organization. A note attached to IEEE Std. 1517 task noted above suggests that reusability criteria for the software parts of the system include their usability, reusability, and reuse.

4.4.12 Adding Consumer Reuse to the Software Installation Activity

The primary function of the Software Installation Activity is to create and execute a plan to install the software product on the target environment. To support consumer reuse, IEEE Std. 1517 adds the requirement to create the installation plan using an installation plan template if possible. Table 4-18 summarizes the tasks that IEEE Std. 1517 adds to the Software Installation Activity to support consumer reuse.

Table 4-18. Extending the Software Installation Activity to Include Consumer Reuse

12207 TASK	1517 TASK	CONSUMER REUSE MINI LIFE CYCLE	DELIVERABLE BUILT / EVALUATED	ASSET REUSED / EVALUATED
5.3.12.1	5.3.12.1	Step 1: Search Step 2: Select Step 3: Build	Installation plan	Installation plan template
—	5.3.12.2 5.3.12.3	Step 4: Evaluate and report	Installation plan	Installation plan template

4.4.12.1 Create and Document an Integration Plan Reusing an Integration Plan Template

Because a software installation plan, like a software integration plan, is a common requirement for all software development projects an organization should consider providing a template to produce a software installation plan. IEEE Std. 1517 requires the use of a template to build and document the software installation plan in the following task:

> *5.3.12.1 The developer shall create and document an installation plan, reusing an applicable installation plan template, if any exists, to define the resources and procedures to install the software product on its target environment(s). (This task defines reuse-related requirements in addition to those requirements specified in IEEE/EIA Std. 12207.0-1996, task 5.3.12.1.)*[96]

Discussion

Building the installation plan from a reusable template ensures that the resources needed to install the software product will be available and that the installation of the software will follow the organization's software installation procedures.

Implementation Considerations

Figure 4-25 illustrates how the Installation Plan Deliverable description from the Implementation Phase of the INVESCO OO methodology is extended to implement IEEE Std. 1517 reuse requirement to develop an installation plan reusing an applicable installation plan template.

4.4.12.2 Evaluate the Installation Plan and the Installation Plan Template

IEEE Std. 1517 also adds the requirements to evaluate and report the reuse potential of the software installation plan and the reusability of the software installation plan template:

> *5.3.12.2 The installation plan and installation plan template shall be evaluated according to reusability criteria. The results of the evaluation shall be documented.[98]*

> *5.3.12.3 The developer shall use the domain engineering feedback mechanism and the asset management communication mechanism to report reuse information about software installation.[99]*

4.5 Reuse Requirements for the Operation Process

The 12207 Standard Operation Process specifies the requirements for operating a software product or system. The main function of the Operation Process is to operate a software product or system. The party responsible for performing the Operation Process is the *operator.*

The 12207 Standard defines the Operation Process as consisting of the following four activities:

1. Process Implementation
2. Operational Testing
3. System Operation
4. User Support

As Figure 4-26, IEEE Std. 1517 adds reuse-related tasks to the Process Implementation Activity to specify the consumer reuse requirements for the Operation Process. Reuse extensions are shown in italic type.

INSTALLATION PLAN DELIVERABLE DESCRIPTION

Deliverable Description: The Installation Plan outlines how and when the project will be installed to the test and production platforms. This document is reviewed and revised before the installation to each platform to explain special procedures that may be required for that platform.

Required or Optional: Required

Supporting Techniques: *Selecting Reusable Assets technique; Identifying New Reusable Assets Technique*[97]

Relationship to Other Deliverables:

Deliverables which contribute to this deliverable:

Risk Analysis; Code; Deferred Event Procedure;

Project Reuse Strategy

Deliverables which this deliverable contributes to:

Installation Plan - Next Phase

Life of Deliverable: Project duration

Review Audience: INVESCO management team; Project team

Producer of Deliverable: Project team

Custodian of Deliverable: Project team

Suggested Tools: Word Processor

Tasks to Produce this Deliverable:

1. Document Installation Plan, *using an Installation Plan Template if an appropriate one is available. If not, consider using this Installation Plan to create an installation Plan Template. Refer to Selecting Reusable Assets Technique, Identifying New Reusable Assets Technique, Guidelines for Preparing an Asset for Reuse Technique.*

2. Review draft with project team.

3. Revise draft based on project team review.

4. Review and revise Installation Plan.

5. Prepare for Installation Plan meeting.

6. Conduct/attend Installation Plan meeting.

7. Follow-up on Installation Plan meeting issues.

Figure 4-25. Example of Adding IEEE Std. 1517 Reuse Requirements to the INVESCO Methodology Installation Plan

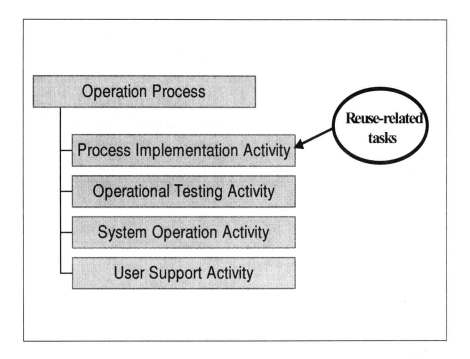

Figure 4-26. IEEE Std. 1517 Extensions to the IEEE/EIA Std. 12207 Operation
Process to Support Consumer Reuse

4.5.1 Adding Consumer Reuse Requirements to the Process Implementation Activity

The primary function of the Process Implementation Activity is to establish procedures for operating a software product in its operational environment(s). IEEE Std. 1517 adds three new tasks to this activity to assure that the operating procedures are defined by reusing existing operational plan and procedure assets whenever feasible.

4.5.1.1 Define Operation Plan

The 12207 Standard requires that an operation plan is created as one of the tasks in the Process Implementation Activity. In addition, IEEE Std. 1517 extends this requirement by specifying that an operation plan template shall be used to create the operation plan:

> *5.4.1.1 The operator shall create and document an operations plan, reusing an applicable operations plan template, if any exists, to define the resources and procedures for operation of the system. (This task defines reuse-related*

requirements in addition to those requirements specified in IEEE/EIA std 12207.0-1996, task 5.4.1.1.)[100]

Discussion

This task is another example of how IEEE Std. 1517 explicitly reminds the user of this Standard to create all project deliverables, including documentation deliverables, from assets whenever possible.

4.5.1.2 Evaluate the Reusability of the Operation Plan and the Operation Plan Template

Whenever an asset is used in a project, it is important to evaluate the quality of the asset in terms of its reusability and usability to the consumer. In this IEEE Std. 1517 task, the operation plan template is the asset to be evaluated:

> *5.4.1.2 The operations plan and the operations plan template shall be evaluated according to reusability criteria. The results of the evaluation shall be documented.*[101]

Discussion

If a template was used to create the operation plan for this system (software product), an assessment of its value to the project in terms of time and cost savings or quality improvements should be made and documented. If an operation plan template was available but was not used to create the system (software product) operation plan, reasons why it could not be used and suggestions for improving the future reusability of the operation plan template should be documented.

Although the project team may not be responsible for creating new assets within the scope of the project, they are responsible for identifying the deliverables they produce that they believe have reuse potential. In this task, the project team is required to evaluate the reuse potential of the system (software product) operation plan.

4.5.1.3 Report Operation Process Reuse Information

Reuse consumers play an important role in improving the quality, reusability and usability of assets, since the proof of the value of an asset lies in its use in an actual project. Therefore, in the following task, IEEE Std. 1517 requires reuse consumers to provide feedback about their use or attempted use of an asset:

> *5.4.1.3 The operator shall use the domain engineering feedback mechanism and the asset management communication mechanism to report reuse information about software operations.*[102]

Discussion

In this task, the operator is the reuse consumer who reports information about the operation plan template and the reuse potential of the operation plan created in this project. Feedback is given to the domain engineer who created the template and to the asset manager who manages the template.

4.6 Reuse Requirements for the Maintenance Process

4.6.1 The Difficulty of Maintaining Software

Although all but ignored by most organizations, software maintenance is usually the dominant phase of the software life cycle. It often claims the majority of the software project resources in terms of effort and budget. Software maintenance refers to changes that are made to an operational software product; that is, software that has been developed and is operational. Software maintenance is performed for a variety of reasons:

- to correct code errors and design defects
- to improve the software design
- to modify the software to meet changes in software requirements
- to make enhancements to the software to add new capabilities
- to migrate the software to different operating environments

A fundamental problem with software maintenance is that when a maintenance change is made to an existing software product for whatever reason, unforeseen side effects are frequently introduced. For example, correcting a defect has a high probability of introducing a new defect. This problem is compounded when assets are involved since a defect in one asset affects all the software products in which the asset is reused.

Many maintenance problems have grown out of a mistaken belief that software maintenance is substantially different and generally easier than software development, and therefore requires less planning, less experienced personnel, less sophisticated tools, and less management control. On the contrary, maintenance work is often more challenging than new software development projects.

Like software development work, software maintenance work should be approached as a project that is guided by the structure of a software life cycle model in which maintenance changes are analyzed, designed, coded, integrated, tested, and installed. In effect then, each maintenance change is implemented by performing a "mini" software development life cycle.

The 12207 Standard Maintenance Process specifies the requirements for maintaining a software product. The main functions of the Maintenance Process are to modify, migrate and retire an existing software product. IEEE Std. 1517 extends the 12207 Standard Maintenance Process by adding the requirements for maintaining a software product with the use of assets; that is, adding the consumer reuse requirements. Also, IEEE Std. 1517 extends the 12207 Standard Maintenance Process to apply to the maintenance of an asset.

The party responsible for performing the Maintenance Process in both the 12207 Standard and IEEE Std. 1517 is the *maintainer*.

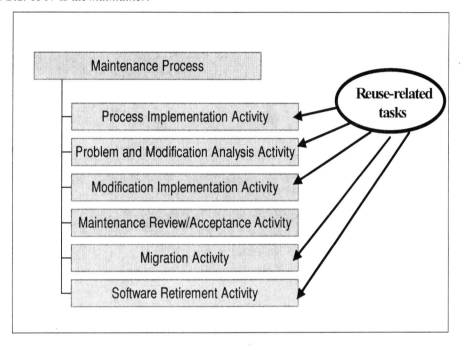

Figure 4-27. IEEE Std. 1517 Extensions to the IEEE/EIA Std. 12207 Maintenance Process to Support Consumer Reuse

4.6.2 Adding Consumer Reuse to the Maintenance Process

IEEE Std. 1517 includes reuse requirements at the very end of the software life cycle by adding consumer reuse tasks to the Maintenance Process. The maintainer is required to search for assets to use in performing maintenance changes to a software product and to consider the wide spread consequences that changing an asset may have.

The 12207 Standard Maintenance Process includes the following six activities:

- Process Implementation
- Problem and Modification Analysis
- Modification Implementation
- Maintenance Review/Acceptance

- Migration
- Software Retirement

As shown in Figure 4-27, IEEE Std. 1517 adds reuse-related tasks to the 12207 Standard Process Implementation, Problem and Modification Analysis, Modification Implementation, Migration, and Software Retirement Activities to specify the consumer reuse requirements for the Maintenance Process. IEEE Std. 1517 does not add any new activities to the Maintenance Process.

4.6.3 Adding Consumer Reuse Requirements to the Process Implementation Activity

Like software development work, maintenance work should be handled as a well managed project in which resources are identified and tasks are planned. The Process Implementation Activity in the Maintenance Process is performed to set up a software maintenance project. This activity requires that the maintainer:

- Create the project plan
- Set up project procedures and communication mechanisms

IEEE Std. 1517 adds three new tasks to the 12207 Process Implementation Activity to support and enable the practice of consumer reuse in a maintenance project.

4.6.3.1 Create Maintenance Project Plan Reusing a Project Plan Template

The primary deliverable produced by the Process Implementation Activity of the Maintenance Process is the maintenance project plan that is used to guide maintenance work on the software product. To produce a high quality project plan that meets the organization's standards, IEEE Std. 1517 requires the use of a project plan template:

> *5.5.1.1 The maintainer shall develop a maintenance plan, reusing an applicable maintenance plan template, if any exists. (This task defines reuse-related requirements in addition to those requirements specified in IEEE/EIA Std 12207.0-1996, task 5.5.1.1.)*[103]

Discussion

Using a plan template offers the advantages of reducing the time needed to produce the plan, ensuring that the plan meets organization's standards, and improving the overall quality and completeness of the plan.

Implementation Considerations

The development project plan template can also be used to create a maintenance project plan since both types of project are based on the software life cycle. An example of a development project plan template was shown in Table 4-4.

4.6.3.2 Establish Asset Manager Feedback Procedures

Normally, the software maintainer responsibilities include not only making maintenance changes but also reporting the changes to the software product users. With reuse, this responsibility may be greatly expanded due to the use of assets in the software product. IEEE Std. 1517 establishes the role of asset manager to handle this expanded reporting responsibility. In the following two IEEE Std. 1517 tasks, the software maintainer is given the responsibility of reporting asset problems and maintenance changes to the asset manager who in turn is responsible for notifying all those affected by the problems/changes:

> *5.5.1.2 The maintainer shall establish procedures for receiving, recording, resolving, and tracking problems, and providing feedback to the asset manager whenever problems are encountered in or change request are made for assets that were reused in the development of the software product.*[104]

> *5.5.1.3 Whenever problems with or change requests for assets are encountered, they shall be recorded in accordance with the IEEE/EIA Std. 12207.0-1996 Problem Resolution Process, so that all other software products that reused these assets can be examined to determine the impact that these problems or change requests may have on these software products.*[105]

Discussion

The 12207 Standard Problem Resolution Process is a general procedure for handling all problems detected in a software product. It is specified as a closed-loop process that entails:

- Prompt reporting of a software problem
- Notification of parties affected by the problem
- Prioritization of the problem
- Identification and analysis of the causes of the problem
- Analysis of possible ways to resolve the problem
- Resolution of the problem (if possible)

IEEE Std. 1517 applies the 12207 Standard Problem Resolution Process to the maintenance of both software products and assets.

4.6.4 Adding Consumer Reuse Requirements to Problem and Modification Analysis Activity

The function of the 12207 Standard Problem and Modification Analysis Activity is to analyze a reported software problem and software change request and to determine how best to address the problem/request, by considering the impact on the organization, the existing software product, and other software products with which it interfaces/interacts.

4.6.4.1 Consider Assets When Performing Maintenance Analysis

IEEE Std. 1517 extends the 12207 maintenance analysis by adding specific considerations for the reuse of assets and the impact on assets in the following three tasks:

> *5.5.2.1 The maintainer shall consider the reuse of assets to implement the maintenance modifications. (This task defines reuse-related requirements in addition to those requirements specified in IEEE/EIA Std. 12207.0-1996, task 5.5.2.3.)[106]*

> *5.5.2.2 The maintainer shall analyze the problem report or modification request for its impact on any assets reused in the development of the system. (This task defines reuse-related requirements in addition to those requirements specified in IEEE/EIA Std. 12207.0-1996, task 5.5.2.1.)[107]*

> *5.5.2.3 The maintainer shall provide the problem/modification request and the analysis results that concern assets to the asset manager.[108]*

Implementation Considerations

First and foremost, software maintenance analysis concerns developing a thorough understanding of the software product—its purpose, internal structure, and operating requirements. If the maintainer does not thoroughly understand the software, there is a much greater risk of jeopardizing software quality and reliability by unknowingly introducing defects when the software is modified. Interactive software maintenance tools, such as code analyzers, restructuring engines, and flow-graphing tools, enable the maintainer to explore the internal structure of the software are an invaluable maintenance analysis aid. They help to identify exactly what parts of the software are affected by the defect or the change. When assets are affected, the asset manager should be notified. The asset manager is responsible for providing information about the status of the asset to all current and potential asset users and to the domain engineer who is responsible for maintaining the asset.

When considering how best to implement a software correction or change, the 12207 Standard requires the maintainer to consider the criticality of the correction (change) as well as the cost and time to implement the correction (change). Based upon an analysis of these considerations, the maintainer chooses an implementation option and then seeks approval for this option before the maintenance change is made. IEEE Std. 1517 adds the requirement that the impact on assets is considered along with these other maintenance considerations. Although not specifically stated in IEEE Std. 1517, it is advisable for the maintainer to seek analysis assistance and approval for an appropriate implementation choice from the domain engineer who is responsible for maintaining the affected assets.

4.6.5 Adding Consumer Reuse Requirements to the Modification Implementation Activity

The purpose of the 12207 Modification Implementation Activity is to implement an approved software correction or change. The 12207 Standard requires the maintainer to follow the 12207 Development Process to implement the change. The IEEE Std. also includes the requirement to follow IEEE Std. 1517 Development Process to implement maintenance changes.

IEEE Std. 1517 adds only one new task to the 12207 Modification Implementation Activity.

4.6.5.1 Receive Modified Assets from the Asset Manager

From the following task, it is clear that in IEEE Std. 1517, the responsibility for modifying an asset is separated from the responsibility for modifying a software product:

> *5.5.3.1 The maintainer shall receive, review, and accept any modified assets from the asset manager and integrate them into the modification implementation of the software product.*[109]

Discussion

According to IEEE Std. 1517, the maintainer implements software product modifications, while the domain engineer implements asset modifications. IEEE Std. 1517 Asset Maintenance Activity in the Domain Engineering Process specifies the asset maintenance responsibilities of the domain engineer. (See Chapter 7.) As shown in Figure 4-28, the asset manager serves as the middleman, first passing asset correction/change requirements from the maintainer to the domain engineer, and then passing the modified asset from the domain engineer to the maintainer for re-integration into the software product.

Implementation Considerations

Modifying software typically involves creating and/or deleting program code to correct a defect or to implement a change or enhancement to an existing software product. The maintainer must make certain that these changes do not destroy the software integrity or decrease the software quality. Whenever software is modified, its correctness should be revalidated. The maintainer should perform selective re-testing to demonstrate that not only is the new code correct but also the unmodified parts of the software remain intact, and the software product as a whole still functions correctly. Assuming that even a small change will work as intended and therefore does not require testing is almost certain to lead to software quality deterioration.

Modifying an existing software product is the most basic maintenance function, and yet is perhaps the most challenging of all software activities. Typically, it involves three steps:

1. Devise a plan for changing the software product (i.e., design the software change/debug the software)

2. Alter the software to incorporate the change

3. Evaluate the impact of the change

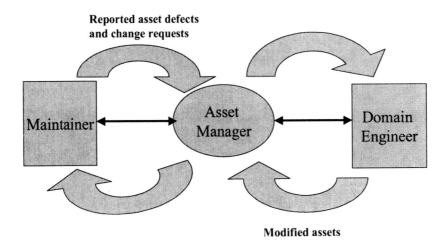

Figure 4-28. Communication Links between Maintainer, Asset Manager, and Domain Engineer

Although altering the software to make the required change may only involve a few lines of code, determining the impact of this change on other portions of the software product may involve a detailed study of the entire software product. Unanticipated and undesired side effects have resulted from even apparently simple software changes. In many cases, the side effect may be so subtle that it remains undetected long after the change has been made. When it is finally noticed, the change that causes the problem may be extremely difficult to pinpoint.

Side effects are a primary cause of software quality deterioration during the maintenance phase. For this reason, the objective of modifying software cannot be simply to make the change correctly, but must include modifying the software in such a way that:

- Software quality is not harmed

- Software style and design integrity are preserved

- Future program changes can be easily made

- Software product users are not adversely affected

If the maintenance work involves correcting a software defect, the maintainer must first locate the cause(s) of the defect and then determine how to rectify the software product by changing the affected software. If the work involves changing or enhancing an existing software product, the maintainer must develop the new software and determine how to integrate it to the existing software product. The top-down approach is recommended for designing a software change is outlined in Table 4-19. Some guidelines for designing a software change are listed in Table 4-20.

Table 4-19. Top-down Approach for Designing a Software Change

1. First, the entire software product is reviewed at a general level by studying each software component, unit, and database

2. Next, in steps, the software components, units, and data structures that are to be changed (and those that are affected by the change) are isolated

3. Then, the internals of each software component, unit, and data structure to be changed (or affected by the change) are studied in detail

4. Finally, the change is designed by specifying the new software to be added and the existing software to be altered

Table 4-20. Guidelines for Designing a Software Maintenance Change[110]

- Examine alternative designs seeking a design for the change that preserves the integrity of the original software product design
- Strive for design simplicity, choosing the design alternative that modifies the least amount (in terms of lines of code or function points) and the least complex parts of the software product
- Choose a design that meets generality/reusability requirements in terms of its ability to be used in different versions and implementations of the software product and in different target operating environments
- Choose a design that meets flexibility/reusability requirements in terms of its ability to isolate specialized functions into separate software components and to provide component interfaces that are insensitive to further changes
- Choose a design that will not degrade software quality, in particular its future maintainability and reusability. Determine the impact that this change may have on other changes that are likely to be needed in the future
- Describe the design in terms that are testable and include test methods, test data and test tools
- Consider changes in performance, storage requirements, and operating procedures
- Consider the effect of the change on users, as well as the time and cost to implement it
- Document the what's and why's behind the design chosen

Since an asset is also software, the requirements for changing a software product also apply to changing an asset. Perhaps it is even more important to enforce these requirements in the case of assets since asset maintenance is likely to be more difficult than software product maintenance. The multi-use capability of an asset means that maintenance tasks such as determining the impact of a defect or a change may require examining not just one, but perhaps many software products—both existing software products and future software products. Keeping track of all reuses of an asset as well as determining all potential asset consumers are essential to being able to effectively perform asset maintenance.

Furthermore, reuse must be a prime consideration when designing a maintenance change to an asset. All the guidelines listed in Table 4-20 should be followed when designing a maintenance change to an asset. In particular, those guidelines that address the impact of the change on the reusability of the asset should be emphasized.

Whenever a software maintenance change is made, the software product should be revalidated to demonstrate that the change has been made correctly and that the software product as a whole still functions correctly. Often, there is a tendency to skip or minimize this maintenance step, especially when the change consists of only a few lines of code. However, this tendency must be avoided because it can quickly lead to the deterioration of even a very reliable, high-quality software product.

A revalidation procedure should be designed for each software product. Software product error histories and complexity measures should be used to identify the most error prone and most complex software components in the product so that the revalidation effort can concentrate on these components as well as the ones in which the changes were made. The procedures should be kept simple and aided by automated testing tools such as test data generators, test coverage analyzers, regression testers, and comparers. Automated testing tools can provide improved organization of the revalidation process, measure the thoroughness of testing, and relieve the maintainer of many routine, tedious chores.

Most important, the revalidation procedure must be used by the maintainer each time the software product is changed. Revalidation should closely resemble the original software validation process reusing the same or similar test cases and test data as those used when the software product was originally developed. The results from the original testing efforts and the re-testing efforts can be automatically compared to reveal any unexpected discrepancies.

Increases in the number of errors detected and in the effort needed to detect and correct errors is often the first sign that software quality is deteriorating and that future maintenance of the software product is likely to require more effort and resources. Error increases may indicate that the maintenance changes were made too hastily or that the testing tools or maintainers' skills were inadequate. Furthermore, they may indicate that the side effects from the change were not recognized, that re-testing was inadequate, or that the quality of the original software product is poor.

Comparing errors discovered during revalidation with previously discovered errors can help identify maintenance problems. This information can be used to suggest improvements in both the software development and maintenance processes as well as the need for more advanced software tools and staff training.

Again, just as for maintenance design, revalidation of an asset may be more difficult than revalidation of a software product. Certainly, it is even more important to thoroughly retest an asset since the ramifications of a poorly tested asset change may have very widespread consequences on many software products and users.

4.6.6 Adding Consumer Reuse Requirements to the Migration Activity

The primary function of the 12207 Standard Migration Activity is to move a software product to a new operating environment(s).

4.6.6.1 Notify Asset Manager of Software Product Migrations

The 12207 Standard includes a user notification requirement when a software product is moved to a new operating environment. In the following task, IEEE Std. 1517 adds an asset manager notification requirement when a software product assembled from assets is migrated to a new operating environment:

> *5.5.4.1 When a system that has been developed from assets is to be migrated to a new environment, migration planning activities shall include notification of the asset manager.*[111]

> *5.5.4.2 After a system that has been constructed from assets has been migrated to a new environment, notifications shall be sent to the asset manager.*[112]

Discussion

Since the asset manager is responsible for managing and controlling use of the assets, it is important that any information that updates how and where an asset is currently being reused or is planned to be reused is promptly given to the asset manager.

4.6.6.2 Provide Migration Feedback to the Asset Manager and Domain Engineer

Fundamental to the quality of an asset is its multi-use capability. This capability includes its usability in different target operating environments. Information about attempts to reuse assets in different target environments in actual practice provides valuable feedback to asset managers and developers. In the following task, IEEE Std. 1517 requires that the asset manger and the domain engineer receive this feedback:

> *5.5.4.3 When the migrated system has been constructed from assets, the results of a post-operation review that assesses the impact of changing to the new environment shall be sent to the asset manager and the domain engineer. (This task defines reuse-related requirements in addition to those requirements specified in IEEE/EIA 12207.0-1996, task 5.5.5.6.)*[113]

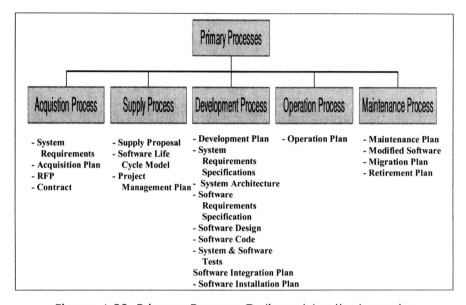

Figure 4-29. Primary Process Deliverables that can be
Produced from Assets

4.6.7 Adding Consumer Reuse Requirements to Software Retirement

The primary function of the 12207 Standard Software Retirement Activity is to handle the cessation of use of and support for a software product. IEEE Std. 1517 adds the following two tasks to the Software Retirement Activity to specify the requirements for notifying the asset manager about the retirement of a software product that was assembled from assets:

> *5.5.5.1 When a system that has been constructed from assets is to be retired, retirement planning activities shall include notifying the asset manager.*[114]

> *5.5.5.2 When a system constructed from assets is retired, notifications shall be sent to the asset manager.*[115]

Discussion

One responsibility of the asset manager is to prune from the organization's asset inventory those assets that are no longer of use to the organization. When a system assembled from as sets is retired, the current and future usefulness of each asset used in the system should be reviewed by the asset manager. The future utility of assets that are not currently used by any operational system should be assessed. If no future reuse of the assets is expected because, for example, they implement outmoded technology or business functions, then the asset manager should consider retiring the assets from the organization's asset inventory.

4.7 Summary

IEEE Std. 1517 primary processes include the Acquisition Process, Supply Process, Development Process, Operation Process, and Maintenance Process. IEEE Std. 1517 defines an agent who is responsible for each primary process. The primary process agents include the acquirer, supplier, developer, operator, and maintainer. The primary processes specify the activities, tasks and deliverables for acquiring, supplying, developing, operating, and maintaining systems, software products, software services, and assets with the use of assets. Figure 4-29 summarizes the primary process deliverables that can be produced from assets when following a consumer reuse strategy. Figure 4-30 summarizes the responsibilities of each primary process agent.

Acquirer
- Define System/Software Requirements
- Choose System/Software Acquisition Approach
- Prepare & Execute Acquisition Plan
- Prepare Request-for-Proposal
- Select System/Software Supplier
- Prepare & Negotiate Contract
- Accept System/Software

Supplier
- Review System/Software Requirements
- Prepare RFP Response
- Select Software Life Cycle Model
- Choose Supply Approach
- Define & Execute Project Management Plan
- Perform Verification & Validation
- Deliver Completed System/Software

Operator
- Develop & Execute Operation Plan
- Establish Software Operating Procedures
- Perform Operational Testing
- Provide User Assistance

Developer
- Select Software Life Cycle Model
- Develop & Execute Development Plan
- Specify System Requirements
- Develop System Architecture
- Specify Software Requirements
- Create Software Architectural Design
- Create Software Detailed Design
- Procedure Software Code
- Integrate Software
- Test System & Software
- Install Software on Target Environment
- Assist Software Acceptance

Maintainer
- Develop & Execute Maintenance Plans
- Establish & Follow Maintenance Procedures
- Process Problems /Change Requests
- Select & Implement Modification Option
- Migrate Software to New Operating Environment
- Retire Software

Figure 4-30. Responsibilities of the Primary Process Agents

4.8 References

1. *IEEE/EIA Std. 12207.0-1996, Standard for Information Technology—Software Life Cycle Processes,* IEEE, Piscataway, N.J., 1996.

2. *IEEE Std. 1517, Standard for Information Technology—Software Life Cycle Processes—Reuse Processes,* IEEE, Piscataway, N.J., 1999.

3. C. Derek et al., *Object-Oriented Development: The Fusion Method,* Prentice- Hall, Upper Saddle River, N.J., 1994.

4. *IEEE/EIA Std. 12207.0 1996, Standard for Information Technology—Software Life Cycle Processes.*

5. IEEE Std. 1517, Standard for Information Technology—Software Life Cycle Processes—Reuse Processes.

6. Ibid.

7. Ibid.

8. Ibid.

9. *IEEE/EIA Std. 12207.0-1996, Standard for Information Technology—Software Life Cycle Processes.*

10. *IEEE Std. 1517, Standard for Information Technology—Software Life Cycle Processes—Reuse Processes.*

11. C. McClure, *Software Reuse Techniques,* Prentice-Hall, Upper Saddle River, N.J., 1997, pp. 159–168.

12. Ibid., pp. 159-168.

13. *IEEE Std. 1517, Standard for Information Technology—Software Life Cycle Processes—Reuse Processes.*

14. Ibid.

15. Ibid.

16. Ibid.

17. Ibid.

18. Ibid.

19. Ibid.

20. Ibid.

21. Ibid.

22. Ibid.

23. Ibid.

24. Ibid.

25. C. McClure, *Software Reuse Techniques*, pp. 148–157.

26. Ibid., pp. 159–168.

27. *IEEE Std. 1517, Standard for Information Technology—Software Life Cycle Processes—Reuse Processes.*

28. C. McClure, *Software Reuse Techniques*, pp. 149–157.

29. Ibid., pp. 149–157.

30. Ibid., pp. 149–157.

31. Ibid., pp. 149–157.

32. *IEEE Std. 1517, Standard for Information Technology—Software Life Cycle Processes—Reuse Processes.*

33. Ibid.

34. Ibid.

35. *IEEE/EIA Std. 12207.0-1996, Standard for Information Technology—Software Life Cycle Processes.*

36. *IEEE Std. 1517, Standard for Information Technology—Software Life Cycle Processes—Reuse Processes.*

37. Ibid.

38. Ibid.

39. Ibid.

40. Ibid.

41. *IEEE/EIA Std. 12207.0-1996, Standard for Information Technology—Software Life Cycle Processes.*

42. *IEEE Std. 1517, Standard for Information Technology—Software Life Cycle Processes—Reuse Processes.*

43. Ibid.

44. Ibid.

45. Ibid.

46. Ibid.

47. *IEEE/EIA Std. 12207.0-1996, Standard for Information Technology—Software Life Cycle Processes.*

48. *IEEE Std. 1517, Standard for Information Technology—Software Life Cycle Processes—Reuse Processes.*

49. Ibid.

50. C. McClure, *Software Reuse Techniques*, pp. 200–237, 279–296.

51. *IEEE Std. 1517, Standard for Information Technology—Software Life Cycle Processes—Reuse Processes.*

52. Ibid.

53. C. McClure, *Software Reuse Techniques*, pp. 279–296.

54. *IEEE Std. 1517, Standard for Information Technology—Software Life Cycle Processes—Reuse Processes.*

55. Ibid.

56. Ibid.

57. *IEEE/EIA Std. 12207.0-1996, Standard for Information Technology—Software Life Cycle Processes.*

58. Ibid.

59. C. McClure, *Software Reuse Techniques*, pp. 201–214, 225–236, 279–296.

60. *IEEE Std. 1517, Standard for Information Technology—Software Life Cycle Processes—Reuse Processes.*

61. Ibid.

62. Ibid.

63. Ibid.

64. Ibid.

65. Ibid.

66. C. McClure, *Software Reuse Techniques*, pp. 201–237, 279–296.

67. *IEEE Std. 1517, Standard for Information Technology—Software Life Cycle Processes—Reuse Processes.*

68. Ibid.

69. *IEEE/EIA Std. 12207.0-1996, Standard for Information Technology—Software Life Cycle Processes.*

70. *IEEE Std. 1517, Standard for Information Technology—Software Life Cycle Processes—Reuse Processes.*

71. Ibid.

72. Ibid

73. Ibid.

74. C. McClure, *Software Reuse Techniques*, pp. 201–237, 279–296.

75. Ibid., pp. 201–237, 279–296.

76. *IEEE/EIA Std. 12207.0-1996, Standard for Information Technology—Software Life Cycle Processes.*

77. Ibid.

78. *IEEE Std. 1517, Standard for Information Technology—Software Life Cycle Processes—Reuse Processes.*

79. Ibid.

80. Ibid.

81. C. McClure, Software *Reuse Techniques*, pp. 279–296.

82. *IEEE/EIA Std. 12207.0-1996, Standard for Information Technology—Software Life Cycle Processes.*

83. *IEEE Std. 1517, Standard for Information Technology—Software Life Cycle Processes—Reuse Processes.*

84. *IEEE/EIA Std. 12207.0-1996, Standard for Information Technology—Software Life Cycle Processes.*

85. *IEEE Std. 1517, Standard for Information Technology—Software Life Cycle Processes—Reuse Processes.*

86. Ibid.

87. Ibid.

88. C. McClure, *Software Reuse Techniques*, pp. 279–296.

89. *IEEE Std. 1517, Standard for Information Technology—Software Life Cycle Processes—Reuse Processes.*

90. Ibid.

91. Ibid.

92. Ibid.

93. Ibid.

94. Ibid.

95. Ibid.

96. Ibid.

97. C. McClure, *Software Reuse Technology*, pp. 201–214, 225–236.

98. *IEEE Std. 1517, Standard for Information Technology—Software Life Cycle Processes—Reuse Processes.*

99. Ibid.

100. Ibid.

101. Ibid.

102. Ibid.

103. Ibid.

104. Ibid.

105. Ibid.

106. Ibid.

107. Ibid.

108. Ibid.

109. Ibid.

110. J. Martin and C. McClure, *Software Maintenance: The Problem and Its Solutions*, Prentice-Hall, Upper Saddle River, N.J., 1983, p. 372.

111. IEEE Std. 1517, Standard for Information Technology—Software Life Cycle Processes—Reuse Processes.

112. Ibid.

113. Ibid.

114. Ibid.

115. Ibid.

Chapter 5.
Asset Management Process

5.1 Introduction

IEEE Std. 1517 views an asset as a software product. Like any software product, an asset must be properly managed throughout its life cycle. For example, information about where it is stored, current version, and history of uses, defects, problems, and modifications should be readily available. However, because it is a multi-use software part, an asset has special management requirements over and above those for normal, single-use software products. For example, modifying an asset has much broader implications than modifying a single-use software product since its modification may affect all the products in which it is currently reused or may be reused in the future.

IEEE Std. 1517 created the Asset Management Process to address asset management requirements. According to IEEE Std. 1517, the Asset Management Process includes activities that specify:

> ...administrative and technical procedures throughout the life of an asset to identify, define, certify, classify, and baseline the asset; track modifications, migrations, and versions of the asset; record and report the status of the asset; and control storage and handling of the asset, delivery of the asset to its reusers, and retirement of the asset.[1]

The Asset Management Process is placed in IEEE Std. 1517's software life cycle framework under the supporting life cycle process category (see Figure 3-1 in Chapter 3). Recall from Chapter 2 that a supporting process is a process that supports another process with a distinct purpose and contributes to the success of a software project.

The standard names the asset manager as the party responsible for the asset management activities. According to IEEE Std. 1517's interpretation of the word "party," a party may be implemented as an individual or group who is assigned the responsibilities of the asset manager. Typically, the role of asset manager is assigned to a reuse library group headed by a reuse library manager.

The activities specified in IEEE Std. 1517 Asset Management Process are listed and summarized in Table 5-1 and presented in detail below.

In the detailed presentation for each activity, the activity is explained in terms of its tasks. Recall that in the standard, a task represents the requirements for implementing the activity in a particular a software life cycle model or methodology.

First, the task is discussed, and then suggestions for how to implement the task are given.

Table 5-1. Activities in IEEE Std. 1517 Asset Management Process

ACTIVITY NAME	ACTIVITY DESCRIPTION
Process Implementation	• Create, document, and review an asset management plan
Asset Storage and Retrieval Definition	• Define, implement, review, and maintain an asset storage and retrieval mechanism • Develop, document, and maintain an asset classification scheme
Asset Management and Control	• Evaluate assets • Accept assets for inclusion in the asset storage and retrieval mechanism • Classify assets • Perform asset configuration management • Track and report use of assets • Monitor, record, and send asset modification request and problem reports to the domain engineers and asset users • Retire assets from the asset storage and retrieval mechanism

5.2 Process Implementation Activity

IEEE Std. 1517 defines an *asset* as:

> *an item, such as design, specifications, source code, documentation, test suites manual procedures, etc., that has been designed for use in multiple contexts.*[2]

The purpose of this activity is to define formal procedures for managing an asset by creating an asset management plan. It consists of three tasks, described below.

5.2.1 Create Asset Management Plan

Organizations often find it is best to evolve their reuse programs over time. They begin on a small scale, experimenting with the reuse of a limited number of assets. When this approach is chosen, it is necessary to create a formal plan for managing the expanding number of assets included in the asset storage and retrieval mechanism.

IEEE Std. 1517 requires the creation of an asset management plan:

> *6.1.1.1 The asset manager shall create and document an asset management plan, reusing an applicable asset management plan template, if any exists, to define the resources and procedures for managing assets. The plan should include the following:*

a) *Defining the requirements for an asset storage and retrieval mechanism;*

b) *Defining the asset storage and retrieval mechanism;*

c) *Establishing the asset storage and retrieval mechanism as an integral part of the software life cycle;*

d) *Naming the organization(s) responsible for managing and maintaining the asset storage and retrieval mechanism;*

e) *Defining asset acceptance, certification, and retirement procedures;*

f) *Defining the relationship of the asset manager to other parties such as developers, maintainers, and domain engineers;*

g) *Promoting the use of the asset storage and retrieval mechanism;*

h) *Defining an asset management communication mechanism;*

i) *Defining an asset classification scheme.*[3]

Discussion

To ensure that all aspects of managing an asset are treated formally, the standard requires the creation of an asset management plan. In accordance with IEEE Std. 1517, the asset management plan must contain several elements, such as the definition of an asset storage and retrieval mechanism. An asset storage and retrieval mechanism is the foundation for formalizing the practice of systematic reuse in an organization. It provides a way to properly manage assets and to distribute them to software system and application developers and maintainers across the organization. To allow for the broadest possible implementation, the standard uses the term "*storage and retrieval mechanism*" rather than a more specific term such as "*library*."

Notice that IEEE Std. 1517 task 6.1.1.1 requires the use an asset management plan template, if one exists, to create the asset management plan. This is an example of the application of consumer reuse where a software process deliverable is created by reusing an existing asset. In IEEE Std. 1517, a *template* is defined as "an asset with parameters or slots that can be used to construct an instantiated asset."[4] In the case of a plan, the template probably is in the form of an outline for a document with the commonly required parts of the document already filled in. Document templates represent an important type of asset that provides valuable reuse benefits to an organization. First, document templates are an excellent way to ensure that organization document standards are followed and that document consistency is enforced across software projects and deliverables. Second, using templates to produce software life cycle document deliverables can greatly reduce the project time and resources required.

Implementation Considerations

The first required element of the asset management plan is to define the requirements for an asset storage and retrieval mechanism. Table 5-2 lists the requirements that an organization should consider for its asset storage and retrieval mechanism.

Table 5-2. Asset Storage and Retrieval Mechanism Requirements

- Ability to accept any asset regardless of size, language, or tool used to generate the asset
- Check-in/Check-out facility
- Import/Export facility to populate the storage and retrieval mechanism from other such mechanisms or development tools
- Classification scheme for identifying and retrieving assets
- Querying capability to locate and retrieve desired assets
- Browsing facility to scan the contents of the storage and retrieval mechanism
- Cataloging facility to catalog assets for browsing and retrieval purposes
- Security to control access to the contents and to restrict ability to add, change, or delete assets to and from the storage and retrieval mechanism
- Validation capability to control asset entry into the storage and retrieval mechanism through rule enforcement
- Versioning to enable multiple versions of assets to be managed by the storage and retrieval mechanism
- Audit trails providing storage and retrieval mechanism contents usage, ownership and status information
- Usage metrics and information about who extracted which assets, when and for which projects
- History information: problem reports and number of times an asset has been selected
- Backup/recovery capability to protect loss of contents
- Open/portable operating on heterogeneous environments
- Extensibility enabling the addition of new types of assets, query methods, relationships, classifications, and data

The major responsibility of the reuse library group is managing and maintaining the asset storage and retrieval mechanism. At least one member of the reuse library group should be an experienced software developer, not simply a library administrator, to ensure the group has the required skills. The responsibilities of the reuse library group are summarized in Table 5-3.

Table 5-3. Reuse Library Group Responsibilities

Establish asset storage and retrieval mechanism	• Determine the types of assets to make available for reuse • Select tools to implement the asset storage and retrieval mechanism • Define the logical and physical structure of the asset storage and retrieval mechanism • Define the asset classification scheme • Populate the asset storage and retrieval mechanism with assets • Create a reuse catalog of assets
Establish access methods for the asset storage and retrieval mechanism	• Assign user IDs • Consult on how to search for and retrieve assets from the asset storage and retrieval mechanism • Advise software project teams on what is available for reuse • Recommend future assets to include in the asset storage and retrieval mechanism
Decide which assets to include in the asset storage and retrieval mechanism	• Estimate the reuse potential of an asset • Estimate the cost to support the asset • Classify and catalog accepted assets
Manage the asset storage and retrieval mechanism	• Perform asset configuration management • Keep track of asset users • Monitor asset searches and retrievals • Assess the quality and value of the asset storage and retrieval mechanism • Add and retire assets from the asset storage and retrieval mechanism • Update the asset classification scheme and catalog • Promote use of the asset storage and retrieval mechanism
Interface with asset consumers	• Consult with reuse consumers about assets available for reuse; • Notify asset consumers of changes, corrections, new versions, and releases of assets they report using

One way to promote the use of the asset storage and retrieval mechanism is for a member of the reuse library group to attend software project reviews. At the review, the reuse library member can inform the project team of what assets currently included in the asset storage and retrieval mechanism may be useful in producing their project deliverables. Also, the reuse library group member may be able to point out project deliverables that have reuse potential and should be submitted for possible inclusion in the asset storage and retrieval mechanism.

5.2.2 Define Documentation, Configuration Management, and Review Procedures

The second task of the Process Implementation Activity uses the 12207 Standard supporting processes to define documentation, configuration management, problem resolution, and review procedures for managing assets:

> *6.1.1.2 The asset manager shall:*
>
> a) *Document this process in accordance with the IEEE/EIA Std 12207.0-1996 Documentation Process;*
>
> b) *Perform configuration management of assets in accordance with the IEEE/EIA Std 12207.0-1996 Configuration Management Process;*
>
> c) *Document and resolve problems and nonconformances found in the assets and the Asset Management Process in accordance with the IEEE/EIA Std 12207.0-1996 Problem Resolution Process,*
>
> d) *Conduct reviews of assets in accordance with the IEEE/EIA 12207.0-1996 Joint Review Process.[5]*

Discussion

This requirement is an example of how IEEE Std. 1517 uses the 12207 Standard to provide the specifications for a reuse process. The Asset Management Process uses the IEEE/EIA Std. 12207.0-1996 supporting processes; namely the Documentation Process, Configuration Management Process, Problem Resolution Process, and Joint Review Process to specify its documentation, configuration management, problem resolution, and review procedure requirements.

Implementation Suggestions

The 12207 Standard Documentation Process is used to record, distribute, and maintain information produced by the Asset Management Process. For, example, information about where the asset is used is particularly important and should be thoroughly documented. Without accurate and up-to-date asset usage information, the quality of the software products using the asset may be jeopardized. Asset usage information is essential to the prompt notification of all asset users whenever a problem in the asset occurs or a new updated version of the asset is contemplated.

The purpose of the 12207 Standard Configuration Management Process is to perform configuration management of the software items (i.e., a software component in the system architecture) in a system. It includes activities to:

1. identify, define, and baseline a software item

2. control modifications and versions of an item

3. report the status of the item

4. manage the storage and delivery of the item

A software item may be composed of assets, or it may be a component of an asset. However, it is not an asset unless it has been designed for reuse. Although a software item and an asset are not one and the same, the general configuration specification requirements defined in the 12207 Standard are not only applicable to, but also absolutely necessary for, assets.

The 12207 Standard Problem Resolution Process provides the general specifications for handling asset and asset management problems. In the case of asset management, the function of the Problem Resolution Process is to address in a timely and responsive manner, any and all problems regarding assets or the execution of IEEE Std. 1517 Asset Management Process.

The 12207 Standard Joint Review Process provides the general specifications for conducting reviews of the asset management activities (such as maintaining the asset storage and retrieval mechanism) and the activity deliverables (such as the asset management plan).

5.2.3 Review Asset Management Plan

The third task in the Process Implementation Activity requires a review of the asset management plan by domain engineers and reuse program administrators:

> *6.1.1.3 The asset management plan shall be reviewed in accordance with the IEEE/EIA Std 12207.0-1996 Joint Review Process. Domain engineers and reuse program administrators shall be included in the review.*

Discussion

In this task, IEEE Std. 1517 applies consumer reuse to itself by reusing the 12207 Standard Joint Review Process to specify the review requirements for the asset management plan.

Implementation Suggestions

The 12207 Standard Joint Review Process is structured as a two party review process. The party responsible for performing the activity and producing the deliverables being reviewed is called the *reviewed party*. The party who evaluates the status of the activity and the quality of the deliverables is called the *reviewing party*. In accordance with IEEE Std. 1517, in an asset management plan review, the role of the reviewed party is assigned to the asset manager and the role of the reviewing party is minimally assigned to the domain engineers and reuse program administrators.

Because the domain engineer developed the asset and is responsible for maintaining the asset, he/she has knowledge of the asset that can be used to ensure that the definitions of the asset storage and retrieval mechanism, asset acceptance and certification procedures, classification scheme, and so forth are appropriate. Because asset management is an important element in a reuse program, the reuse program manager (who typically implements the role of reuse program administrator) is an interested, as well as required, reviewing party.

5.3 Asset Storage and Retrieval Definition Activity

A prerequisite for practicing software reuse is having something to reuse, i.e., an inventory of high-quality, well-managed assets such as code, templates, design models, etc. The primary functions of an asset storage and retrieval mechanism are to organize, store, and manage assets, often supporting multiple versions of the components. This activity consists of the three tasks described below.

5.3.1 Implement and Maintain Asset Storage and Retrieval Mechanism

The mechanism for asset storage and retrieval was selected as part of the asset management plan. The first task of the Asset Storage and Retrieval Definition Activity requires implementing and maintaining the asset storage and retrieval mechanism:

> *6.1.2.1 The asset manager shall implement and maintain an asset storage and retrieval mechanism.[6]*

Discussion

An important element in establishing a successful, formalized software reuse program in an organization is to implement an asset storage and retrieval mechanism. This entails:

- Defining the types of assets to be reused
- Defining the physical and logical organizational structure for the asset storage and retrieval mechanism
- Selecting support tools such as a repository, cataloging tool, configuration management tool, classification tool, and browsers
- Defining a classification scheme for identifying and retrieving assets
- Defining ways and sources for populating the asset storage and retrieval mechanism with assets
- Cataloging, classifying, and certifying assets

Implementation Considerations

As Table 5-4 shows, there are five types of tools that support the creation and use of an asset storage and retrieval mechanism: repositories, classification tools, browsers, system configuration management systems, and cataloging tools. The principal tool is the repository, which provides the automated mechanism for storing, accessing, and managing a variety of types of assets ranging from code to project documents/deliverables.

Table 5-4. Tools that Support an Asset Storage and Retrieval Mechanism

Repository	Stores, retrieves, and manages assets	Reuse consumers select assets from the repository for reuse Reuse producers add new assets to the repository
Classification Tool	Classifies assets	Reuse library group classifies assets to be stored in the asset storage and retrieval mechanism
Configuration Management Tool	Manages versions and releases of assets	Reuse library group performs asset version control and change management
Browser	Examines the repository for available assets	Developers and maintainers scan the contents of the asset storage and retrieval mechanism
Cataloging Tool	Stores a reference to an asset that is stored somewhere else	Reuse consumers select assets to examine further for possible reuse

A repository is a tool for defining, storing, accessing, and managing information that describes an enterprise and its software systems during each phase of the software life cycle.

A *classification tool* provides automated support for building a classification scheme for an asset storage and retrieval mechanism and for classifying assets.

A very important function of the asset storage and retrieval mechanism is to manage and keep track of each asset in terms of its versions, changes to the asset, and users of the asset. This function is supported by *configuration management tools* that interface with the repository.

A *browser* is a tool that assists with the retrieval of assets from the asset storage and retrieval mechanism and provides a variety of different views of assets. Browsers are able to look through an asset storage and retrieval mechanism to obtain information about any asset it contains. They scan the contents of the asset storage and retrieval mechanism to examine assets, their classification information, or relationships to other assets. For example, an object-class library can be browsed by type, classification, or relationship. Often, browsers are not stand-alone tools, but rather a feature of another tool, such as repository or a cataloging tool.

A *cataloging tool* is used to automatically scan a library/file of existing assets and extract some descriptive information about the asset that is used to build a reuse catalog.

A *reuse catalog* is a set of asset descriptions with a reference or pointer to where the assets are actually stored or information about how they can be acquired.

5.3.2 Develop, Document, and Maintain a Classification Scheme

IEEE Std. 1517 defines *classification* as:

> *"the manner in which the assets are organized for ease of search and extraction within a reuse library."*[7]

The second task of the Asset Storage and Retrieval Definition Activity recommends, but does not require, the development of an asset classification scheme. Note that the word "should" is used to indicate that the requirement is optional:

> *6.1.2.2 The asset manager should develop, document, and maintain a classification scheme to be used in classifying an asset.*[8]

Discussion

If assets are stored in the reuse library (i.e., asset storage and retrieval mechanism) without being organized, they will not only be difficult to find, but also difficult to understand. Classifying assets into meaningful structures allows reuse consumers to easily search the asset storage and retrieval mechanism by matching their needs to those provided by assets contained in the asset storage and retrieval mechanism.

A *classification scheme* is a representation method for an asset to enable reuse consumers to easily and quickly find and understand assets.

Implementation Considerations

Classification schemes typically are based on three kinds of representation methods:[9]

1. Library and information science
2. Artificial intelligence
3. Hypertext systems

Fortunately, experience to date has shown that simple representation methods are as effective as the more complex ones using more advanced technology in retrieving assets from asset storage and retrieval mechanisms.[10] This is especially true where the asset storage and retrieval mechanisms are small (i.e., contain less than a few hundred components) and are divided into reasonably sized application domains.

Today most classification schemes for asset storage and retrieval mechanisms that are in use in industry are based on library and information science methods. Library and information science methods are divided into two categories:

1. *Controlled Vocabulary*: Limits are placed on the number of classification terms and on the syntax used to combine terms
2. *Uncontrolled Vocabulary*: No limits placed on the number of classification terms

There are examples of reuse classification schemes that fall into both categories. Most reuse classification schemes are based on either uncontrolled—free text; or controlled—enumerated, faceted, or attribute-value methods.

Implementation Considerations

In a *free-text classification scheme*, assets are described by keywords or phrases. This is similar to asset descriptions typically used for reuse catalogs that contain lists of assets. Keyword indexing terms and descriptions are extracted automatically from asset documentation or entered by a person who is classifying the asset. This is the same process used to create a reuse catalog. It is the cheapest and fastest way to classify assets because it can be automated through the use of cataloging tools.

The problem to watch for with this method is that multiple assets that each provide a different function could have the same description; or on the other hand, different assets that provide the same function may have different descriptions. This may lead to ambiguity and redundancy among assets. For example, software assets used to calculate discounts may be described using similar terms, when in fact some of the described assets reference different situations, or are at a different stage of the software life cycle. On the other hand, two assets that calculate discounts may have a totally different description.

In an *enumerated classification scheme*, assets are organized into a class hierarchy. The Dewey Decimal system is an example. Searching for an asset to reuse is done by following the class hierarchy. The hierarchy makes it easy to understand the classification terms by which the asset is classified. However, an enumerated classification scheme is difficult to change since the hierarchy must be divided into exclusive classifications. Another disadvantage is that the ambiguity of the asset may allow it to fit into multiple places in the hierarchy.

For example, a classification scheme might be developed for a homogeneous hardware environment, and not include the concept of platform in the hierarchy. When the organization moves to open systems and multiple sources for platforms, the classification scheme no longer works. Also, when data-oriented assets are differentiated from process-oriented assets, some things such as business objects, or data derivation rules, could fit in to either classification.

In a *faceted classification scheme*, the classification is defined in terms of a set of ordered facets. Classification facets describe various properties of an asset. Each facet has a finite set of valid terms or values. An example of a facet is *operating system* with the allowable values being AIX, VM, MVS, OS/2. To classify an asset, a facet term (or the null value, 0, if the term is not applicable) is chosen for each facet. It is a good idea to limit the number of facets to seven or less. Most faceted classification schemes have from five to ten facets.

The advantages of a faceted classification scheme are: (1) it is easy to modify and (2) having a limited number of valid facet terms eliminates the ambiguity problem. The disadvantage is the effort to create and maintain facet term lists. For example, when programming language is one of the facets, the list of legal languages must be kept up to date.

The *attribute-value classification scheme* is similar to faceted classification but instead of facets, it uses attribute-value pairs. Attributes are unordered and there can be as many as needed. Each attribute has values. To classify an asset, a valid value is chosen for each attribute. Examples of possible attributes are *functional area* or *language*. One value for a functional area is "financial." One value for a language is "C++." The attribute of an asset can take on any value that the person classifying the component chooses.

Attribute-value classification is easy to use and can be partially automated. An asset is located in the asset storage and retrieval mechanism by specifying a value or range of values for each attribute in the classification. The shortcoming of this method is that because there is no way to control attribute values, different values can be used for the same thing causing ambiguity and redundancies. For example, one classifier may use the term *programmer* and another *developer* when describing the author of an asset. Either might choose to use only the last name, or a set of initials, as the value.

Studies have not shown that any one of these classification scheme methods is superior to the others. This means that whichever representation method best suits an organization's needs, preferences, and tool set can be chosen. However, when making a choice, both the strengths and weaknesses of the classification scheme should be kept in mind and weighed.

5.3.3 Review Asset Storage and Retrieval Mechanism

The third task of the Asset Storage and Retrieval Definition Activity requires a review of the asset storage and retrieval mechanism:

> *6.1.2.3 The asset manager shall conduct joint review(s) of the asset storage and retrieval mechanism in accordance with the IEEE/EIA 12207.0-1996 Joint Review Process. Reuse program administrators and domain engineers shall be included in the review(s).[11]*

Discussion

It is important to carefully evaluate the asset storage and retrieval mechanism, since it is the key enabler of communication and sharing of software system information and assets across software tools, life cycle activities, teams, and applications. It simplifies software work and improves the quality of system information and assets by controlling access to information and assets and by eliminating redundant definitions. The asset storage and retrieval mechanism houses the asset inventory and provides a means of easily accessing and understanding the assets.

Implementation Considerations

The asset storage and retrieval mechanism is usually implemented with repository, browser, and classification tools. Many organizations already have a repository as part of their software development tool environment. This repository also may be suitable for the asset storage and retrieval mechanism. In some cases, the organization may have mandated that this repository is used to house the asset inventory.

Some important considerations that an organization should include in the review of the repository chosen to implement the asset storage and retrieval mechanism are listed in Table 5-5.

Table 5-5. Repository Selection Considerations

QUESTIONS REGARDING THE TYPES OF ASSETS THAT CAN BE STORED IN THE REPOSITORY:

- How well do the types of assets that can be stored in the repository match the organization's list of desired types of assets to be stored and managed by its asset storage and retrieval mechanism?
- If code is one type of asset, does this repository support the required languages and versions?
- If design models are one type of asset, does the repository support the design model format? Remember that many design models are in a tool-specific form. Even when they conform to standards such as CDIF or UML, they may need to be converted before they can be placed in the repository.

QUESTIONS REGARDING THE PHYSICAL ORGANIZATION OF THE REPOSITORY:

- Is it centralized or distributed? Does this fit how and where the organization plans to practice reuse? For example, will one centralized or multiple distributed software development groups have access to the repository?
- Does the physical organization of the repository support the logical organization of the asset storage and retrieval mechanism? For example, the plan may be to divide the asset storage and retrieval mechanism into domains or layers with each layer signifying an asset's certification level. (e.g., undocumented, non-certified, "use-at-your- own-risk" assets are placed at the lowest level; documented, non-certified assets at the next level; and documented, certified assets at the highest level).

Browsers are very important reuse support tools because they help the reuse consumer locate desired assets. However, by themselves they do not make assets fast and easy to find. If assets are not named in a meaningful way, described in terms of what they do and what they need to be used, and organized into meaningful groupings to shorten the searching time, they will be difficult to find—regardless of the browsing tool.

Catalogs and classification schemes make it much easier to find and understand assets stored in an asset storage and retrieval mechanism.

A reuse catalog is used to assist the identification and retrieval of candidate assets and does not require the creation of an asset storage and retrieval mechanism. A reuse catalog is usually set up as a separate database or file that contains descriptions of the assets. It does not contain the asset but often has pointer information to where the asset is actually stored. A reuse consumer searches the catalog for candidate assets that meet his/her current needs by creating a search request or pattern that is compared to the asset descriptions stored in the catalog.

During the early stages of its software reuse program, an organization may choose to set up a reuse catalog before building a full asset storage and retrieval mechanism in order to learn about the types of assets that may be most beneficial to reuse. A catalog is much faster and cheaper to create than an asset storage and retrieval mechanism.

Cataloging tools can be used to automatically scan a library/file of existing assets and extract some descriptive information about the asset used to build a catalog. This approach makes existing software assets immediately available for reuse. However, because these assets most likely were not designed with reuse in mind (i.e., sufficiently generalized or documented), they may not be in the best form for reuse. Therefore, the reuse consumer may need to re-engineer or redesign the asset before it can be reused. Even in this case, it may be better, cheaper, and faster to reuse and alter an existing asset rather than to build one from scratch. The existing asset is a working example that has already been implemented and proven to work.

Features that an organization should look for when selecting a cataloging tool are listed in Table 5-6.

Table 5-6. Catalog Tool Features

- Automatic scanning of existing files and libraries to extract descriptive information such as keywords to create the catalog entries
- Pointers to or retrieval of assets selected from the catalog
- Access to distributed, remote files and libraries
- Searching of local and distributed files and libraries to locate candidate assets that match the reuse consumer's search request
- Assessing the quality of the assets to be listed in the catalog
- Creating and publishing catalog entries
- Keeping track of the number of times an asset is reused/requested for reuse

5.4 Asset Management and Control Activity

Procedures that manage assets throughout their life cycle provide an organization with a powerful means to assure the quality of assets as well as controlled access to assets. Asset management and control procedures are used to manage code modules, requirements specifications, test scripts, test data, test results, designs, etc. Through the use of configuration management tools, they provide a means of keeping track of all associated information (such as which version of the runtime library, which compiler version, which versions of tools or DBMS are used to create the asset, and on which operating system the asset was created). This information is invaluable to a reuse consumer who is trying to evaluate how closely an existing system and its assets match the new system's requirements. It is also useful to be able to recreate an environment when tracking down an asset problem.

By keeping tack of its assets, an organization can provide a level of safety and control that is vital to the success of its reuse program. This activity consists of nine tasks that are described below.

5.4.1 Evaluate Assets

In this IEEE Std. 1517 task, an asset is evaluated to determine if it should be accepted for inclusion in the asset storage and retrieval mechanism:

> *6.1.3.1 For each asset submitted to the asset manager, the asset shall be evaluated based on the asset acceptance and certification criteria.*[12]

Discussion

Software developers, software maintainers, domain engineers, software system users, and others may know of assets that they believe should be available for reuse. However, IEEE Std. 1517 does not permit any of these parties to directly add assets into the asset storage and retrieval mechanism. The reason is that to assure that the level of general quality and reusability, assets must first be submitted to a formal asset acceptance and certification procedure.

In IEEE Std. 1517, the asset manager is responsible for the asset acceptance and certification procedure. The asset manager is the only party permitted to add assets to or retire assets from the asset storage and retrieval mechanism.

Implementation Considerations

Reuse consumers will not want to utilize assets from the asset storage and retrieval mechanism unless they are confident in the asset's validity. Every asset should be subjected to a certification procedure. The particulars of the procedure depend upon the kind of assets (e.g., different procedures are appropriate for source code vs. software designs). Certification information should be "carried along" with the reusable asset as part of its documentation.

Asset acceptance procedures should include criteria that address:

1. the reuse potential of the asset, noting specific projects and software products in which the asset may be used

2. the cost and resources needed to create/acquire/prepare the asset for reuse

3. the potential benefits that the asset can deliver to the organization

4. the quality of the asset (e.g., error history of the asset)

5. the asset's compliance to organization standards

An organization should develop asset acceptance and certification criteria for assets developed in-house as well as assets acquired from outside sources. For example, consider acceptance criteria for vendor-supplied class libraries. Vendor-supplied class libraries are readily available to assist object-oriented programming. Most are code-level libraries that support a specific programming language such as Smalltalk or C++. They contain foundation classes (i.e., low-level classes) which make programming easier. Examples include foundation classes for data structures such as String, Date, Time, Regular Expression and Tokenizers. The following types of class libraries are currently being marketed: data structures and programming classes, mathematical classes, graphical user interfaces classes, database classes, and graphics classes.

Class-library acceptance criteria should address the use of a particular class library (the quality, compatibility, legal issues, and support provided for the classes).

5.4.2 Include Asset in the Asset Storage and Retrieval Mechanism

In this IEEE Std. 1517 task, an asset that passes the asset acceptance and certification criteria is added to asset storage and retrieval mechanism:

> *6.1.3.2 For each asset accepted, it shall be made available for reuse though the asset storage and retrieval mechanism.*[13]

Discussion

Although not stated explicitly in the standard, it is assumed that the asset manager is responsible for including the asset in the asset storage and retrieval mechanism.

Implementation Considerations

The reuse library group should be responsible for initially populating the asset storage and retrieval mechanism with an inventory of approved assets and updating the inventory over time as new assets become available.

5.4.3 Classify Assets

This IEEE Std. 1517 task specifies the requirement of classifying an asset approved for inclusion in the asset storage and retrieval mechanism according to the organization's asset classification scheme:

> *6.1.3.3 The asset shall be classified in accordance with the reuse classification scheme, if any exists.*[14]

Discussion

Recall that in IEEE Std. 1517 task 6.1.2.2, the development of a reuse classification scheme is stated as an optional requirement. Therefore, only if the organization has developed an asset classification scheme does the standard require an approved asset to be classified in accordance with this classification scheme.

Implementation Considerations

The reuse library staff should be responsible for classifying an approved asset as part of the asset storage and retrieval mechanism. For example, when using a faceted classification scheme, an asset is classified by selecting a facet value for each of the facet terms. The procedure follows:

- Review the asset and its associated documentation to fully understand the asset

- For each facet, choose from its facet term list, the term that best describes the asset

- Consider the facet term and its related synonyms when selecting a facet term, but use the facet term not the synonym to classify the asset

- If a new synonym comes to mind, suggest it for possible addition to the classification scheme by the asset manager

- If no facet term fits the description of the asset, suggest a new term to be added to the facet term list by the asset manager

- Note that not all facets need to be used in classifying a particular asset

The asset classification is used by reuse consumers to identify and locate the asset for possible reuse in their projects. When the asset stored in the asset storage and retrieval mechanism is described in terms of a set of classification facets, the facets are used to identify and locate the asset. The asset sought by a reuse consumer is called the *target*. To search the asset storage and retrieval mechanism for one or more assets that match the target, the reuse consumer forms a query that specifies the facet value for each facet for the target. Not all facets need to be assigned a value. The search and retrieval tool then uses this query to search the asset storage and retrieval mechanism for all available assets that match the target and returns all matching assets to the reuse consumer.

5.4.4 Perform Asset Configuration Management

In this IEEE Std. 1517 task, the requirement for asset configuration management is specified:

> *6.1.3.4 The asset manager shall perform configuration management for the asset using the IEEE/EIA 12207.0-1996 Configuration Management Process.*[15]

Discussion

Configuration management is the process of identifying, organizing, and controlling changes to software; in other words, it is change management throughout the software life cycle.

Configuration management maintains the current version of any asset for shared use and reuse. All the related parts of the asset (e.g., source code, object code, executable image) can be managed as one software unit, enabling faster and better understanding of the asset whenever it is reused and/or changed. Configuration management allows controlled variation for an asset or a system. For example, an existing system with similar functionality can be reused to create a variant that runs on a different platform or conforms to a somewhat different set of requirements (e.g., conforms to a particular state's regulations).

Table 5-7 summarizes the benefits that configuration management offers. The configuration management functions that are especially important to support a reuse program are listed in Table 5-8.

Table 5-7. Configuration Management Benefits

- Provides a standard way to store and access software versions
- Provides a database to store software
- Enables recovery of previous versions
- Allows sharing and reuse of the latest version
- Manages all related parts
- Allows controlled variants

Table 5-8. Configuration Management Functions Needed to Support Reuse

- Security functions that ensure assets stored in the asset storage and retrieval mechanism will not be changed outside of the controlled environment
- Version control to allow controlled change for specific reuse applications of an asset without actually changing the core asset
- System builds that manage variants of a system to support multiple platforms or minor variations for implementing specific business rules without changing the core functionality
- Relationship management that connects documentation and test programs to other software assets
- Reporting functions to track asset usage patterns to provide documentation that makes it easier to find and reuse an asset

One important function of configuration management is the ability to relate assets to one another. Configuration management tracks which assets are used by other assets and thereby have an effect on the other assets. By storing and understanding asset relationships, configuration management has information needed for impact analysis.

Knowing *how assets are related* as well as what they do enhances the reuse consumer's understanding and confidence when attempting to reuse the asset and may aid them in finding additional assets to reuse.

Also, configuration management is of great importance to reuse because it can be used to create variants of a system. In this way, a generic base system can be created and then reused and changed to create similar new systems while allowing the central core functionality of the generic version to remain intact. Configuration management can manage the core or kernel of the system and the variants. When a change is needed to the kernel, it can be migrated to all variants by the configuration management tools.

Managing variants is also useful to supporting system portability and flexibility. Software developers often need to build software that runs on a multitude of operating systems, LAN services, and DBMS's. Using configuration management, they can create one functional kernel system in which technology-specific functions are placed into separate assets and then vary the technology-related assets as needed.

Implementation Considerations

Configuration management tools are used to automate the various configuration management functions. For example, configuration management tool features can be categorized into storage, version control, system build and reporting support functions (Table 5-9).

Table 5-9. Configuration Management Tool Support Functions

STORAGE FEATURES

- Store assets in a secure database environment
- Provide security and access control for assets
- Maintain an asset inventory
- Check-in and check-out an asset

VERSION CONTROL FEATURES

- Manage the modification of an asset, providing revision/version control
- Ensure that when a developer is working on an asset that no one else can change the asset
- Support procedures to merge shared work back together
- Re-create versions of an asset
- Ensure that everyone using the asset has the correct version

SYSTEM BUILD FEATURES

- Maintain a map of how assets fit together into a system
- Track which versions of assets are in a particular configuration
- Manage variants of a system
- Analyze the impact of an asset change on other assets in the system
- Manage associated files for an asset: source, binary design, documentation
- Provide automatic rebuild of a system when an asset changes

The storage features of a configuration management tool ensure that an asset is not misplaced or inadvertently destroyed. It does this by providing a common secure storage area for managed assets. The environment should protect assets from "back door" access, in which assets are accessed directly and not through the intervening configuration management software that provides control.

Part of the storage management feature provides an inventory of what is stored. This in itself supports reuse by making assets more accessible. Finally, the storage feature is controlled by the check-in/check-out feature that protects assets from uncontrolled access and possible contamination.

Managing versions of assets without a configuration management tool is almost impossible. Possibly the biggest problem for reuse consumers is finding the correct version to work with. During development and revision activities, overlapping work can be very complex, and the configuration management tool protects one person's work from being destroyed by another's. It is often difficult to know which version of an asset is the currently most correct version to use. Configuration management tools can recognize the most current version, as well as recreate previous versions.

The third big usage of a configuration management tool is managing the system build. Various ways are used to retain the connections among assets of a system. In addition, different versions of the entire system contain different versions of their assets. Configuration management tools keep track of these complex relationships.

When selecting configuration management tools, an organization should take into consideration the repository, browsers, classification tools, and cataloging tools that it uses or plans to use to implement the asset storage and retrieval mechanism. Since these tools will be used together, their features and functions should compliment one another.

5.4.5 Track Asset Use

In this IEEE Std. 1517 task, asset use is tracked and reported:

> *6.1.3.5 The asset manager shall keep track of each reuse of the asset and report to the domain engineer information about actual reuses of the asset. Asset reuse information should include the reuser's name, project name, original developer or owner of the asset, cost of reusing the asset, and the savings and benefits derived from reusing the asset.[16]*

Discussion

The proof of the value of an asset to an organization lies in its actual reuse. The standard requires that usage information is recorded and, in particular, is reported to the domain engineer who developed or reengineered and prepared the asset for reuse. The domain engineer can learn valuable lessons from asset usage information that can be applied to the identification and development of future assets or future versions and implementations of the asset. For example, if it is more costly than anticipated to reuse the asset, the domain engineer may find that asset generalization techniques should be revised.

Implementation Considerations

The organization's reuse library group should keep track of asset use and record and distribute asset usage information to reuse program manager, reuse program sponsor, as well as the appropriate domain engineering teams.

A configuration management tool can report information about changes, versions, and configurations by automatically annotating change activities as they occur. When an asset is changed, the reason for the change, the name of the responsible person, and the time of the change can be recorded. Configurations can be identified by level of completion.

Also, a wide range of reports is available, including impact analysis, archive history revisions, check-outs, check-ins, file attributes, and comparisons. This information supports reuse by enabling an organization to track how a particular asset is reused as well as how many times it has been reused and to what extent it is changed when it is reused. Table 5-10 lists some examples of typical configuration management reports that support asset management in a reuse program.

Table 5-10. Examples of Configuration Management Reports

Asset Status Report	Status information about an asset or group of assets
Impact Analysis Report	List of all the systems in which this asset is used and would be affected by a change to the asset
History of Reuse Report	List of when and by whom the asset is being used (i.e., checked out of the library)
Asset Inventory Report	List of all the assets stored in the library sorted by characteristics that help identify their use
Difference between Versions Report	Report that presents an analysis of the differences between versions of the asset

5.4.6 Handle Asset Modification Requests and Problem Reports

In this IEEE Std. 1517 task, the responsibility of processing asset modification requests and problem reports is assigned to the asset manager and the domain engineer:

> *6.1.3.6 The asset manager shall forward asset modification requests and problem reports received from asset reusers to the domain engineer for review and correction/modification plans and actions. Actions planned and taken to meet requests or to correct problems shall be reported to the asset reuser making the request or filing the problem report.*[17]

Discussion

The responsibility for handling asset modification request and problem reports is split between the asset manager and the domain engineer. The asset manager serves as the middle-man between the reuse consumer and the reuse producer to collect and disseminate asset status and usage information. The domain engineer modifies and maintains assets by determining how to address an asset modification request or reported problem.

Implementation Considerations

The reuse library group should be responsible for collecting and distributing information regarding assets. This information should include the current status of the asset and the asset modification requests and problem reports. As Table 5-10 shows, a configuration management tool can be used to provide up-to-date information about an asset to all interested parties.

5.4.7 Record Asset Modification Requests and Problem Reports

In this IEEE Std. 1517 task, the asset manager is assigned the responsibility of monitoring and recording asset modification requests and problem reports:

> *6.1.3.7 The asset manager shall monitor and record these asset requests/reports and the subsequent actions taken. Whenever, problems with an asset are encountered, they should be recorded and entered into the Problem Resolution Process, as specified in the IEEE/EIA Std 12207.0-1996.[18]*

Discussion

The standard uses the 12207 Standard Problem Resolution Process to specify the requirements for monitoring and recording asset modification requests and problem reports. The 12207 Standard requires that a closed loop process is established and executed to handle asset requests and problem reports. The closed loop process entails:

- prompt entry of the request/problem into the process
- categorization and prioritization of the request/problem
- contacting of the relevant parties about the existence of the request/problem
- analysis and resolution of the problem
- tracking, recording and reporting of the request/problem

Implementation Considerations

The reuse library group should be assigned the responsibility of defining and executing the process to address asset modification requests and problem reports. Configuration management tools can be used to provide automated support to execute the problem resolution process especially in the area of tracking, recording, and reporting asset request and problems.

5.4.8 Notify Asset Reuses and Domain Engineers

In this IEEE Std. 1517 task, the asset manager is assigned the responsibility of notifying asset reusers and domain engineers about problems detected in and modifications made to assets:

> *6.1.3.8 The asset manager shall notify all asset reusers and the domain engineer of the problems detected in the asset, modifications made to the asset, new versions of the asset, and deletion of the asset from the asset storage and retrieval mechanism.[19]*

Discussion

To ensure confidence in the quality of assets, reuse consumers must be promptly notified about changes to assets. Also, domain engineers need feedback about the use of assets they have developed.

Implementation Considerations

The reuse library group should notify all asset reusers and domain engineers, who have either reported developing or reusing the asset, about changes, corrections, or new versions of asset. Configuration management tools can be used to identify all users of the asset and the relationship of the asset to other assets. E-mail messages can be used as the notification mechanism.

5.4.9 Retire Assets

In this task, the asset manager is assigned the responsibility of retiring assets from the asset storage and retrieval mechanism:

> *6.1.3.9 The asset manager shall retire assets from the asset storage and retrieval mechanism according to the asset retirement procedures and criteria.*[20]

Discussion

Assets that are never used or have serious quality deficiencies should be removed from the asset storage and retrieval mechanism to control the size and quality of the organization's asset inventory.

Implementation Considerations

Configuration management tools can be used to automatically track the use of assets, relationships of assets to other assets, and reported asset problems. The reuse library group can use this information to make appropriate and practical asset retirement decisions.

5.5 Summary

IEEE Std. 1517 Asset Management Process defines the requirements for managing an organization's asset inventory. It is categorized as a supporting life cycle process in the software life cycle process framework. Figure 5-1 shows the activities that specify, and the major deliverables produced by, the Asset Management Process. The party responsible for the Asset Management Process is the asset manager. Figure 5-2 summarizes the areas of responsibility for the asset manager.

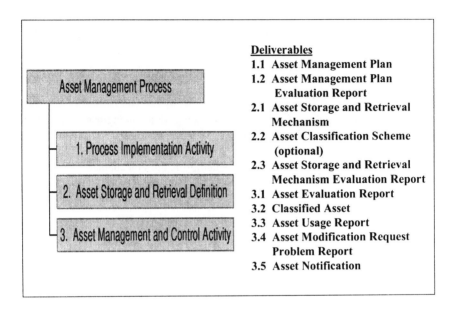

Figure 5-1. Asset Management Process Activities and Deliverables

Figure 5-2. Responsibilities of the Asset Manager

5.6 References

1. *IEEE Std. 1517, Standard for Information Technology—Software Life Cycle Processes—Reuse Processes*, IEEE, Piscataway, NJ, 1999.

2. Ibid.

3. Ibid.

4. Ibid.

5. Ibid.

6. Ibid.

7. Ibid.

8. Ibid.

9. D. Hofman, "A Major Change in Software Delivery," *Managing Software Development.* vol. 15, no. 11, Nov. 1995, pp. 1–4.

10. C. McClure, *Software Reuse Techniques: Adding Reuse to the Systems Development Process.* Prentice-Hall, Upper Saddle River, N.J., 1997, pp. 239–264.

11. *IEEE Std. 1517, Standard for Information Technology—Software Life Cycle Processes—Reuse Processes.*

12. Ibid.

13. Ibid.

14. Ibid.

15. Ibid.

16. Ibid.

17. Ibid.

18. Ibid.

19. Ibid.

20. Ibid.

Chapter 6.
Adding the Reuse Program Administration Process to the Software Life Cycle Process Framework

6.1 Introduction to the Reuse Program Administration Process

Reuse is a unique software paradigm in that it normally requires adoption above the single project level. To position itself to reap the maximum benefits that reuse promises, an organization must establish a technical, management, and cultural environment where assets can be shared across project teams and software organizations, as well as reused in multiple software products and systems over time. Ideally, the scope for a reuse initiative covers the entire enterprise.

6.1.1 Reuse Adoption Strategy

Initiatives with such a broad scope require careful planning, management commitment, and good communication channels among software groups and teams. If an organization relies solely on an informal adoption strategy for reuse, it runs a great risk of failing to achieve any substantial benefits from reuse. To combat this risk, the reuse initiative must be formalized in a reuse program endorsed by management, adequately funded, and supported by the software organization, infrastructure, and culture.

6.1.2 Reuse Program

The Random House Dictionary defines the word *program* as a "plan of action to accomplish a specified end; schedule of activities, procedures, etc., to be followed; a planned, coordinated group of activities, procedures, etc., often for a specific purpose."[1]

Thus, a reuse program is the plan of action or activities through which an organization manages assets and provides the processes that enable the practice of inter-project reuse. The reuse program provides the structure and discipline needed to manage and use assets effectively during the software life cycle.

As Figure 6-1 shows, IEEE Std. 1517 extends the IEEE/EIA 12207 software life cycle process framework by adding a new organizational life cycle process called the *Reuse Program Administration Process*. This process is a requirements specification for a reuse program that supports the adoption of systematic reuse at the organization-level. In the context of the standard, the term *organization* may be used refer to an entire enterprise, a national or industrial association, a company, or an organization or group within a company or enterprise. Therefore, the Reuse Program Administration Process may be used to establish and implement a reuse program that ranges from supporting one software development group to an entire corporation.

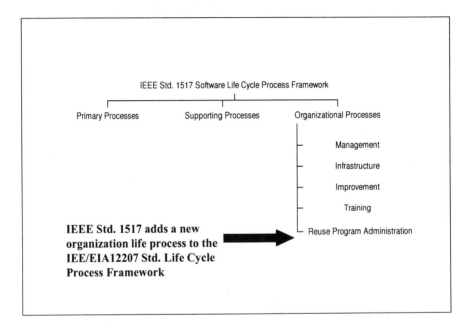

Figure 6-1. Adding the Reuse Program Administration Process to the IEEE/EIA 12207 Organizational Life Cycle Process

The standard recommends that the following elements be included in the reuse program:

- Reuse sponsor
- Reuse infrastructure (the hardware, software, tools, techniques, standards, metrics, and facilities for practicing reuse)
- Reuse funding and other resources
- Reuse program support function
- Reuse communication, feedback, and notification mechanisms

From this list, it is clear that IEEE Std. 1517 recognizes technology as only one of several essential elements in a reuse program. Non-technical elements, such as a reuse sponsor and proper funding, play a very instrumental role in successfully adopting systematic reuse. Furthermore, systematic reuse requires cooperation, communication, teamwork, and sharing across software project teams and perhaps across different corporate groups. Practicing reuse across team and even organizational boundaries maximizes the base on which reuse costs can be spread and enables better recognition of reuse opportunities in the organization.

The standard names the *reuse program administrator* as the party responsible for establishing, managing, and supporting the practice of systematic reuse.

The Reuse Program Administration Process specifies the activities required for planning, establishing, managing, executing, monitoring, and improving an organization's reuse program. These activities are listed and summarized in Table 6-1 and presented in detail below, explained in terms of its tasks. Recall that, in the standard, a task represents the requirements for implementing the activity. First, the task is discussed, and then suggestions for how an organization may implement the task are presented.

6.2 Initiation Activity

The purpose of IEEE Std. 1517 Initiation Activity is to lay a proper foundation for a successful reuse program. The strength of this foundation depends upon a clear understanding of what the organization believes software reuse is and why the organization wants to adopt a reuse approach for software development and maintenance. This foundation is established by defining the organization's reuse strategy.

6.2.1 Define Reuse Strategy

The first task that IEEE Std. 1517 includes in the Initiation Activity of the Reuse Program Administration Process establishes the organization's reuse strategy and recommends, at a high level, what elements should be contained in the organization's reuse program:

> *The reuse program for an organization shall be initiated by establishing the organization's reuse strategy that includes its reuse goals, purposes, objectives, and scope. Elements of the reuse program should address the following:*
>
> *a) Reuse sponsor*
>
> *b) Reuse infrastructure (hardware, software, tools, techniques, standards, metrics, and facilities for practicing reuse)*
>
> *c) Reuse funding and other resources*
>
> *d) Reuse program support function*
>
> *e) Reuse communication, feedback, and notification mechanisms[2]*

Table 6-1. Activities in IEEE Std. 1517 Reuse Program Administration Process

Initiation	• Establish reuse strategy • Name reuse sponsor • Identify reuse program participants/roles • Establish reuse steering function • Establish reuse program support function
Domain Identification	• Identify, evaluate, and refine the organization's reuse domains
Reuse Assessment	• Assess organization's systematic reuse capability • Assess reuse potential of organization's domains • Recommend refinement of organization's reuse strategy and reuse program implementation plan • Improve organization's reuse infrastructure
Planning	• Create, document, evaluate, review, get approval for, and maintain organization's reuse program implementation plan
Execution and Control	• Execute activities defined in organization's reuse program implementation plan • Monitor progress of reuse program • Report reuse program problems • Reaffirm management's reuse program support
Review and Evaluation	• Periodically assess achievements of organization's reuse program • Report reuse program results and lessons learned • Recommend changes to improve organization's reuse program

Discussion

It is important to clarify and agree upon the organization's reuse expectations up-front since they will help shape a reuse program that has the ability to achieve these expectations, as well as help determine how the organization will define and measure reuse success. For example, one organization may emphasize software quality improvements as its primary reuse objective, while another may choose reducing product time-to-market as its reuse objective. By defining its reuse goals and objectives, all reuse program participants have a common understanding of the organization's reasons for adopting reuse. Without knowing these reasons, an organization cannot define an effective reuse program.

To increase management's interest and acceptance of reuse, the reuse strategy should address not only technical goals and objectives but also the needs of the business. For example, one company planned to implement an enterprise-wide reuse program with the goals of reducing product time-to-market by increasing software productivity and increasing client satisfaction by improving software quality.

Also, the scope of the reuse effort should include only areas where there are known opportunities to reuse specific assets that are or could easily be made available and where their reuse would result in significant business benefits to the organization. By limiting the reuse scope in this manner, an organization greatly increases it chance for reuse success (i.e., achieving sufficient reuse benefits).

The standard recognizes that those who participate and are affected by the reuse program may have different job functions and roles as well as be members of different organizational groups. As Figure 6-2 shows, the standard suggests the establishment of communication channels between various groups.

Implementation Suggestions

The reuse strategy should be developed using enterprise models, strategic system plans, product lines, and organizational structure to identify areas where there are reuse opportunities.

An organization is not expected to completely define the elements of its reuse program at the initiation stage. More information must be known about the organization's reuse strategy, the general software engineering maturity of the organization, and the availability of resources before the program can be fully defined.

Since adopting systematic reuse across an organization can be a very expensive venture, it is important that the cost of reuse is well understood at the beginning of any attempt to establish a reuse program. The following observations from industry should be kept in mind.

First, there is a cost associated with practicing reuse. For example, creating a component for reuse can cost 25 percent to 13 times more than creating it for a single use.[3] The major elements contributing to reuse costs are:

- Establishing and supporting a reuse infrastructure

- Acquiring, building, re-engineering, and managing assets

- Establishing and supporting a reuse program support function

- Changing the organization to enable the acceptance and practice of systematic reuse

Second, management must realize that reuse will not succeed unless the reuse program is adequately funded. How much is needed and when it is needed depends upon the scope of the reuse strategy and the pace at which the organization plans to introduce reuse.

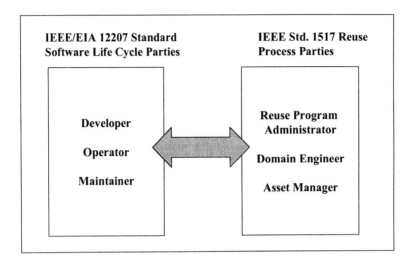

Figure 6-2. Communication Channels between the
Reuse Program Participants

When the goal is to practice reuse across the enterprise, the reuse program is typically supported with a general fund. Some suggestions are:

1. Fund the reuse program via a tax paid by all projects whether or not the project practices reuse. For example, at one company each project is charged a reuse tax at the rate of 2% of the project budget.[4] All projects that contribute assets for reuse are given a tax refund.

2. Fund the reuse program through all divisions or organizations that wish to participate in the reuse program.

3. Allocate a specific percentage of the entire Information Technology budget to the reuse program. For example, at one organization 20% of the IT budget is allocated to setting up the reuse program. Once the program is established, this percentage will be lowered substantially.[5]

4. A fee is charged to use the reuse program's assets.

5. The cost of the reuse program is amortized over the software products expected to be developed using the reuse program's assets.

It is advisable to reconcile funding issues early in the reuse program to assure its success. Consider taking the following actions to address reuse program funding issues:

1. Obtain a firm, long-term commitment from management.

2. Make the reuse sponsor(s) responsible for funding.

3. Define reuse cost/benefit analysis methods to estimate the cost of reuse and the savings and other benefits the organization expects to obtain from the reuse program.

4. Expect to see the need for funding change depending upon the stage of maturity of the reuse program. For example, when the reuse program is initiated, it probably will take the form of a pilot in a few projects before it becomes more widely spread throughout the organization. This means that less funding is needed at first but then, as the program grows, more funding will be needed to conduct training and to enlarge the reuse program support function. Experience from industry has shown that in the second or third year of the reuse program, the organization should be prepared to see costs rise. Then, probably by the fourth or fifth year, the costs will drop as the practice of reuse in the organization matures.[6]

6.2.2 Name Reuse Sponsor

In the second Initiation Activity task, IEEE Std.1517 recommends, but does not require, that an organization name a reuse sponsor for the reuse program:

7.1.1.2 A Reuse Sponsor should be named.

Discussion

A reuse sponsor is preferred, but not necessarily required, because some organizations may not have a management structure that allows them to satisfy this requirement. However, it is important to note that organizations that have succeeded with reuse usually have a reuse sponsor whose job is to authorize, approve, promote, and generally help provide resources for the reuse program. The reuse sponsor has been found to be an effective way to ensure that reuse will be taken seriously by both management and software staff and that the commitment needed for reuse is not beyond the scope of influence of the reuse program manager.

The reuse sponsor has particularly critical responsibilities during the initiation of the reuse program. This is the point at which the reuse sponsor incorporates management's vision into the reuse strategy and links reuse to other important and already accepted management initiatives. In addition, the reuse sponsor outlines how reuse can help attain important business objectives, and determines how well the organization can handle the changes that reuse requires.

Implementation Suggestions

Table 6-2 lists the responsibilities that an organization should consider assigning to its reuse sponsor. An organization that is implementing IEEE Std. 1517 should consider appointing a reuse sponsor as early as possible during the initiation of the reuse program to give the program more credibility. The reuse sponsor should be an individual or group from management ranks (the higher, the better). One possible candidate is the Chief Information Officer.

Another implementation suggestion is to assign each software development unit or product-line manager responsibility for sponsoring reuse in his/her group to ensure that reuse opportunities are actually pursued. Unit and/or product-line reuse sponsors should be encouraged to work together to communicate reuse opportunities and sharing across unit/product-line boundaries.

Table 6-2. Responsibilities of the Reuse Sponsor

- Creating the corporate reuse vision
- Introducing reuse into the organization and encouraging and mandating its practice
- Determining how the corporation will handle any organizational and cultural changes required by reuse
- Authorizing, approving, promoting and providing resources for the reuse program
- Ensuring the success of reuse as a business strategy by determining how reuse can help attain corporate business objectives

6.2.3 Identify Reuse Program Participants

In third task of the Initiation Activity, IEEE Std. 1517 requires the identification of the reuse program participants and roles:

> *7.1.1.2 Reuse program participants shall be identified and their roles shall be assigned.*[8]

Discussion

IEEE Std. 1517 does not, however, specify who the participants must be or what their roles are. These details are left to each individual organization that is implementing the standard. It can be assumed that the reuse sponsor and members of the reuse program support function are some of the participants in the reuse program. It can also be assumed that some reuse program participants will assume the role of reuse producers who are responsible for building and maintaining assets; and other participants will assume the role of reuse consumers who use assets to build software products and systems. In some cases depending upon the particular project or structure of their organization, the same participant may assume both roles of reuse producer and reuse consumer.

Implementation Suggestions

Although not mentioned specifically in the standard, an organization should also consider including reuse champion and reuse program manager roles in the reuse program. A *reuse champion* is an individual or small group of individuals that investigate and experiment with reuse and promote the concept of reuse within the organization.[9] A *reuse program manager* is responsible for defining, implementing, and providing ongoing support for a reuse program.[10]

An organization should choose as its reuse champion an individual or group who is respected by both management and software professionals, is a good communicator, is trained in reuse, and is excited about reuse. The role of the reuse champion is to help initiate the program, light the spark of interest in reuse throughout the organization, and promote the practice of systematic reuse.

While it is the role of the reuse sponsor to create a business vision for reuse, it is the role of the reuse program manager to establish and manage a reuse program that can transform that vision into actual, meaningful benefits delivered to the organization. The reuse program manager is usually chosen from the ranks of software technology management. The role of the reuse program manager should include responsibilities such as those listed in Table 6-3.

Table 6-3. Role of the Reuse Program Manager

- Perform strategic reuse planning for the organization
- Define, implement, and provide ongoing support for the reuse program.
- Manage the day-to-day details of the reuse program
- Assume the responsibility for the reuse infrastructure
- Measure and report the impact of the reuse program on the organization

6.2.4 Establish a Reuse Steering Function

IEEE Std. 1517 specifies the establishment of a reuse steering function as another required Initiation Activity task:

7.1.1.4 A reuse steering function shall be established to assume the authority and responsibility for the organization's reuse program. Its functions should include the following:

a) investigation of the practice of reuse in the organization

b) identification of the areas in the organization where there are potential reuse opportunities

c) assignment of the responsibilities for reuse in the organization

d) redefinition of the organization's incentives, disincentives, and culture to support and encourage reuse.[11]

Discussion

The standard suggests that members of the reuse steering function include the reuse sponsor (if one has been named), the software development manager, the operations manager, the maintenance manager, and a reuse expert. Of course, if a reuse program manager has been appointed, he/she should be a member of the reuse steering function.

Implementation Suggestions

When implementing this task, consider implementing the reuse steering function as a committee composed of managers from the different business units/departments that are interested in practicing reuse. The members should have a solid understanding of the business, both where it is today and where it is going in the future. Also, the reuse champion(s) and any other internal/external reuse experts should work with the committee to identify all the elements necessary to create a successful reuse program.

Participation in the reuse steering committee may be voluntary or mandatory. Mandatory participation is more likely to lead to real results.

The purpose of reuse steering committee is to gain a consensus of opinion from the managers about how to implement the reuse initiative in the organization. A reuse steering committee is especially important in companies whose management style is "consensus-by-committee."

One important area of responsibility for the reuse steering function is promoting the reuse program. A major part of introducing reuse into an organization is promoting the concept to management, software users, and the software staff. Reuse represents a fundamental change in the way software professionals work; and like any change, it will be resisted if not properly promoted. In general, management, software users, and software professionals need to understand the reasons why the organization has chosen to adopt reuse; how reuse changes the organizational structure, values, and reward systems; and what the rewards for adopting reuse are to be. Commonly used methods to promote reuse are:

1.   Active information campaigns to explain the purposes and benefits of reuse

2.   Reuse education and training programs for management and the software staff

3.   Reuse incentive programs to recognize high achievers

Without the buy-in and support from the reuse program participants, even the most carefully planned and well-managed reuse program is likely to fail. Promoting reuse is essential, especially in the early stages of implementing the reuse program. After reuse has become a normal software practice, some promotional activities, such as incentives programs, may no longer be necessary; while others, such as training, will continue to be critical to the survival of the program.

6.2.5 Establish a Reuse Program Support Function

The responsibility for systematic reuse is a big one because reuse fundamentally changes the software life cycle. It takes persistent effort and special skills to introduce the practice of systematic reuse into an organization's software procedures and personnel structures. New roles, responsibilities, and job functions are essential in practicing systematic reuse.

In task 7.1.1.5, IEEE Std. 1517 specifies the requirement to establish a reuse program support function. Also, task 7.1.1.5 recommends some of the responsibilities that an organization should consider assigning to the reuse program support function:

> *7.1.1.5 A reuse program support function shall be established. The responsibilities of the reuse program support function should include the following:*
>
> *a)   Participating in the creation and implementation of a reuse program implementation plan*
>
> *b)   Identifying, documenting, and conveying the reuse strategy to all reuse program participants*

    c)   *Promoting the practice of reuse to encourage a reuse-positive soft-ware culture*

    d)   *Seeking out opportunities to practice reuse in current and future software projects*

    e)   *Establishing and maintaining the reuse infrastructure*

    f)   *Providing reuse consulting support to software projects that practice reuse*

Discussion

The purpose of the reuse program support function is to make the practice of reuse proactive in an organization. The reuse program support function is the means by which to move reuse beyond a grass-roots or committee effort where reuse is mostly talk and little action to where systematic reuse is a normal, accepted practice in the organization's software projects. If management does not provide sufficient resources to support the reuse program support function, it is unlikely that the practice of reuse will ever mature beyond a poorly defined practice that only occasionally occurs within projects and only occasionally delivers benefits.

Implementation Suggestions

The reuse program support function may be implemented in the form of a reuse program support group. When the organization's reuse goal is to practice systematic reuse across multiple software systems and projects, management should assign representatives from the various development projects/units and product-line groups expected to practice reuse to be the members of the reuse program support group.

The reuse program support group may begin with a reuse champion who is active during the startup stages of the program. Often, the reuse initiative evolves from one reuse champion in the early stages to a formally established reuse program support group headed by a reuse program manager.

An organization should address the following aspects when forming the reuse program support group:

- Size
- Skill Set
- Location in organizational structure
- Funding
- Responsibilities

What is considered an appropriate size for the reuse program support group depends upon: the scope of the reuse program (i.e., the number of projects following a reuse-driven development approach); the level of maturity of the reuse program (e.g., Initial Startup Stage, Ongoing Support Stage); and the size of the software staff to be supported by the reuse program support function.

In the early stages of the reuse program, when the reuse is being planned and when reuse is being attempted on an experimental/pilot project basis, only a small group is needed. As the practice of reuse grows, spreading throughout the organization, the size of the reuse program support group will need to grow accordingly. More support must be provided to design and populate the asset storage and retrieval mechanism with assets. Also, enough support must be available to provide reuse consulting to every project in which reuse is being practiced. In general, the size of the reuse program support group should be in the range of 1-to-2 percent of the software staff it supports.[12]

The function of the reuse program support group is to drive reuse and make it happen at the project level. The reuse program support group should be staffed with reuse experts who go out and "work" the projects by promoting the benefits of reuse to the project team, learning what the project is building that may be of use elsewhere, and supplying projects with assets. Only if the reuse program support group brings to a project everything it needs to practice reuse, (e.g., assets, methods, standards, and tools) can project teams be expected to apply systematic reuse. Teams with no previous experience must be lead step-by-step through the details of practicing reuse by a skilled reuse expert. Table 6-4 lists the skill set required for a reuse expert.

It is important to define an initial proposed structure, placement, and responsibilities for the reuse program support group. This is an essential element of a stable infrastructure needed to support reuse, especially if the organization's ultimate goal is to practice systematic reuse across the entire enterprise.

One choice is to define reuse support as a centralized function if the group is to serve different software development organizations. In this case, the most natural place for the reuse program support group is as a subgroup within the central information resource management group. A second choice is to form the reuse program support group as subgroup within a high productivity/advanced technology group, the data administration group, repository administration group, or software re-engineering group. In this case, it is important that at least one member of the group is assigned reuse as his/her primary job function.

As Figure 6-3 shows, one possible structure for the reuse program support group, based on the structure used at GTE Data Services, is to divide it into the following three subgroups reflecting the basic functional areas of reuse support provided: [13]

1. The *Management Subgroup* defines the elements of the reuse program, obtains reuse funding, and administers the reuse program.

2. The *Library Administration Subgroup* identifies potential assets, creates and certifies assets, and manages the asset storage and retrieval mechanism.

3. The *Consulting Subgroup* guides project teams in the application of reuse.

6.3 Domain Identification Activity

The second activity that IEEE Std. 1517 specifies in the Reuse Program Administration Process is Domain Identification. The standard defines a *domain* as "a problem space."[14] Examples of a domain are a particular business function such as aircraft maintenance or a product line such as 35mm cameras.

Table 6-4. Reuse Expert Skill Set

- Strong technical skills to gain respect of the software staff
    - Good organizational skills
    - Ability to adapt to a new way of thinking and working
    - Self-motivating personality
- Interested in and enthusiastic about reuse
- Knowledgeable software methodologist
- Knowledgeable user of re-engineering tools, repositories, testing tools, and library/configuration management tools
- Good understanding of the business and business directions
- Experienced in developing software with assets and developing assets
- Working knowledge of software testing and configuration management principles
- Ability to apply software metrics and measurements and compile and analyze data
- Ability to guide project team members in the practice of reuse
- Ability to recognize opportunities for reuse
- Ability to use abstraction to create an asset for reuse

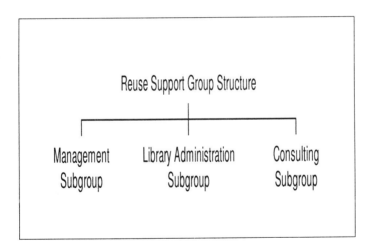

Figure 6-3. Possible Structure for Reuse Program Support Group

In this activity, the standard further explains that a domain "characterizes a set of systems in terms of common properties that can be organized into a collection of reusable assets."[15] For example, common properties might refer to common designs, common capabilities or services, common technology, or a common information architecture that are shared by a set of systems.[16] Assets that implement these common properties may be used to build systems in the domain.

By associating assets with domains, the reuse program can be divided into focus areas where reuse is easier to manage, where reuse opportunities are easier to identify, and where reuse can be more easily adopted.

6.3.1 Identify Domains

The first task in the Domain Identification Activity requires the identification of the domains to include in the scope of the reuse program:

> *7.1.2.1 The reuse program administrator, aided by the appropriate management, domain engineers, users, and software developers, shall identify and document the domains in which to investigate reuse opportunities or in which the organization intends to practice reuse.*[17]

Discussion

This task implies that an organization may have to perform an exercise in which it divides itself into a set of domains. Also, this task implies that an organization may not plan to practice reuse in every one of its domains and that all domains do not have the same reuse potential.

There are several reasons why an organization may choose to limit the scope of its reuse program to cover only a subset of its domains:

1. There may not be enough common properties among the systems in the domain to enable adequate payback from the cost of practicing reuse.

2. The domain may be too unstable to identify domain assets.

3. Very little software systems work is planned for this domain.

4. Software systems in this domain are not considered of great enough strategic value to the organization to merit the inclusion of this domain in the reuse program.

It is important to note that domain identification cannot be done solely by the reuse program administrator. The organization's management, software system users, software system developers, and domain engineers must also be involved in identifying the domains that offer the best reuse potential to the organization. Management provides valuable strategic information about what system capabilities are most important to achieve business objectives. System users provide valuable knowledge about their current and future system needs. System developers provide information about the assets they would find most useful in building software systems. Domain engineers provide information about the effort and cost associated with building and managing particular assets.

All of this information and all of these perspectives are needed to determine the domains in which the organization's reuse program should be focused.

Implementation Suggestions

If enterprise models have been built, they should be used to identify business areas, functions, and possible domains where there are opportunities for reuse. Commonalities that recur across the models should be used to determine areas to focus reuse efforts. Characteristics that help identify the domains most appropriate for practicing reuse are: (1) narrow, not too broad, (2) mature, stable and well-defined, and (3) independent of technology.[18] One insurance company used its enterprise information architecture, which consisted of eleven families or subject areas that represent basic data and processes, to initially define eleven domains for the company.

If there are no enterprise models, the product lines or the organizational structure may be used to identify areas where there are reuse opportunities.

A domain should be defined in terms of its scope and it relationship to other domains. The scope of a domain should be defined in terms of the functions and capabilities or services that are included in the domain, as well as those are excluded from the domain. A context model, data flow model, or object model can be used to document the scope of the domain.[19] The relationship of the domain to other domains can be documented using a data flow model or structure chart.[20]

6.3.2 Evaluate Domains

In the second task of the Domain Identification Activity, IEEE Std. 1517 requires an evaluation of the domains that are included in the scope of the reuse program:

> *7.1.2.2 The reuse program administrator, aided by the appropriate management, domain engineers, users, and software developers, shall evaluate the domains to assure that they accurately reflect the organization's reuse strategy. The results of the evaluation shall be documented.[21]*

Discussion

Reuse is not an end in itself. Although it may be easy to forget when immersed in the details of establishing a reuse program, reuse must be seen as a means to achieve the objectives of an organization. Usually, these objectives are rooted in crucial business goals, not merely in new technology directions.

Recall that the reuse strategy expresses an organization's reuse goals, purposes, objectives, and scope. Reuse should not be practiced in a domain unless this contributes to the achievement of the organization's reuse strategy.

Implementation Suggestions

For each domain that has been identified for inclusion in the scope of the reuse program, an organization may determine how well it satisfies the reuse strategy by performing the following evaluation steps:

1. List the systems and software products in this domain for which there are known development or enhancement plans

2. Identify assets, including common architectures and designs, that could be used to develop or enhance these systems and products; determine whether these assets are currently available or must be developed or acquired

3. Determine the benefits, such as cost or times savings, that may expected from practicing reuse in this domain using the assets identified above

4. Determine if any these expected benefits can be mapped to the reuse goals and objectives included in the organization's reuse strategy

5. Finally, if the benefits can satisfy a reuse goal, will management consider the benefit great enough to off set the effort of practicing reuse in this domain

6.3.3 Conduct a Domain Review

IEEE Std. 1517 requires that the results of the domain evaluation be formally reviewed:

> *7.1.2.3 The reuse program administrator shall conduct joint reviews in accordance with the IEEE/EIA 12207.0-1996 Joint Review Process. Software developers, domain engineers, and users shall be included in the reviews.*[22]

Discussion

All the participants in the reuse program should be in agreement concerning the scope of the reuse program. A formal review of the results of the evaluation of the domains is an opportunity to obtain that agreement or to uncover conflicting positions on the reuse scope. If not detected and resolved, such conflicts may result in serious implementation problems and even the eventual failure of the reuse program.

Implementation Suggestions

In this task, IEEE Std. 1517 refers to the IEEE/EIA 12207 Standard to specify the requirements for conducting a joint review. The Joint Review Process is defined as one of the supporting life cycle processes in the IEEE 12207 Standard. According to the IEEE/EIA 12207 Standard, the Joint Review Process may be used to evaluate the status and products of an activity, as a project management review or as a technical review.

Since IEEE Std. 1517 does not specify the purpose of the joint view in the context of the Domain Identification Activity, the organization may choose to conduct the joint review for any one or all of these purposes. For instance, the Domain Identification Activity may be viewed as a project whose status and problems should be reviewed; or the domain definitions and the domains selected for inclusion in the scope of the reuse program as a products that may be technically reviewed.

6.3.4 Refine Domains

In the fourth task in the Domain Identification Activity, IEEE Std. 1517 recognizes that an organization's domains may change over time and therefore specifies the option—but not the requirement to refine its domains:

> *7.1.2.4 As more information about the organization's domains and plan for future software products becomes available or when the domains are analyzed, the domains may be refined and rescoped by the reuse program administrator.*[23]

Discussion

Since an organization is a fluid structure that is likely to change over time, its domains are also fluid and must be allowed to change. Furthermore, since there is no order of execution implied in the list of tasks included in the standard, it is possible that the identification and analysis of domains can occur simultaneously with each affecting the results of the other. To accommodate such interaction, the standard allows for refining the domains identified in an organization and the domains in which an organization practices reuse.

Implementation Suggestions

A common reason for refining a domain is that its scope is too broad, thus the domain is very difficult to analyze and manage. If this is the case, then either do a high-level analysis of the whole domain, especially if the purpose is to gain an understanding of the domain; or narrow the reuse focus for the domain down to a sub-domain.[24]

6.4 Reuse Assessment Activity

Introducing the practice of systematic reuse in an organization is a large, complex undertaking. There are many ways in which an organization can fail in its attempts to adopt reuse, such as:

- Not being properly prepared in terms of tools and skill sets
- Trying to do too much too soon
- Not understanding what benefits the organization is seeking from reuse
- No way to measure the impact of reuse or the extent to which it is practiced
- Insufficient understanding of reuse/lack of management commitment

To ensure success, an organization needs to determine how ready, willing, and able it is to practice systematic reuse, and what actions to take to prepare to implement its reuse strategy. A reuse assessment can help identify the risks for failure and how to avoid or compensate for them. A reuse assessment can help an organization define a more realistic reuse strategy.

The reuse assessment is performed to measure the potential for practicing systematic reuse in an organization, determine if the organization is ready to embark on a reuse program, and define where to focus its reuse efforts to gain the maximum benefit from practicing reuse. The emphasis is on a business viewpoint, looking at the reasons for applying reuse and the expected business value to be gained from reuse. The result of the reuse assessment can be used as the basis for defining the organization's reuse goals, reuse adoption approach, the domains in which to practice reuse, and the reuse program implementation plan.

This activity provides an understanding of the reuse maturity of the target organization, assesses the target domains for reuse potential, and uses the information obtained to make recommendations on how to proceed noting possible risks for failure of the reuse program and recommending ways to overcome or minimize the impact of these risks. This activity also can help motivate and direct incremental improvements in many areas of the reuse program, such as training and infrastructure.

6.4.1 Assess Organization's Systematic Reuse Capability

The first task in IEEE Std. 1517 Reuse Assessment Activity assesses the organization's systematic reuse capability:

> *7.1.3.1 The reuse program administrator shall assess the organization's systematic reuse capability. The results of the assessment shall be documented and provided to the reuse steering function.*[25]

Discussion

The reuse capability is used to determine:

- how well prepared an organization is to assimilate the practice of systematic reuse
- what are the actions that the organization should take to improve its ability to successfully adopt reuse

As Figure 6-4 shows, there is often a gap between an organization's current capabilities to practice reuse and the capabilities it needs to succeed with systematic reuse. The assessment helps define how to close this gap.

Implementation Suggestions

An assessment team should be formed to perform the reuse assessment. At least one member of the team should have previous experience in performing a reuse assessment; and at least one member should be an experienced software developer familiar with assets currently available in the organization. Also, the reuse program manager, if there is one, and the reuse champion, if there is one, should be included in the assessment team.

The reuse assessment should be conducted as a combination interviewing and reviewing exercise. Key personnel from each group expected to participate in the reuse program should be interviewed to learn about their reuse suggestions or reservations. In addition, key software material (such as strategic software system plans, enterprise models and architectures, and software standards) should be reviewed during the assessment. Since different organizations and groups within an organization are likely to have different reuse capabilities, they should be assessed separately. There are five suggested dimensions used to measure reuse capability:

1. Reuse Opportunities

2. Investment in Reuse

3. Reuse Skills and Experience

4. Reuse Infrastructure

5. Organization's Culture

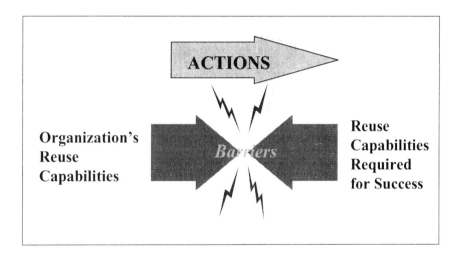

Figure 6-4. The Reuse Capability Gap

One possible method to use to assess an organization's reuse capability is the Software Engineering Capability Maturity Model (CMM) developed by the Software Engineering Institute at Carnegie Mellon University.[26] As Figure 6-5 shows, the CMM divides the quality of the software life cycle process into five maturity levels; with the first level representing the least mature process and the fifth level representing the most mature process. Typically, organizations use the CMM as a guide in improving their software life cycle processes.

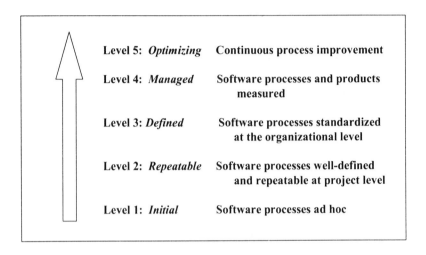

Figure 6-5. Framework for the Software Engineering Institute's
Software Engineering Capability Maturity Model

The minimum level of maturity an organization should have to successfully adopt software re-use is Level 2. At Level 2, there is a well-defined, repeatable process in place at the project level. However, to successfully adopt systematic reuse, the minimum level of process maturity must be Level 3. At Level 3, the software life cycle process is well-defined, repeatable, and standardized across the organization.

If an organization is below Level 2, it should take steps to introduce a well-defined, repeatable process before it attempts to introduce reuse.

Although the CMM offers some guidance in assessing an organization's reuse capability, it should not be used as the sole assessment method. This is because the current version (at the time of writing this book) of the CMM, Version 1.1, does not address reuse activities in sufficient detail (discussed further in Chapter 9).

Another method that may help an organization measure its reuse capability is the Reuse Maturity Model, shown in Figure 6-6.[27,28] The CMM was used as the basis for creating the Reuse Maturity Model. Like CMM, the Reuse Maturity Model has five levels or stages. Successive stages represent more mature practices of reuse. An organization may use the five stages as a basis for creating a reuse program implementation plan. Also, an organization can use this model to identify those groups or project teams that are more likely to succeed with reuse because their reuse capability is better. Initially, an organization should focus its reuse efforts in the most reuse mature groups/teams to ensure early reuse successes.

It is highly recommended that an organization use IEEE Std. 1517 to help assess it reuse capability since it offers a comprehensive and standardized description of systematic reuse (Figure 6-7). By using the standard as a requirements specification for reuse capability, an organization can determine which requirements it has met and which it needs to implement.

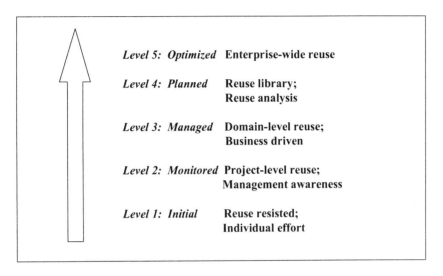

Figure 6-6. Reuse Maturity Model

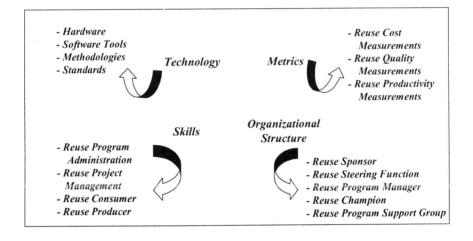

Figure 6-7. Elements of IEEE Std. 1517 Infrastructure

Also, according to task 7.1.3.1 in IEEE Std. 1517, an organization must document the results of the reuse assessment. It is a good idea to prepare a formal reuse assessment report that states the areas where the reuse opportunities were identified; reasons and evidence that supports these choices, constraints on the reuse program; expected value to be gained from the reuse program; actions to take to fulfill reuse goals; and risks for failure.

Figure 6-8 shows an example of the Executive Summary from a Reuse Assessment Report for one company.

INVESCO GOALS	RECOMMMENDED ACTIONS
1. Coordinate reuse in and across projects	• Enforce current corporate Standards and Global Naming Conventions • Using Reuse Standards from Reuse Task Force, create corporate Reuse Standards • Follow the new GUI Standards from the Usability Group • Follow the OO Modeling Standards from the OO Forum Project Management Subgroup • Get consensus from projects and set direction for adhering to platforms, tools and methods standards • Increase size of currently established Reuse Group to include a manager and two members (Currently one person is assigned to the reuse support function) • Train Reuse Group staff in reuse and enhance their reuse responsibilities • Introduce a reuse consultant function
2. Build and provide reusable components that give immediate benefit	• Use Corporate Systems Lotus Notes prototype to create a reuse catalog • Implement a classification scheme covering use cases, class descriptions, design models, code and subroutines • Populate catalog with descriptions of subroutines, analysis/design documents, test scripts, CBO GUI modules and telephone exchange business objects, use cases, object models and class descriptions, and C++ class library • Inventory and buy additional useful class libraries and frameworks • Make a prototype of the reuse catalog available for use in a pilot project

Figure 6-8 Continued

3. Incorporate reuse into methodologies	• Add reuse extensions to OO Development methodology • Include reuse considerations and checks in project reviews, inspections and JAD sessions • Complete and add reuse extensions to OO methodology defined by OO Forum Project Management Subgroup • Develop reuse guidelines for creating and using reusable components • Complete and add reuse extensions to OO methodology defined by OO Forum Project Management Subgroup • Develop reuse guidelines for creating and using reusable components for use with the IE and OO methodologies • Pilot the OO methodology in pilot projects • Pilot the IE methodology in selected IE projects • Create reuse training for software project managers and personnel
4. Practice enterprise-wide reuse	• Investigate and develop enterprise-wide reusable components in the following areas: security, customer, date routines, address, legal owner, widgets for building GUIs, recovery, and audit • Perform domain analysis on all INVESCO Products to identify and build or locate reusable components that can be shared across these systems. Define who will build the components, when they are needed and how the cost will be shared • Appoint a INVESCO enterprise reuse sponsor and a reuse sponsor for each major INVESCO product • Mandate the practice of reuse having management include reuse in its policy and invest in INVESCO's Reuse Program • Establish reuse funding sources/procedure

Figure 6-8. Example of Executive Summary from a
Reuse Assessment Report

The INVESCO Reuse Program implementation actions recommended by the reuse assessment are summarized below.

6.4.2 Assess Domain Reuse Potential

In addition to assessing the systematic reuse capability of the organization, IEEE Std. 1517 assesses the reuse potential of each of the organization's domains:

7.1.3.2 The reuse program administrator shall assess each domain being considered for reuse to determine the potential for reuse success in the domain. The results of the assessment shall be documented and provided to the reuse steering function.[29]

Discussion

Because resources for the reuse program and management's ability to wait for results are usually limited, the potential for reuse success in the domain may be based on:

- how much time will be needed to deliver reuse benefits in the domain
- the strategic importance of the systems and software products in the domain.

Domains that offer the best potential for reuse success should be the focus, at least initially, of the organization's reuse program.

Implementation Suggestions

To assess the reuse potential of the domain and determine whether it makes good technical and business sense to perform an analysis of this domain, an organization should address the considerations [30] listed in Table 6-5.

Table 6-5. Ways to Determine the Reuse Potential of a Domain

- What is the potential for reuse of assets from this domain? How many software projects could use the domain assets and what is the number of future software products to be built in this domain? (For the domain to be considered viable, the number of future systems to be developed in the domain should be greater than one.)
- Are there any existing assets that are available for use in this domain?
- Is the domain stable? Are the majority of the essential concepts that describe the domain unlikely to change much during the time period covered by the Strategic Systems Plan for the organization?
- It the domain mature? Can the essential concepts in the domain be well defined and are they known to domain experts?
- Who are the consumers for the domain assets and what is their reuse capability?
- Are systems in the domain of strategic importance to the business?[32]
- What is the feasibility of developing the domain assets based on available information about the domain and the resources and level of expertise available?
- Consider environmental differences. Identify any environmental differences (e.g., target environments) for systems planned for the domain. If these differences cannot be abstracted away, there may not be enough commonality across systems in the domain to justify the practice of reuse in this domain. If this is the case, consider reducing the scope of the domain to a subdomain in which environmental differences do not exist, or not attempting to practice reuse in this domain.

6.4.3 Make Reuse Assessment Recommendations

IEEE Std. 1517 requires that the results of the reuse assessment be used to re-examine and, if necessary, refine the organization's reuse strategy and reuse program implementation plan:

> *7.1.3.3 The reuse program administrator shall make recommendations for refining the organization's reuse strategy and reuse program implementation plan based on the results of the reuse assessments. The recommendations shall be documented and provided to the reuse steering function.[32]*

Discussion

The reuse assessment is an essential instrument in creating a viable reuse program for an organization. For example, the results of the assessment may show that the organization's original reuse strategy was too broad or that the time it allowed for implementing the reuse program was too short. Therefore, the results of the assessment should be used as the basis for more realistically defining the elements of the reuse program and creating a reuse program implementation plan that has a high probability of leading to reuse success.

Implementation Suggestions

If the results of assessing the reuse potential of a domain showed that reuse success is questionable, then a recommendation should be made to delete this domain from the scope of the reuse strategy.

In addition to providing the report with recommendations, the reuse assessment team should orally present the findings in the reuse assessment report to the reuse sponsor, reuse steering committee, and other key management and software staff members as a means to gain their acceptance and support for a reuse program and execution of the recommended actions.

Underestimating the importance of promoting the concept of reuse could severely hamper the success of the reuse program. Cultural and management problems often outweigh technical problems when attempting to introduce systematic reuse into an organization. Armed with specific facts about how to effectively implement a successful reuse program, the reuse assessment presentation offers an excellent opportunity to firmly plant the reuse concept in the organization's culture.

6.4.4 Improve the Reuse Infrastructure

The final task in IEEE Std. 1517 Reuse Assessment Activity focuses on the requirement to improve the reuse infrastructure:

> *7.1.3.4 The reuse program administrator, in conjunction with appropriate acquirers, suppliers, developers, operators, maintainers, asset managers, and domain engineers, shall use the IEEE/EIA Std 12207-0.1996 Improvement Process to incrementally improve the skills, technology, reuse processes, organizational structure, and metrics that together comprise the reuse infrastructure.*

Discussion

Without a reuse infrastructure (Figure 6-7) there will be no foundation for coordinating efforts to practice reuse with the use of the same tools, methods and assets across projects. Also, the organization's investment in assets may be jeopardized if the supporting infrastructure that enables the reuse of assets is not in place.

It is apparent from reading this requirement that the standard views almost everyone involved in a software organization as sharing the responsibility for reuse infrastructure. This global responsibility is due to the global nature of practicing systematic reuse.

It is also apparent from this requirement that an organization is not expected to put in place a complete reuse infrastructure in one step. Rather, it is viewed as an incremental task that continues over time as management makes the necessary resources available, as the reuse program is implemented, as the organization's needs change, and as technology advances.

Although most organizations tend to emphasize the technology element of the reuse infrastructure, the standard clearly points out the many other elements that must be addressed, such as skills, the organizational structure, and metrics. For example, a major risk in adopting reuse is that software professionals will be expected to practice reuse without knowing how. To combat this problem, reuse training should be treated as an important element of the reuse infrastructure.

Implementation Suggestions

One essential element of the technical infrastructure is tools. Assets must be fast and easy to find, understand, and modify or specialize for a particular use. The following tools assist in these activities and therefore should be included in the reuse infrastructure:

1. *Repository*: Tool to store and manage assets

2. *Browser*: Tool to search for assets

3. *Configuration Management Tool*: Tool to manage and control multiple asset

4. *Code Analyzer*: Tool to aid in understanding an asset and finding where it has been used

5. *Restructuring Tool*: Tool to change the format of an asset

6. *Reverse Engineering Tool*: Tool to product a description of the asset at a higher level of abstraction

7. *Catalog*: Tool to keep a list of the description of and location of assets

Another essential element of the reuse infrastructure is a software life cycle model that includes reuse processes to enable the practice of reuse throughout the life cycle. An organization's software life cycle model should support the following four aspects of reuse:

1. *Reuse Consumer Support*: Software development and maintenance with assets

2. *Reuse Producer Support*: Assets developed and maintained for reuse

3. *Project Management Support*: Managing the practice of reuse in projects

4. *Process/Methodology Reuse Extensibility*: Extending the software life cycle processes to include reuse related activities and tasks

The reuse infrastructure should be established as early as possible in the reuse program. Although its elements may change over time, an initial definition is needed to guide the selection of tools and development of reuse standards and methodologies.

6.5 Planning Activity

Practicing systematic reuse is expensive, time-consuming, and often takes two-to-five years before the full benefits of reuse are realized by the organization. As with any complex technology, its introduction into an organization should be carefully planned to ensure that reuse delivers its promised benefits in a timely and cost-effective fashion.

Introducing reuse too quickly can lead to culture shock and resistance to the very idea of reuse. To minimize this risk, most organizations use an incremental approach to implement systematic reuse. The reuse program initially covers only one or two domains and a few of the software teams. It should be attempted with a few assets that are known to be of immediate use in particular software projects/products that have identified a need for these assets. Gradually as experience is gained and successes occur, the reuse program can be expanded across the organization.

Management's expectations must be properly prepared for an evolutionary reuse adoption strategy. The approach should be planned in a way in which valuable benefits and payback from the investment in reuse can be reaped along the adoption road.

The purpose of the reuse program implementation plan is to define and schedule the activities that comprise the reuse program.

The reuse program implementation plan is created, evaluated, reviewed, and approved as part of IEEE Std. 1517's Planning Activity.

6.5.1 Create Reuse Program Implementation Plan

In the first task in IEEE Std. 1517 Planning Activity, a reuse program implementation plan is created, documented, and maintained. IEEE Std. 1517 specifies the required contents of the plan, some of which is defined in the IEEE 12207 Standard.

> *7.1.4.1 A reuse program implementation plan shall be created, documented, and maintained, reusing an applicable reuse program plan template, if any exists, to define the resources and procedures for implementing a reuse program. The plan shall describe the following:*
>
> a) *the reuse program activities*
>
> b) *procedures and schedules for performing these activities*
>
> c) *the parties responsible for performing these activities*
>
> d) *the relationships with other parties, such as software developers or domain engineers*

e)   the resources needed for the reuse program

f)   all other items of the IEEE/EIA Std. 12206.1 Clause 5.2 Plan-
     generic content guidelines[33]

Discussion

This task is an example of incorporating consumer reuse into the software life cycle. The standard user is required to search for and, if appropriate, use a template to create the reuse program
implementation plan. In addition, the standard user is directed to use the guidelines from the IEEE
12207.1 Standard to create the contents of the plan. The IEEE 12207 plan content guidelines are
specified below:

5.2 Plan—generic content guidelines
Purpose: define when, how, and by whom specific activities are to be
performed, to include options and alternatives, as required.

5.2.1 A plan should include:
a)   Date of issue and status;

b)   Scope:

c)   Issuing organization;

d)   References;

e)   Approval authority;

f)   Planned activities and tasks;

g)   Macro references (policies or laws which give rise to the need
     for this plan);

h)   Micro references (other plans or task descriptions which elabo-
     rate details of this plan);

i)   Schedules;

j)   Estimates;

k)   Resources and their allocation;

l)   Responsibilities and authority;

m) Risks;

n)   Quality control measures;

o)   Cost;

p)   Interfaces among parties involved;

q)   Environment/infrastructure (including safety needs);

r)   *Training;*

s)   *Glossary;*

t)   *Change procedures and history.*[34]

Implementation Suggestions

The standard assigns the responsibility for creating and implementing the reuse program implementation plan to the reuse program support function. If the group has not yet been formed, then it should be assigned directly to the reuse program manager. If there is no reuse program manager, the reuse steering function should assign reuse as someone's official job function before the company embarks on the creation of a reuse program implementation plan.

Creation of the reuse program implementation plan should be one of the first tasks performed by the reuse program support group. It should be done following a reuse assessment. The initial, high-level reuse implementation plan produced by the reuse assessment, which defines the organization's reuse strategy, a description of the elements of the reuse program, and a proposed reuse implementation schedule, should be used as a basis for creating a comprehensive reuse program implementation plan.

The information gathered from interviews of reuse program participants and reviews of software system material during the reuse assessment should also be used. This information will serve as invaluable input for creating a realistic reuse program implementation plan that meets the expectations and needs of the organization. The reuse assessment is the primary source of input from all those expected to fund and participate in the reuse program.

The first required element of the reuse program implementation plan is a list of the reuse program activities. The activities to be included in the reuse program implementation plan can be categorized into three basic implementation stages:[35]

1.   Introducing Reuse

2.   Institutionalizing Reuse

3.   Sustaining Reuse

This categorization scheme helps an organization define the implementation sequence and schedule for performing the activities, as well as plan the resource needs of the reuse program. To define the activities at a level of detail that allows for easy estimating of costs and resources, an organization should identify activities whose duration time is in the range of one-to-three staff months of effort.[36]

The activities listed in Table 6-6 should be considered for inclusion in the introduction stage of the reuse program. Table 6-7 lists some suggested activities to include in the institutionalization stage of the reuse program. Table 6-8 lists some suggested activities to include in the on-going support stage of the reuse program.

Table 6-6. Suggested Activities to Include in the Reuse Program Introduction Stage

- Activities to get management support, a reuse sponsor, and funding for the reuse program and activities to establish a reuse steering committee
- Activities to clearly define the organization's reuse goals, objectives, and measures of success
- Activities to survey software professionals and management about reuse to determine possible causes for reuse program failure and opportunities for practicing reuse within projects, functional areas (domains), and organizations
- Activities to form a reuse program support group and to appoint a reuse program manager
- Activities to assess current software practices, the organization's reuse capability, and reuse potential of domains
- Activities to determine the types of assets that are to be stored in the organization's asset storage and retrieval mechanism initially and added later on as the program matures (e.g., code, design models, documentation, test suites, software architectures)
- Activities to determine the tools needed to support reuse. Include tools that are most essential to reuse such as repositories, re-engineering tools, and configuration management tools
- Activities to establish the organization's asset storage and retrieval mechanism
- Activities to experiment with reuse on a small scale, such as in a pilot project

Table 6-7. Suggested Activities to Include in the Reuse Program Institutionalization Stage

- Activities to promote reuse across the organization, such as through the use of newsletters or on-line bulletin boards, reuse incentive programs, reuse special interest groups, etc.
- Activities to establish and/or standardize the software life cycle models and methodologies, extending them to incorporate consumer reuse, producer reuse and reuse project management practices
- Activities to introduce reuse standards and to incorporate them into the organization's software standards
- Activities to create and present reuse training programs for managers, software professionals, and end users who are expected to participate in the reuse program
- Activities to expand and improve the organization's asset storage and retrieval mechanism and classification scheme
- Activities to create certification procedures for assets
- Activities to record reuse lessons learned and to gather, analyze and report on feedback from projects that have practiced reuse
- Activities to establish a reuse metrics program to measure productivity and quality improvements that have resulted from employing reuse; include economic models to measure expected and actual reuse costs and savings

Table 6-8. Suggested Activities to Include in the Reuse Program On-going Support Stage

- Activities to provide on-going support and maintenance for the organization's asset storage and retrieval mechanism and entire reuse infrastructure

- Activities to provide consulting support for project teams practicing reuse

- Activities to report on reuse practices in the organization

- Activities to further expand the practice of reuse across the organization

- Activities to continually improve the practice of reuse in software projects, the quality and reusability of assets and the software life cycle processes

The second required element in the reuse program implementation plan is the schedule for performing the plan's activities. When defining the schedule for performing the plan's activities, an organization should specify the predecessor/successor relationships between activities and which activities can be performed in parallel. Then, based on the duration defined for the activity, the sequence suggested for performing activities and the activity predecessor/successor relationships, start and finish dates for each activity can be defined.

In addition, major review points and milestones for the reuse program implementation plan should be defined. Review points should be inserted at critical points in the plan to enable periodic evaluation and possible adjustments to the plan to minimize the risk of failure of the reuse program, management disappointment, or software staff disillusionment with reuse. For example, a review point should be inserted after a reuse pilot project to incorporate the findings of the pilot into the plan.

The schedule should be divided into one-year-size blocks of activities to make the plan consistent with the organization's annual planning and budgeting procedures. When scheduling activities, the reuse program budget constraints, the level of reuse expertise and experience available to the organization, and the pace at which management has chosen to introduce reuse should be taken into account.

Figure 6-9 is a template for a three-stage, three-to-five-year reuse program implementation plan. [37,38]

Another required element of the reuse program implementation plan is the resources needed for the reuse program. Adequate, skilled personnel are just as important to assuring success in adopting reuse as is adequate funding. Areas of concern that may put a reuse program at risk are:

1. Inadequate staffing for the reuse program support function

2. Resistance to changing the organizational structure to enable the addition of a reuse program support function

3. Lack of reuse training for reuse program participants

To provide the resources needed for reuse training, an organization should include the personnel and other resources expected from the corporate training department or an external training source in its reuse program implementation plan.

6.5.2 Evaluate Reuse Program Implementation Plan

In the second task in IEEE Std. 1517 Planning Activity, the reuse program implementation plan is reviewed and evaluated:

> *7.1.4.2 The plan shall be reviewed and evaluated considering the following criteria:*
>
> *1. Completeness*
>
> *2. Ability to realize the organization's reuse strategy*
>
> *3. Feasibility of implementing the plan*
>
> *The results of the evaluation shall be documented. Those evaluating the plan should include members of the reuse steering function.*

Discussion

Reuse experience from industry has shown that the most critical elements leading to a successful reuse program are:

1. Management leadership and support
2. Creation of a reuse-positive organizational culture
3. Establishment of a reuse infrastructure

When evaluating the completeness of the reuse program implementation plan, an organization should check that each of the above critical elements is adequately covered in the plan.

Implementation Suggestions

Although IEEE Std. 1517 specifically mentions only the members of the reuse steering function, an organization should encourage representatives of every group expected to contribute to and participate in the reuse program to review the plan and make suggestions on how to improve it based on their needs. If every group has the opportunity to review the plan, it is more likely that they will accept the plan and actively participate in its implementation.

The various participants in the reuse program should review the plan from different perspectives to ensure that the program has the greatest chance to succeed and fulfill the organization's reuse strategy. For example, the reuse program manager should review the plan to ensure that it is complete and viable. The reuse sponsor should review the plan to ensure that the level of management commitment that is expected and the resources needed for the program are feasible and that the anticipated benefits to be delivered meet management's needs and expectations. The representatives and/or manager of each software organization that is expected to participate in the reuse program should help insure the feasibility of the plan by asking questions, voicing unaddressed concerns, and making suggestions for improving the plan.

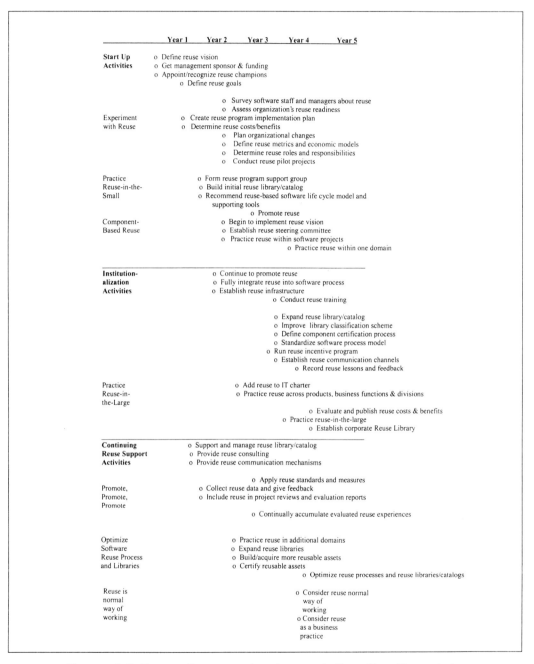

	Year 1	Year 2	Year 3	Year 4	Year 5
Start Up Activities	o Define reuse vision				
	o Get management sponsor & funding				
	o Appoint/recognize reuse champions				
	o Define reuse goals				
		o Survey software staff and managers about reuse			
		o Assess organization's reuse readiness			
Experiment with Reuse	o Create reuse program implementation plan				
	o Determine reuse costs/benefits				
		o Plan organizational changes			
		o Define reuse metrics and economic models			
		o Determine reuse roles and responsibilities			
		o Conduct reuse pilot projects			
Practice Reuse-in-the-Small		o Form reuse program support group			
		o Build initial reuse library/catalog			
		o Recommend reuse-based software life cycle model and supporting tools			
			o Promote reuse		
Component-Based Reuse		o Begin to implement reuse vision			
		o Establish reuse steering committee			
		o Practice reuse within software projects			
				o Practice reuse within one domain	
Institution-alization Activities		o Continue to promote reuse			
		o Fully integrate reuse into software process			
		o Establish reuse infrastructure			
			o Conduct reuse training		
			o Expand reuse library/catalog		
			o Improve library classification scheme		
			o Define component certification process		
			o Standardize software process model		
			o Run reuse incentive program		
			o Establish reuse communication channels		
				o Record reuse lessons and feedback	
Practice Reuse-in-the-Large			o Add reuse to IT charter		
			o Practice reuse across products, business functions & divisions		
					o Evaluate and publish reuse costs & benefits
				o Practice reuse-in-the-large	
				o Establish corporate Reuse Library	
Continuing Reuse Support Activities		o Support and manage reuse library/catalog			
		o Provide reuse consulting			
		o Provide reuse communication mechanisms			
			o Apply reuse standards and measures		
Promote, Promote, Promote		o Collect reuse data and give feedback			
		o Include reuse in project reviews and evaluation reports			
			o Continually accumulate evaluated reuse experiences		
Optimize Software Reuse Process and Libraries		o Practice reuse in additional domains			
		o Expand reuse libraries			
		o Build/acquire more reusable assets			
		o Certify reusable assets			
				o Optimize reuse processes and reuse libraries/catalogs	
Reuse is normal way of working				o Consider reuse normal way of working	
				o Consider reuse as a business practice	

Figure 6-9. Reuse Program Implementation Plan Template

6.5.3 Obtain Approval for Reuse Program Implementation Plan

IEEE Std. 1517 specifies a requirement to obtain approval for the reuse program implementation plan:

> *7.1.4.3 Approval and support for the reuse program implementation plan shall be obtained from the reuse steering function, and appropriate managers.*

Discussion

Introducing systematic reuse across an organization is likely to take three to five years. If management is not willing to make such a long-term commitment, the reuse program is almost certainly doomed to failure. If the reuse fails, it will be very difficult to convince either the software staff or the organization's management to give reuse a second chance.

Implementation Suggestions

To ensure that management's commitment to reuse is real, it is of the utmost importance to obtain formal approval for the reuse program implementation plan from management and those expected to sponsor and supply the resources for the reuse program before beginning to formally implement a reuse program.

6.5.4 Conduct a Reuse Program Implementation Plan Review

IEEE Std. 1517 requires a formal review as part of the Planning Activity of the Reuse Program Administration Process:

> *7.1.4.4 The reuse program administrator shall conduct joint review(s) in accordance with the IEEE/EIA Std 12207.0-1996 Joint Review Process. Members of the reuse steering function and the appropriate managers shall be included in the reviews.*

Discussion

The reuse program implementation plan is the blueprint for how to introduce, practice, and manage systematic reuse in an organization. Because it is the guiding document for the entire reuse program, is should be viewed as the major deliverable produced by the Reuse Program Administration Process. A formal review of this document is required to assure that a viable reuse program can be established, managed, and maintained based on this plan.

Implementation Suggestions

The format for the formal review is specified in the IEEE 12207 Standard Joint Review Process.[39] Since the purpose of the review is to evaluate the reuse program implementation plan, the review should be conducted as a technical review. According to the IEEE/EIA 12207 Standard, the Joint Review Process is applied by two parties, where one party is the reviewer and the other is the party reviewed. In this case, the reuse program support group is the party reviewed and the steering committee and appropriate management comprise the reviewers.

Based on a review of the evaluation information, the reuse steering committee should direct revisions to the reuse program implementation plan to incorporate the approved suggestions and changes.

6.6 Execution and Control Activity

This activity describes the requirements for executing the reuse program implementation plan and tracking progress.

6.6.1 Execute Reuse Program Implementation Plan

The first requirement in the Execution and Control Activity is to execute the reuse program implementation plan:

> *7.1.5.1 Activities in the reuse program implementation plan shall be executed in accordance with the plan.[40]*

Discussion

A plan is of little value to an organization unless it is implemented.

Implementation Suggestions

The responsibility for implementing the reuse program implementation plan should be assigned to the reuse program manager.

6.6.2 Monitor Reuse Program Progress

IEEE Std. 1517 assigns the responsibility of monitoring the progress of the reuse program and adjusting the reuse program implementation plan to the reuse program administrator:

> *7.1.5.2 The reuse program administrator shall monitor the progress of the reuse program against the organization's reuse strategy, and make and document as necessary adjustments to the plan to realize the strategy.[41]*

Discussion

The progress of the reuse program is monitored to determine if the program is on track in terms of schedule, budget, allocation, and utilization of resources. Monitoring is also done to determine how well the program is meeting its objectives as defined in terms of the organization's reuse strategy.

Implementation Suggestions

Reuse data should be collected, and reuse metrics should be applied to evaluate the data against the reuse strategy and determine the current level of success or failure of the reuse program. Actuals should be compared to plan estimates to determine the status of the reuse program. Status information should be reported to the reuse program manager, the reuse sponsor, the reuse steering committee, and the participating software groups. Providing feedback to the reuse program participants periodically will help sustain their interest in reuse and motivate them to continue their efforts to adopt reuse.

Based on reuse program status information, a determination as to whether continue implementing the current reuse program implementation plan, revise the plan, or cancel the reuse program should be made by the reuse program manager. Any recommendations should be made first to the reuse steering committee and then to the appropriate management.

6.6.3 Record Reuse Program Problems

IEEE Std. 1517 requires recording problems encountered with the execution of the reuse program implementation plan:

> *7.1.5.3 Problems and nonconformances that occur during the execution of the reuse implementation plan shall be recorded and entered into the Problem Resolution Process, as specified in the IEEE Std 12207.0-1996.*[42]

Discussion

Systematic reuse is a formal approach to adopting software reuse. Part of this formality includes a formal way to track and record problems. The standard uses the Problem Resolution Process, a supporting life cycle process defined in the IEEE/EIA 12207 Standard, to specify the requirements for analyzing and resolving problems and recognizing trends.[43] According to the 12207 Standard, problem resolution must be treated as a "closed loop" where detected problems are promptly reported and actions are promptly taken to resolve problems and record their history.

Implementation Suggestions

Implementation problems that occur with the plan should be identified and reported as soon as possible to minimize any negative impact they may have on the reuse program.

To help quickly put the reuse program back on track, the problem report should also contain suggestions for correcting the problem or an alternative approach that avoids the problem.

6.6.4 Reaffirm Management's Reuse Commitment

The final requirement in IEEE Std. 1517 Execution and Control Activity is to reaffirm management's commitment to the reuse program:

> *7.1.5.4 The reuse program administrator shall periodically reaffirm management sponsorship, support, and commitment to the reuse program.*[44]

Discussion

Management commitment to reuse must be vocal, active, and ongoing for the duration of the reuse program to ensure that the organization's reuse strategy is achieved. Of course, commitment for funding and resources is needed since a reuse program can cost millions of dollars over its lifetime. In addition to providing the funding, management support is also needed to change the organization's structure, culture, and incentives to encourage the practice of systematic reuse.

Implementation Suggestions

To ensure the continued interest of management in the reuse program, the reuse sponsor should periodically present to management a report on the current status and accomplishments of the reuse program. The presentation should explain how reuse is tied to the achievement of important business goals and strategies; explain the benefits that reuse has delivered thus far, using reuse metrics and measurements; and advise about any adjustments to the reuse strategy or reuse program that may become necessary.

Management can show its continued commitment to reuse with actions such as the following:

1. Assigning reuse as an action item to one or more executives

2. Approving changes to the organizational structure to better support reuse

3. Including reuse in management policies, mission statements, and performance reviews

4. Encouraging the practice of reuse by participating in reuse recognition and award programs

6.7 Review and Evaluation Activity

IEEE Std. 1517 includes an activity in the Reuse Program Administration Process for periodic assessment and improvement of the reuse program. It is unrealistic for an organization to expect that a large, lengthy undertaking, such as introducing reuse, will go according to plan. Factors such as changes in the organization's structure or business, advances in technology, and experiences in practicing reuse are likely to impact the reuse program. Unless these factors are taken into account to make adjustments to the reuse program, the program may lose its effectiveness and overall value to the organization.

6.7.1 Assess the Reuse Program

IEEE Std. 1517 requires a periodic assessment of the reuse program to determine its effectiveness and suitability:

> *7.1.6.1 The reuse program administrator shall periodically assess the reuse program for achievement of the organization's reuse strategy, and the continued suitability, and effectiveness of the reuse program.*[45]

Discussion

This task serves as an explicit reminder that the reuse program is not an end in itself, but rather has been established to deliver some specific results to the organization. Since the value of the reuse program lies solely in its ability to achieve the reuse strategy, its suitability and effectiveness should be evaluated against the reuse strategy.

Implementation Suggestions

A periodic assessment of the reuse program should be performed on an annual basis. In the first year or two of the reuse program, an assessment should be done every six months to detect and address any problems as soon as possible. For most organizations, the introduction of reuse will brings some very dramatic changes which may cause some unexpected problems, especially in the early stages when there is little previous experience with reuse to draw upon.

The periodic assessment can take the form of a mini version of the assessment that was performed during the initiation stage. Interviews of key reuse program participants should be conducted to gather their reactions to and criticisms of reuse, as well as the concerns or suggestions they may have. Also, reuse data should be gathered and analyzed to demonstrate achievement of the reuse strategy.

6.7.2 Provide Assessment Results to Reuse Steering Function

> *7.1.6.2 The reuse program administrator shall provide assessment results and lessons learned to the reuse steering function, and the appropriate managers.[46]*

Discussion

A major reason for failure of a complex technical initiative is that management is kept in the dark about achievements and/or problems. If they are informed about problems in a timely manner, they are better able to make changes to minimize their impact, provide the resources to address the problems, and to adjust their expectations accordingly. On the other hand, delaying the presentation of bad reuse program news to management is likely to cause certain death to the program.

Implementation Suggestions

IEEE Std. 1517 task 7.1.5.4 suggests that a periodic presentation should be given to management as a way to continue their interest in the reuse program. This presentation should be used as a forum to provide reuse program assessment results and lessons learned to management. A very effective motivation mechanism is to allow the top reuse achievers to directly present their reuse achievements to management.

Of course, the presentation should also highlight the bad news as well as the good news. If the presentation of problems is accompanied with proposals for solving the problems, management is more likely to take the bad news well and to continue its commitment to the reuse program.

6.7.3 Improve the Reuse Program

> *7.1.6.3 The reuse program administrator shall recommend and make changes to the reuse program, expand the reuse program, and improve the reuse program in accordance with the IEEE/EIA Std 12207.0-1996 Improvement Process.[47]*

Discussion

The standard uses the Improvement Process, which is an organizational life cycle process defined in the IEEE/EIA 12207 Standard, to specify the requirements for improving the reuse program.[48] The purpose of the Improvement Process is to assess, measure, control, and improve a life cycle process. In this case, it is applied to the Reuse Program Administration Process.

The Improvement Process specifies that an assessment procedure is developed and applied to the process and that the assessment results (including historical, technical, and evaluation data that have been collected and analyzed) are used to guide improvements to the process. The Improvement Process also specifies that cost of both the prevention and resolution of problems is used in the determination of how to improve the process.

Implementation Suggestions

Based on the results of the reuse program assessment and reuse lessons learned, recommendations for changes and improvements to the reuse program should be given to the reuse steering function. The reuse steering function should decide what improvements are to be made to the reuse program and present these recommendations to management for its approval.

6.8 Summary

The Reuse Program Administration Process specifies the activities required for planning, establishing, managing, executing, monitoring, and improving an organization's reuse program.

Figure 6-10 summarizes the activities in the Reuse Program Administration Process and the life cycle deliverables produced by each activity.

The party responsible for the Reuse Program Administration Process is the reuse program administrator. Figure 6-11 summarizes the areas of the responsibility for the reuse program administrator.

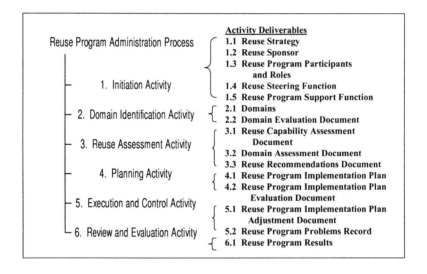

Figure 6-10. IEEE Std. 1517 Reuse Program Administration Process
Activities and Deliverables

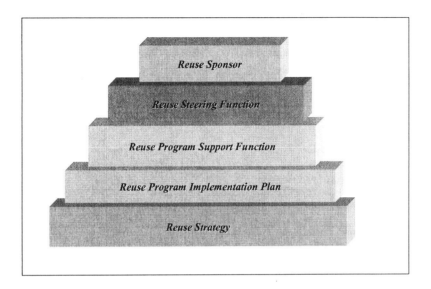

Figure 6-11. Responsibilities of the Reuse Program Administrator

6.9 References

1. *Random House Webster's College Dictionary*, Random House, Inc, New York, N.Y., 1992.

2. *IEEE Std. 1517, Standard for Information Technology—Software Life Cycle Processes—Reuse Processes*, IEEE, Piscataway, N.J., 1999.

3. W. Lim, "Effect of Reuse on Quality, Productivity and Economics," *IEEE Software,* vol. 11, no. 5, Sept. 1994, pp. 23–30.

4. B. Meyer, *Object Success*, Prentice-Hall, Englewood-Cliffs, N.J., 1995, pp. 127–128.

5. D. Hofman, "A Major Change in Software Delivery," Managing Software Development, Nov. 1995, pp.1–4.

6. R. Prieto-Diaz, "Making Software Reuse Work," SPC-92031-CMC, Version 01.00.00, Software Productivity Consortium, Herndon, Va., p. 25.

7. *IEEE Std. 1517, Standard for Information Technology—Software Life Cycle Processes—Reuse Processes.*

8. Ibid.

9. C. McClure, *Software Reuse Techniques: Adding Reuse to the Software Development Process*, Prentice-Hall, Upper Saddle River, N.J., 1997, p. 118.

10. Ibid., p. 118.

11. *IEEE Std. 1517, Standard for Information Technology—Software Life Cycle Processes— Reuse Processes.*

12. R. Prieto-Diaz, "Making Software Reuse Work," p. 25.

13. Ibid., p. 25.

14. *IEEE Std. 1517, Standard for Information Technology—Software Life Cycle Processes— Reuse Processes.*

15. Ibid.

16. F. Maymir-Ducharme and S.M. Webb, "CARDS: A Comprehensive Approach To Reusable Defense Software," Multiple Perspectives on Domain Engineering Tutorial, presented at the Software Reuse Workshop, Morgantown, W.Va., July 29–August 1, 1996.

17. *IEEE Std. 1517, Standard for Information Technology—Software Life Cycle Processes— Reuse Processes.*

18. R. Prieto-Diaz, "Making Software Reuse Work," p. 17.

19. Kang et al., *Feature-Oriented Domain Analysis Feasibility Study*, tech. report CMU/SEI-90-TR-21 EDS-90-Tr-21, Software Engineering Institute, Carnegie Mellon Univ., Pittsburgh, Pa., Nov. 1990, pp. 31–34.

20. Ibid., pp. 31–34.

21. *IEEE Std. 1517, Standard for Information Technology—Software Life Cycle Processes— Reuse Processes.*

22. Ibid.

23. Ibid.

24. Kang et al., *Feature-Oriented Domain Analysis Feasibility Study*, pp.31–34.

25. *IEEE Std. 1517, Standard for Information Technology—Software Life Cycle Processes— Reuse Processes.*

26. "Capability Model Summary," Software Engineering Institute, Carnegie Mellon Univ., Pittsburgh, Pa., SEI Web Page: sei.cmu.edu.

27. K. Bourgeois, "Technology Transfer of Mature Reuse Practices," Proc. Fifth Annual Workshop Software Reuse, 26 Oct. 1992.

28. A. Hydson, "Draft Stages of Reuse Maturity," Report on Fourth Software Productivity Consortium TAG Meeting, Melbourne, Fl., Nov. 1990.

29. *IEEE Std. 1517, Standard for Information Technology—Software Life Cycle Processes—Reuse Processes.*

30. *Reuse Adoption Guidebook,* SPC-92051-CMC, Version 02.00.24, Software Productivity Consortium, Herndon, Va., Nov. 1993, pp. A-1–A-10.

31. Ibid., p. Opp 27.

32. *IEEE Std. 1517, Standard for Information Technology—Software Life Cycle Processes—Reuse Processes.*

33. Ibid.

34. *IEEE/EIA Std. 12207.1-1998, Guide for Information Technology—Software Life Cycle Processes—Life Cycle Data,* IEEE, Piscataway, N.J., 1996.

35. M. Griss and W. Tracz, "5th Annual Workshop on Software Reuse Working Group Reports," *SIGSOFT Software Engineering Notes,* vol. 18, no. 2, Apr. 1993, pp. 74–85.

36. *Reuse Adoption Guidebook,* p. 3–38.

37. M. Griss and W. Tracz, "5th Annual Workshop on Software Reuse Working Group Reports," pp. 74–85.

38. R. Joos, "So Much for Motherhood, Apple Pie and Reuse," Proc. 5th Annual Workshop on Software Reuse, Univ. of Maine Department of Computer Science, Oct. 26–29, 1992.

39. *IEEE/EIA Std. 12207.1-1998, Guide for Information Technology—Software Life Cycle Processes—Life Cycle Data.*

40. *IEEE Std. 1517, Standard for Information Technology—Software Life Cycle Processes—Reuse Processes.*

41. Ibid.

42. Ibid.

43. *IEEE/EIA Std. 12207.1-1998, Guide for Information Technology—Software Life Cycle Processes—Life Cycle Data.*

44. *IEEE Std. 1517, Standard for Information Technology—Software Life Cycle Processes—Reuse Processes.*

45. Ibid.

46. Ibid.

47. Ibid.

48. *IEEE/EIA Std. 12207.1-1998, Guide for Information Technology—Software Life Cycle Processes—Life Cycle Data.*

Chapter 7.
Adding Domain Engineering to the Software Life Cycle Process Framework

7.1 Introduction to the Domain Engineering Process

A prerequisite for practicing reuse is a collection of high quality, highly reusable assets (i.e., reusable software parts such as a software design model). Domain Engineering is a process for supplying these assets for use in a particular domain. The notion of domain is used to narrow the practice of reuse to a size that is conceptually easier to understand, technically easier to implement, and organizationally easier to manage.

Typically, a domain, which IEEE Std.1517 defines as "a problem space,"[1] represents one segment of an organization in which there is potential to practice reuse. How an organization chooses to segment itself for reuse—whether by product lines, by business functions, by technology platforms, or whatever else—is left to the discretion of the user of the standard. However, the intention of the standard is that a domain should be defined broadly enough to encompass assets that are applicable to multiple software products over a period of time. Also, since it is expected that an organization will choose to practice reuse in multiple domains, it is expected that the domain engineering process will be applied multiple times within the organization.

7.1.1 Supplying Assets

The notion of domain is also used to lift the Domain Engineering Process above the project level. The Domain Engineering Process supplies assets that are intended for use by multiple software projects in which multiple software products are developed or maintained. In order to meet the requirements of multiple projects, assets must possess common properties that can be shared and reused by the software products produced in these projects. IEEE Std. 1517 categorizes Domain Engineering as a cross project life cycle process because this process exists beyond the boundaries and duration of one project.

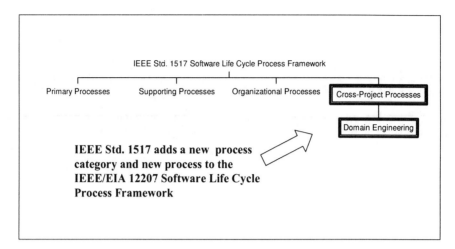

Figure 7-1. Adding the Cross-Project Process Category and the
Domain Engineering Process to the IEEE/EIA Std. 12207
Software Life Cycle Process Framework

7.1.2 Producer Reuse

Recall from Chapter 3 that producer reuse is concerned with how to provide assets for reuse. In effect, producer reuse is the life cycle for assets. Producer reuse is called domain engineering when applied within a domain. In general, producer reuse is concerned with how to analyze, design, create, and maintain assets. When applied in a domain, producer reuse is concerned with the analysis, design, creation, and maintenance of assets for the domain.

As Figure 7-1 shows, IEEE Std. 1517 extends the 12207 Standard software life framework by adding the process category called *cross-project processes*. In the cross-project category, IEEE Std. 1517 defines the process Domain Engineering to specify the requirements for performing producer reuse at the domain level. The Domain Engineering Process covers the development and maintenance of assets for the domain.

In IEEE Std. 1517, *domain engineering* is defined as:

> *A reuse-based approach to defining the scope (i.e., domain definition), specifying the structure (i.e., domain architecture), and building the assets (e.g., requirements, designs, software code, documentation) for a class of systems, subsystems, or applications. Domain engineering may include the following activities: domain definition, domain analysis, developing the domain architecture, and domain implementation.[2]*

The standard names the *domain engineer* as the party responsible for the domain engineering activities. A domain engineer may be either an individual or a group of individuals according to the standard's interpretation of a "party." Most likely, an organization will implement the domain engineer in the form of a project team that is assembled at the initiation of the domain engineering project and remains in existence throughout the domain engineering life cycle.

Table 7-1. Activities in the Domain Engineering Process

ACTIVITY NAME	ACTIVITY DESCRIPTION
Process Implementation	• Create, document, and execute domain engineering plan • Select representation forms for the domain models and domain architectures
Domain Analysis	• Define domain boundaries and relationships with other domains • Identify needs of domain software developers; • Build, document, classify, evaluate, and submit domain models • Construct, evaluate, and submit domain vocabulary
Domain Design	• Create, document, classify, evaluate, and submit domain architectures • Develop, document, and evaluate asset specifications
Asset Provision	• Develop, document, classify, evaluate, and submit assets
Asset Maintenance	• Analyze request for asset modification, choose and get approval for asset modification option, implement asset modification, and submit modified asset

IEEE Std. 1517 Domain Engineering Process activities are listed and summarized in Table 7-1. These activities may be mapped to the phases in the reuse producer life cycle. They are presented in detail below.

In the detailed presentation for each activity, the activity is explained in terms of its tasks. Recall that in the standard, a task represents the requirements for implementing the activity. The task is first discussed and then suggestions for how an organization may implement the task are presented.

7.2 Process Implementation Activity

The purpose of this activity is to formally prepare for domain engineering by creating a domain engineering plan, defining the format to be used to represent the domain engineering products, and defining technical and management procedures to be used by a domain engineering effort.

7.2.1 Create Domain Engineering Plan

The first requirement (i.e., task) that IEEE Std. 1517 includes in the Process Implementation Activity is to create and execute a domain engineering plan.

> *8.1.1.1 The domain engineer shall create and document a domain engineering plan, reusing an applicable domain engineering plan template, if any exists, to define the resources and procedures for performing domain engineering. The plan should include standards, methods, tools, activities, assignments, and responsibilities for performing domain engineering. To create the domain engineering plan, the domain engineer should consult with domain experts, developers, and users of software products within the domain. The domain engineering plan shall be executed.[3]*

Discussion

Depending upon the size of the domain, domain engineering may be a lengthy, complex effort. Treating domain engineering as a carefully planned project is essential to ensuring that it is a useful exercise resulting in the production of valuable assets for the domain.

Implementation Suggestions

One important element in the domain engineering plan is the domain engineering method. To select an appropriate domain engineering method, an organization should:

1. Make a choice that is based on the domain goals, the output deliverables to be produced by the domain engineering effort, the tools available, and skills of the domain engineering team

2. Consider using a method that incorporates well established domain analysis methods such as:

   - Feature-Oriented Domain Analysis from SEI4

   - STARS Reuse Library Process Model (commonly known as the "sandwich" approach)5

   - Domain Analysis and Design Process from the Defense Information Systems Agency/Center for Information Management (DISA/CIM)[6]

3. Review the selected domain engineering method with domain engineers and domain experts in the domain engineering team

4. The domain goals refer to the purpose for performing the domain engineering effort. Some typical purposes for performing domain engineering are to:

   - Gain an understanding of the domain, i.e., its basic common concepts and vocabulary

   - Determine if there is sufficient commonality in this domain to warrant practicing systematic reuse in this domain

- Supply a set of highly reusable assets that can be used to build software products in this domain

Although not mentioned specifically in the standard, an organization is advised to explicitly define its goals for a domain engineering effort as part of the domain engineering process implementation activity. A clear definition of the domain goals is essential to developing an appropriate domain engineering plan. Including the domain goals in the domain engineering plan will ensure that all members of the domain engineering team and those impacted by the domain engineering effort will share a common understanding of its purpose.

Also, the domain engineering plan should treat domain engineering as a project that must be properly managed. Thus, the domain engineering plan should include project constraints such as budget, schedule, and resources. Resources should include both the technical and non-technical resources needed to perform domain engineering. On the technical side, the standard requires that tools, methods, and standards are identified. On the non-technical side, activities, assignments, and responsibilities must be defined.

Responsibilities for the domain engineering project should be assigned to a domain engineering team (Figure 7-2). The members of the domain analysis team should provide the following roles and skills. Some of these roles and skills may be covered by the same team member:

1. A systems/business analyst who is an expert in analysis modeling and data synthesis

2. A data administrator who is responsible for corporate data dictionary and naming standards

3. An information architect who is knowledgeable of the Information/Enterprise Architecture for the enterprise or business unit to which this domain belongs

4. A domain expert who has expert-level knowledge and understanding of the domain

5. End users and software developers who are knowledgeable about their current and future system needs

6. A reuse facilitator who is experienced in performing domain analysis

IEEE Std. 1517 defines a *domain expert* as "an individual who is intimately familiar with the domain and can provide detailed information to the domain engineers."[7] Domain experts may include knowledgeable end users and software professionals (i.e., software system developers and maintainers who have experience working on software products that are similar to the software products to be built for this domain). They should know what properties are important in future systems planned for the domain. Domain experts are a critical source of information about the domain and therefore a critical component of the domain analysis team.

Finally, the domain engineering plan should identify the tools that will be used to support the domain engineering project. Different types of tools are needed to support the analysis, design, and implementation activities. For example, tools that support the building and analysis of strategic planning models and information architectures, such as entity relationship, data flow, and object modeling diagramming tools, and dictionary tools, are useful in performing domain analysis. Data synthesis tools, data and process reverse engineering tools, program code analyzers, flow graphing tools, complexity metrics tools, and process logic and data rationalization restructuring tools are also useful in performing domain analysis. In addition, repositories, browsers, cataloging tools and configuration management tools are needed to store and mange the domain model, the domain architectures and assets. Of course, what specific tools are appropriate for a particular domain engineering project depend on the types of models and code to be analyzed and the representation forms chosen for the domain models and domain architectures.

Business	Data	End	Information	Software	Reuse
Analyst	Administrator	User	Architect	Developer	Facilitator

Figure 7-2. Members of the Domain Engineering Project Team

7.2.2 Select Domain Model and Domain Architecture Representation Forms

In the second task in the Process Implementation Activity of the Domain Engineering Process, IEEE Std. 1517 requires the selection of the representation forms for the domain models and domain architectures:

> *8.1.1.2 The domain engineer shall select the representation forms to be used for the domain models and domain architectures, in accordance with the organization's reuse standards, and by consulting domain experts and developers and users of software products within the domain.*[8]

Discussion

According to IEEE Std. 1517, the definitions for a domain model and domain architecture are:

> *Domain model: a product of domain analysis that provides a representation of the requirements of the domain. The domain model identifies and describes the structure of data, flow of information, functions, constraints, and controls within the domain that are included in software systems in the do-*

main. The domain model describes the commonalities and variabilities among requirements for software systems in the domain.[9]

Domain architecture: a generic, organized structure or design for software systems in a domain. The domain architecture contains the designs that are intended to satisfy requirements specified in the domain model. The domain architecture documents design, whereas the domain model documents requirements. A domain architecture: 1) can be adapted to create designs for software systems within a domain, and 2) provides a framework for configuring assets with individual software systems.[10]

The domain model is a generic analysis model and the domain architecture is a high-level design model. Together they serve as a starting point and guide for building assets and software products within the domain. Therefore, the representation forms used for the domain models and domain architectures impact the choice of domain engineering methods used to supply assets for the domain, software development methods used to build software products within the domain, and the choice of domain engineering and software development tools.

Implementation Suggestions

The representation forms selected for the domain model and the domain architecture should fit the domain analysis and design approaches and the tools available to use in this domain engineering project. For example, the Features-Oriented Domain Analysis (FODA) approach uses of set of models (entity relationship model, data flow diagram and state transition diagram and structure diagram)[11] to represent the domain model and another set of models (process interaction model and module structure chart) to represent the domain architecture.[12]

Also, the representation forms for the domain model and the domain architecture should fit the development methodologies and the corresponding analysis and design models that will be used to develop software products within this domain. Using the same kinds of representation forms in both places reduces the learning curve, the need to convert from one representation form to another, and the need to acquire different tools to support domain engineering and software product development.

A common modeling language such as the Unified Modeling Language (UML) from the Object Management Group should be considered for both the domain model and the domain architecture representation forms.[13] A combination of UML models (class model, use case model, and sequence/collaboration model) are used to represent the domain model. For more information about the UML, see Chapter 10.

7.2.3 Define Technical and Project Management Procedures

In the third task of the Process Implementation Activity in the Domain Engineering Process, domain engineering procedures are established in accordance with the IEEE/EIA Std. 12207 procedure specifications. In addition, there is a requirement for the establishment of communication procedures between the domain engineer and the asset manager.

8.1.1.3 The domain engineer shall:

a) *Document this process in accordance with the IEEE/EIA Std 12207.0-1996 Documentation Process;*

b) *Perform configuration management of the domain engineering outputs in accordance with the IEEE/EIA Std 12207.0-1996 Configuration Management Process;*

c) *Document and resolve problems and nonconformances found in the assets and domain engineering process in accordance with the IEEE/EIA Std 12207.0-1996 Problem Resolution Process;*

d) *Conduct joint reviews in accordance with the IEEE/EIA 12207.0-1996 Joint Review Process and include in the review experts of the domain, and software developers and users of the software products within the domain;*

e) *Establish procedures for receiving, resolving and providing feedback to the asset manager whenever problems or change requests occur for assets developed by the domain engineer[14]*

Discussion

This requirement is an example of how IEEE Std. 1517 uses the existing IEEE/EIA 12207 Standard to provide the specifications for a reuse-related process. As shown in Figure 7-3, the Domain Engineering Process uses the IEEE/EIA 12207 Standard supporting processes; namely the Documentation Process, Configuration Management Process, Problem Resolution Process, and Joint Review Process to specify its documentation, configuration management, problem resolution, and review procedure requirements.

An additional required domain engineering procedure is specified to provide the means for communicating with the asset manager. This requirement is made explicit because IEEE Std. 1517 separates the development of assets and the management of assets into two distinct roles as a means of balancing the responsibility for and control over domain assets. The domain engineer assumes the role of asset development and maintenance, while the asset manager assumes the role of asset management. A communication channel between the two parties is needed in order for each to effectively perform its assigned responsibilities.

Implementation Suggestions

Figure 7-4 shows the communication of domain information between the domain engineer and the asset manager.

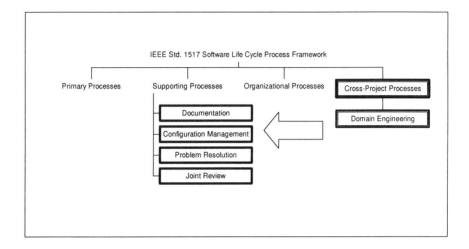

Figure 7-3. The IEEE/EIA 12207 Standard Supporting Processes
used by the IEEE Standard 1517 Domain Engineering Process

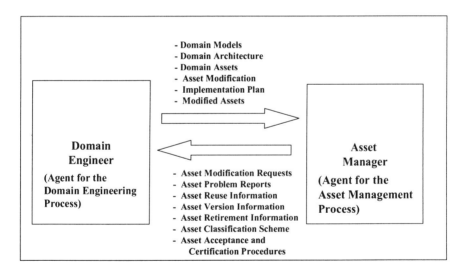

Figure 7-4. Communication Channels between the
Domain Engineer and Asset Manager

7.3 Domain Analysis Activity

Like the traditional software system life cycle, the domain engineering life cycle covers analysis, design, implementation, and maintenance activities. In this case, however, the cycle is applied to assets, which include domain models, domain architectures, and other types of software parts that are used to build software products in the domain. Domain analysis is the analysis phase in the asset life cycle.

IEEE Std. 1517 defines *domain analysis* as:

> *(A) The analysis of systems within a domain to discover commonalities and differences among them.*
>
> *(B) The process by which information used in developing software systems is identified, captured, and organized so that it can be reused to create new systems, within a domain.*
>
> *(C) The result of the process in (A) and (B).*[15]

Domain analysis analyzes, abstracts, and models the characteristics of existing and envisioned software products within a domain to determine what the products have in common (their commonality) and how they differ (their diversity). This information is captured in a set of domain models during domain analysis.

The purposes of the domain models are to:

1. Aid in the understanding of the domain's essential common elements and the relationships that exist between these elements

2. Define a domain vocabulary to create a common understanding of the domain

3. Capture the essential common and differentiating features, capabilities, concepts, and functions in the domain

7.3.1 Define Domain Boundaries

IEEE Std. 1517 requires that one output of the domain analysis activity is a definition of boundaries of the domain in which the domain engineering process is being performed:

> *8.1.2.1 The domain engineer shall define the boundaries of the domain and the relationships between this domain and other domains.*[16]

Discussion

The domain boundaries should be defined in terms of which functions, features, properties, and capabilities to include in the domain and which to exclude from the domain. Also, relationships, such as one domain is a subset of another domain, should be established. This information, which the standard defines as the *"domain definition,"* is needed to produce and, if necessary, redefine the domain models.

Implementation Suggestions

The domain boundaries should be refined in an iterative manner through a comparison with other existing domains defined in the organization. Information from market analysis, customer requirements, software developers, and domain experts can be used to determine the boundaries of the domain. Also, the reuse program implementation plan should be reviewed since one component of the plan is an identification of the organization's domains. The boundaries for this domain should agree with those specified in the reuse program implementation plan. If they do not, then either or both the boundaries for this domain should be redefined and/or the reuse program implementation plan's domain definitions should be adjusted accordingly.

A context model, data flow model, or object model may be used to show the boundaries of a domain.[17] A data flow model or structure chart may be used to show relationships between domains.[18] The models used to show the boundaries of the domain should be the same representation forms selected for the domain models and domain architectures, respectively.

7.3.2 Identify Developers' Needs

Another domain analysis task required by IEEE Std. 1517 is the identification of the needs of the software developers who build software products in the domain:

> *8.1.2.2 The domain engineer shall identify the current and anticipated needs of developers of software products within the domain.*[19]

Discussion

The developers of the software products belonging to the domain are expected to be the primary users of the domain engineering deliverables. Based on their experience, these software developers may be in the best position to identify the assets that will be most useful in performing their software development work. There is a strong possibility that assets they used in the development of previous software products will also be needed in future versions and implementations of these products, as well as in new products that share similar features or capabilities with the existing products.

Assets that software developers consider useful in building current and future software products for the domain should be used to help define or refine the boundaries for the domain.

Implementation Suggestions

Developers and maintainers of software products for the domain should be interviewed to identify the assets that they believe would be most useful in their software projects. Also, the reuse experience and expertise of the domain software developers should be evaluated to determine if they have the skills needed to use the assets in their work. Based on this information, the boundaries of the domain may need to be adjusted to ensure that a domain engineering project performed for this domain will produce assets that can actually be used by the domain software developers and maintainers in their work.

7.3.3 Build Domain Models

In this task in the Domain Analysis Activity, the domain engineer is required to build the domain models:

> *8.1.2.3 The domain engineer shall build the domain models using the representation forms selected in the process implementation activity for this process.*[20]

Discussion

The domain models capture the static and dynamic characteristics and the vocabulary of the domain. Their purpose is to aid in the understanding of the domain's essential concepts, features, capabilities, and functions, and the relationships that exist between them. The domain models serve as the foundation specifications for the domain assets.

Domain analysis produces the domain models and can be viewed as a form of requirements analysis for the set of current and future software products within the domain.

Implementation Suggestions

Typically, domain analysis is performed in an iterative fashion as a combination top-down/bottom-up analysis activity. During the top-down analysis portion, exiting systems and models are studied to identify common structures. Similar common structures are grouped together for further study. The common and variable aspects of the group are identified and used as the basis for creating a generic structure that represents the properties of the group.

During the bottom-up portion of domain analysis, common assets that occur in the systems and models studied are identified. Also, relationships such as generalization ("is a") and aggregation ("consists of") that exist between common assets are identified. Common assets are mapped to a generic structure defined during top-down analysis.

7.3.4 Construct Domain Vocabulary

In this task in the Domain Analysis Activity, the domain engineer is required to construct the domain vocabulary:

> *8.1.2.4 The domain engineer shall construct a vocabulary that provides the terminology to describe the important domain concepts and the relationships among similar or common assets of the domain.*[21]

Discussion

The domain vocabulary is the foundation for recognizing commonalities that exist between software products within a domain. The domain vocabulary enables domain engineers and software developers to speak the same language and therefore more easily recognize and understand which assets may be used as the common building blocks in constructing software products within a domain.

Implementation Suggestions

The domain vocabulary may be created by discussing the domain with the domain experts and by analyzing concepts, keywords, nouns, and verbs contained in the existing software system documentation and analysis and design models, and in the enterprise and business models that pertain to this domain.

The domain vocabulary should be refined during the iterative process in which the domain models are created.

7.3.5 Classify and Document Domain Models

In this task in the Domain Analysis Activity, the domain engineer is required to classify and document the domain models:

8.1.2.5 The domain engineer shall classify and document domain models.[22]

Discussion

Any type of asset, including a domain model, cannot be reused unless the reuse consumer understands the asset. The function of documentation is to provide that understanding in a fashion that clearly identifies and explains the asset to the reuse consumer. The domain engineer who builds the domain architecture and other domain assets and the developers and maintainers of software products within the domain are the principal reuse consumers of the domain models.

Even though an asset is well documented, it still may be difficult to reuse if it is difficult to find. Therefore, assets must be not only well documented, but also well organized. Classifying assets into meaningful structures allows reuse consumers to find assets easily and quickly.

IEEE Std. 1517 defines *classification* as "the manner in which the assets are organized for ease of search and extraction within a reuse library."[23]

Implementation Suggestions

For any asset, including a domain model, its documentation should include information about what the asset does, its properties, and its usage requirements. In addition, information more specific to reuse, such as under what conditions it can be reused and how to adopt it for use in a particular software product, should be included in the documentation. Table 7-2 lists the suggested categories of information to include in an asset's documentation.

A classification scheme can be as simple as the asset's name or more complex, such as a faceted classification scheme which consists of a set of facet values. Classification schemes are discussed further in Chapter 5. The standard assigns the responsibility of creating a classification scheme for the domain to the asset manager, and the responsibility of using that classification scheme to classify the asset to the domain engineer who creates or acquires the asset.

Table 7-2. Categories of Asset Documentation Information

- Asset name, following the organization's naming conventions
- Short description of what the asset does
- Domain to which the asset belongs
- Instructions about using the asset, including technical environment requirements, performance constraints, and legal restrictions
- Test suite, including test plan, test cases, test scripts, test data, test results, and test tools
- Quality of the asset (e.g., error rate)
- Recommendations for improving the asset and putting it into a more reusable form
- History of the asset's use
- Classification for the asset

7.3.6 Evaluate Domain Models and Vocabulary

IEEE Std. 1517 requires an evaluation of the domain models and domain vocabulary:

> *8.1.2.6 The domain engineer shall evaluate the domain models and domain vocabulary in accordance with the provisions of the modeling technique selected and in accordance with the organization's asset acceptance and certification procedures. The results of the evaluation shall be documented.*[24]

Discussion

This task provides an explicit reminder to check the overall quality of the domain models. As the generic analysis models for the entire domain, domain models play an important role in both consumer and producer reuse. On the producer side, they influence the development of the domain architectures and other domain assets. For example, the domain models are used to determine the reuse potential of assets (i.e., what are the most valuable assets that may be used to develop software products in the domain). Assets that have the greatest reuse potential become the focus of later domain engineering creation or acquisition activities.

On the consumer side, the domain models influence the development of software products in the domain. For example, the domain models can be used when creating a software product project plan to initially identify opportunities for reuse and set reuse target levels for the software project. Also, they can be used during the analysis phase of a software product life cycle to check the completeness and consistency of the software requirements specified for the software product.

The creation and management of the organization's asset acceptance and certification procedures are the responsibility of the asset manager.

Implementation Suggestions

After completing top-down/bottom-up domain analysis activities used to create the domain models, the domain models can be evaluated by performing the following:

1. Check that all common assets and relationships defined during the domain analysis activity are included in the domain models.

2. Perform a redundancy check on the domain models to ensure that none of the assets or relationships are redundant. If any redundancies in the models are discovered, eliminate them by replacing the redundant assets with a generic version of the asset.

3. Check that the domain models comply with all modeling standards and naming standards of the organization.

4. Check that the domain models have been properly classified and documented.

7.3.7 Conduct Domain Analysis Joint Reviews

IEEE Std. 1517 requires a formal domain analysis review:

> *8.1.2.7 The domain engineer shall conduct domain analysis joint review(s) in accordance with the IEEE/EIA Std 12207.0-1996 Joint Review Process. Software developers, asset managers, domain experts, and users shall be included in the review.*[25]

Discussion

Since the domain model is a major deliverable of the domain engineering process, the domain models should be formally reviewed from the various perspectives of those impacted by the domain models. For example, software developers will be reuse consumers of the model and asset managers will manage the models over their lifetime.

Domain experts and users are also included in the review to ensure that the domain models correctly capture all the known key concepts in the domain.

Implementation Suggestions

The format for the domain analysis review is specified in the IEEE/EIA 12207 Standard Joint Review Process. When used to evaluate a software product such as a domain model, the IEEE/EIA 12207 Standard Joint Review Process is conducted as a technical review. Its function is to evaluate the software product to ensure its:

1. Completeness
2. Compliance to standards
3. Adherence to plans and approved changes

The IEEE/EIA 12207 Standard Joint review Process involves two parties: (1) the reviewed party and (2) the reviewing party. In the case of a domain analysis joint review, the domain engineer assumes the role of the reviewed party and the domain expert, user, and software developers assume the role of the reviewing party.

7.3.8 Submit Domain Models to Asset Manager

IEEE Std. 1517 requires that assets developed or acquired and approved during the Domain Engineering Process are given to the asset manager whose role is to manage the use of the domain assets:

> *8.1.2.7 The domain engineer shall submit domain models to the asset manager.*[26]

Discussion

The domain engineer's responsibility lies in the realm of producing and maintaining assets for the domain, but not in managing the use of the assets. When the domain engineer completes the asset production or maintenance function, the management responsibility for the asset is turned over to the asset manager.

Implementation Suggestions

The approved domain model(s), like any domain asset, should be submitted for inclusion in the organization's reuse catalog and/or reuse library where it can be accessed by reuse consumers, updated, and properly maintained over its lifetime.

7.4 Domain Design Activity

The purpose of IEEE Std. 1517 Domain Design Activity is to produce the design specifications for the domain architecture and domain assets. The domain architecture provides a common generalized framework for building software products with assets. While the domain model can be thought of as a definitional device for understanding domain commonalities, the domain architecture can be thought of as an implementation vehicle for building software products in the domain with the use of assets. The domain architecture provides:

1. The general structure for assembling assets into a software product

2. The impetus to use existing assets

3. A guide to creating new assets

4. An aid in understanding the domain's essential common assets and the relationships that exist between assets

Domain assets are designed to fit with the domain architecture. In this way, the domain architecture acts as the "glue" to integrate assets into a software product. Also, the standard intends that each software project in the domain is based upon the domain models and is derived from the domain architecture.

7.4.1 Create Domain Architecture

In this task of the Domain Design Activity, the domain architecture is selected or, if none exists, is created:

> *8.1.3.1 The domain engineer shall create and document the domain architecture, consistent with the domain model and following the organization's standards.*[27]

Discussion

The domain architecture is intended to serve as a high-level "starter" design specification that is used to create the design for each software product within the domain. It provides a standardized framework in which component interfaces are formally defined to guide the design of domain assets and software products.

Many of the architecture decisions concerning the operation of the system are made when the domain architecture is created. Then, when the architecture is reused in the development of domain software products, these decisions need not be made. This speeds up the development process and eliminates building redundant software parts.

Implementation Suggestions

It may be necessary to develop more than one domain architecture for the domain if different target environments are required for software products in the domain. For example, a different architecture is needed for distributed applications versus uni-process or host-based applications.

The knowledge and experience of architecture experts and software developers who are experienced in building this kind of software architecture should be used to help design the domain architecture. Also, the domain model should be considered an important input in domain design. The generic structures of the design models are used as the basis for creating the domain architecture. They will either become the domain architecture or a subsystem within the domain architecture.

Like a domain model, a domain architecture must also be generalized, standardized, and documented to enable its use in building multiple software products. Suggested ways to generalize the domain architecture:

1. Isolate implementation dependencies to enable their easy recognition and the ability to change implementation (environment) details to suit the requirements of a particular software product or to satisfy new environment and technology requirements when they occur in the future.

2. Layer the architecture to separate assets (e.g., processes and services) that are application-specific, operation-system-specific and hardware-platform specific into "layers." In this way, it will be easy to adapt the architecture to the specific requirements of a particular software product in the domain.[28]

3. At each layer, look for common assets to use as the basis for specifying assets that fit into the architecture. For example, processes and services supporting communications, user interface, windows management, information management, transaction

management, and batch process control should be defined as architecture assets. Many of these assets are environment-dependent and are examples of "horizontal" reuse since they can be used across domains that share the same system environment requirement.

Suggested ways to standardize the domain architecture:

1. Standardize the interfaces between assets (e.g., standard interface between the application system and the database management system, standard protocol between the application system and the communications software)[29]

2. Focus on subsystems (e.g., communications subsystem) and their interactions

3. Use a standardized modeling language such as UML

Documentation for the domain architecture should include information regarding reuse adaptation of the architecture, when to reuse the architecture, and classification of the architecture. Documentation suggestions for the domain architecture are listed in Table 7-3.

Table 7-3. Domain Architecture Documentation

- Reuse adoption information that guides the reuse consumer in modifying or specializing the domain architecture to build a particular software product[30]
- When-to-reuse information that describes the particular hardware target environments and particular development tools (e.g., code generators, GUI builders) for which the domain architecture was designed
- Classification of the domain architecture using the classification scheme specified by the domain asset manager (for details on classification schemes, see Chapter 5)

7.4.2 Evaluate Domain Architecture

In this task of the Domain Design Activity, IEEE Std. 1517 requires an evaluation of the domain architecture:

> *8.1.3.2 The domain architecture shall be evaluated in accordance with the provisions of the architecture design technique selected and the organization's asset acceptance and certification procedures. The results of the evaluation shall be documented.[31]*

Discussion

Since the domain architecture is used to guide the development of software products and assets for the domain, its overall quality, completeness, consistency, and compliance to standards must be carefully evaluated.

Creation and management of the organization's asset acceptance and certification procedures used to evaluate the domain architectures are the responsibility of the asset manager.

Implementation Suggestions

To validate its usability, the domain architecture should be compared with the design of at least one existing software product belonging to this domain (but not studied during the domain engineering analysis activity) to determine if the domain architecture could have been used as a starter design for this product.

Also, a domain expert, who is not a member of this domain engineering team, should review the domain architecture.

7.4.3 Develop Asset Specification

In this task of IEEE Std. 1517 Domain Design Activity, the focus is on creating design specifications for the domain assets:

> *8.1.3.3 For each entity selected to be designed for reuse, the domain engineer shall develop and document an asset specification.*[32]

Discussion

In this requirement, the standard implies that only a subset of all possible assets in the domain are likely to be designed for reuse. In domain engineering, a *selective reuse strategy* is usually followed. Selective reuse singles out for development or acquisition those assets that have the highest reuse potential, in that they:

1. Can be used the most frequently in software product development and maintenance projects within the domain

2. Provide the greatest benefits (e.g., cost savings, time savings, reducing the risk for project failure, enforcing standards) to the organization

3. Can be used to build and maintain software products that are of the greatest strategic importance to the organization

4. Have been requested by reuse consumers (e.g., software developers and software maintainers); that is, there is a known demand for the asset

To control the cost and length of a domain engineering project, design specifications are created only for assets with a high reuse potential

Implementation Suggestions

For ideas on which particular asset design specifications to create, organizations should study commonalities (e.g., common features or services) in software products in the domain that are currently being built or re-engineered. They also should ask software developers for their suggestions and contributions, and review vendor-supplied assets that are currently offered in the marketplace.

Table 7-4 shows the design specification information that should be provided for an asset. In addition, organizations should consider the following to identify which assets that have the highest reuse potential in the domain:

1. The potential number of times the asset can be used in building or maintaining software products in the domain

2. The strategic business importance of each software product in which the asset can be used

3. The similarities and differences expected in these software products

4. The impact of these differences on the reuse potential of the asset and the reuse benefits of the asset

5. The ability to create the asset in a way to accommodate expected differences and capture expected similarities over its reuses

6. The ease of certifying the reusability and overall quality of the asset

7. The cost to create/re-engineer/acquire the asset

8. The life expectancy of the asset compared against the time to produce/supply the asset

9. The cost to manage and maintain the asset over its lifetime

10. The number of times the asset must be used to recover its lifetime cost

11. The business benefits that use of the asset may provide (e.g., faster time to market)

12. The ease of fitting the asset into the domain architecture

Table 7-4 Asset Design Specification Information

• The function performed by the asset 　o What the asset expects from its clients 　o What the asset produces for its clients 　o Performance characteristics of the asset 　o The extent of commonality and variability required by the asset 　o Assumptions about the target environments of the asset • Limitations on the use of the asset

7.4.4 Evaluate Asset Specification

IEEE Std. 1517 includes a requirement for the evaluation of asset specifications:

8.1.3.4 For each asset specified, the specification shall be evaluated in accordance with the provisions of the IEEE/EIA Std 12207.0-1996 subclause 5.3.6.7, and in accordance with the organization's asset acceptance and certification procedures. The results of the evaluation shall be documented.[33]

Discussion

In addition to specifying that the organization's asset acceptance and certification procedures will be used to evaluate the asset specification, the standard also specifies the use of software evaluation requirements from the IEEE/EIA 12207 Standard. In the Software Detailed Design Activity in the Development Process of the IEEE/EIA 12207 Standard, the required areas for evaluating a detailed software design include:

1. Traceability of the design to the requirements specification

2. Consistency with the architectural design and between parts

3. Appropriateness of design methods and standards used

4. Feasibility of testing and maintaining the software

Implementation Suggestions

Traceability of the asset can be demonstrated by mapping the asset to its appropriate place in the domain model. Asset consistency can be shown by demonstrating where the asset fits into the domain architecture and by showing that the asset interface complies with the domain standards. Appropriateness of the design methods and standards used can be shown by demonstrating that the asset specification meets the asset acceptance and certification procedures as provided by the domain asset manager. Testability and maintainability of the asset can be shown by demonstrating the completeness of the asset documentation.

7.4.5 Conduct Domain Design Joint Review

The IEEE 1517 Std requires a formal domain design review:

> *8.1.3.5 The domain engineer shall conduct domain design joint review(s) in accordance with the IEEE/EIA 12207.0-1996 Joint Review Process. Software developers, domain experts, and asset managers shall be included in the reviews.*[34]

Discussion

The deliverables produced by the domain design are key to the success of the domain engineering project and to the ability to develop software products using domain assets.

A formal review of the domain design activity and its outputs helps ensure that the domain engineering project is on track and that the domain design outputs have been completed and are of high quality.

Implementation Suggestions

This IEEE Std. 1517 uses the IEEE/EIA 12207 Standard Joint Review Process to specify the requirements for a domain design review. The Joint Review Process is used to evaluate the status and products of the Domain Design Activity. A project management review of the activity is performed to determine if the activity is progressing according to the domain engineering plan, if adequate resources are available to satisfy activity requirements, and if there are any problems that may put the domain engineering project at risk.

In addition, a technical review of the domain architecture and asset design specifications is performed to ensure that they are complete, comply with standards, and are ready to be used as inputs in the development of domain assets and software products.

7.4.6 Submit Domain Architecture

IEEE Std. 1517 requires the submittal of the approved domain architecture(s) to the asset manager responsible for its management:

> *8.1.3.6 The domain engineer shall submit the domain architecture to the asset manager.[35]*

Discussion

The domain architecture must be properly managed since its function is to be used in development of all software products within the domain. Also, it is germane to employing a reuse-based development approach such as component-based development.

The management responsibility for the domain architecture is assigned to the asset manager.

Implementation Suggestions

The domain architecture should be submitted for inclusion in the organization's reuse catalog and/or reuse library where it can be accessed by software developers, maintainers, and other domain engineers and where it can be updated and maintained over its lifetime.

7.5 Asset Provision Activity

In this activity of IEEE Std. 1517 Domain Engineering Process, assets that have been determined to have potential for reuse in the domain software products are provided through an Acquisition Process or a Development Process. These assets are intended for use as building blocks to assemble software products in the domain. These assets may already exist or may need to be developed. For those assets that must be developed, a specification should have been created.

7.5.1 Develop or Acquire Assets

IEEE Std. 1517 requires assets to be provided through one of two means: either through development or through acquisition:

> *8.1.4.1 The domain engineer shall develop the asset executing the Acquisition Process (clause 5.1) to cause a contract for the asset to be put in place*

if the asset is to be acquired, or executing the Development Process (clause 5.3) if the asset is to be developed internally.[36]

Discussion

Recall that IEEE/EIA Std. 12207 defines a software product as a "set of computer programs, procedures, and possibly associated documentation and data."[37] IEEE Std. 1517 recognizes an asset as a special type of software product because its primary function is to be used as a building block in constructing other software products. Although an asset is special, the general requirements for developing or acquiring software products also apply to assets. Therefore, IEEE Std. 1517 uses the Development Process and Acquisition Process (see Chapter 4) to specify the general requirements for developing and acquiring software products. In addition, this activity adds tasks related specifically to developing or acquiring assets.

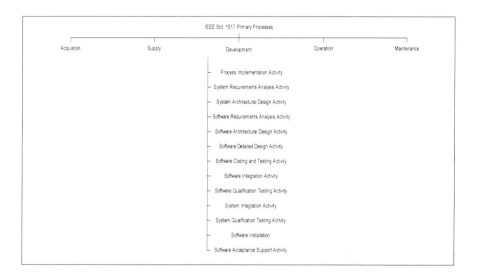

Figure 7-5. Activities in the IEEE Std. 1517 Development Process

Figure 7-5 shows the activities that comprise IEEE Std. 1517 Development Process as it applies to a software product developed with the use of assets. Figure 7-6 shows the activities that comprise IEEE Std. 1517 Acquisition Process as it applies to the acquisition of a software product acquired with the use of assets. It is important to note not all of these activities need be performed to comply with IEEE Std. 1517 when developing or acquiring an asset. The standard allows the user to tailor these processes by eliminating some of the activities in order to better meet the scope, magnitude, complexity, and criticality of a project concerned with the special case of assets rather than software products.

Implementation Suggestions

While it is true that an asset is a software product, it is also true that because of its multiple-use capability, an asset should be viewed as a special kind of software product that possesses properties over and above those normally expected in a software product. For example, any software product is expected to be of high quality. Requiring an asset to be thoroughly specified, documented, efficient, and tested will help ensure that the asset's quality is sufficient to qualify it as being basically reusable.38 However, to further ensure its reusability, an asset must also exhibit other characteristics, such as portability, interoperability, understandability, and maintainability.

IEEE Std. 1517 defines reusability as:

> *The degree to which an asset can be used in more than one software system, or in building other assets. In a reuse library, the characteristics of an asset that make it easy to use in different contexts, software systems, or in building assets.39*

Table 7-5 lists the characteristics commonly sought in an asset to ensure its reusability. If the asset is to be developed, then the domain engineer should build the reusability characteristics into the asset. If the asset is to be acquired, then the domain engineer should include reusability characteristics in the selection criteria for an acquired asset.

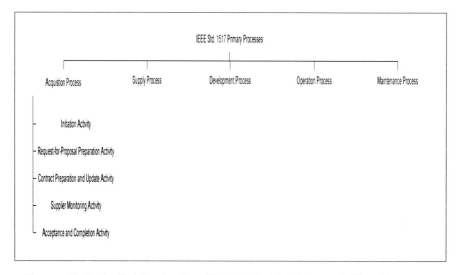

Figure 7-6. Activities in the IEEE Std. 1517 Acquisition Process

Table 7-5. General Reusability Characteristics

- Generalized with built-in adaptability/specialization
- Widely applicable
- Modular/self-contained
- Complete and consistent
- Machine independent
- Implementation/application independent
- Reliable
- Robust (Asset has safety built in through good error/exception handling)
- Understandable/well-documented
- Adaptable/extensible
- Standardized
- Portable (Can be used across various hardware and operating systems; dependent features are minimized and isolated)
- Certified/testable
- Maintainable
- Encapsulated (Details are isolated and hidden from the user to minimize effects of change)

It may not be feasible or even necessary to incorporate all of the characteristics shown in Table 7-5 into an asset. At the very least, however, the following characteristics should be present in a software product that is to be used as an asset:

1. Generalized

2. Standardized

3. Documented

When developing an asset, the domain engineer should generalize the asset to enable its use in multiple products. A generalized asset captures the common characteristics of the domain, but also allows for expected diversity. Generalization is a technique for abstracting the commonalities and stripping away the differences (i.e., ignoring the details of how, when, where, and conditions) from an asset to make it generally usable and reusable. Table 7-6 lists some commonly used asset generalization techniques.

Software reuse is made easier by standardization. When software features such as menus, GUIs, help functions, and error handling are standardized, opportunities for reuse are created. Assets that implement features in accordance with the standards can be used to enforce the standards. Also, if an asset complies with the organization's documentation, interface design, and testing standards, its reusability is increased because it is of better quality and general usefulness. Table 7-7 lists some of the common areas in which assets are standardized.

Table 7-6. Generalization Techniques

- Separating out the internal/implementation details/dependencies such as language or host/target environment dependencies[40]
- Separating the abstract common behavior/functionality from the application-specific business rules, logic and procedures
- Broadening the asset by adding additional features[41]
- Separating the information needed to use the asset (i.e., its specification from the information needed to implement it)
- Converting the asset to a higher level of abstraction (e.g., design, rather than code)[42]
- Not splitting a concept across assets but rather layering assets if needed in order to make the asset conceptually self-contained[43]
- Keeping the component interface implementation independent, explicit, and simple[44]
- Practicing information hiding and encapsulation[45]
- Identifying commonalities and isolating differences through techniques such as parameterization and abstract classes[46]
- Leaving small details uncommitted
- Describing assets in terms of requirements that are fixed (i.e., do not change from software product to software product) and are variable (i.e., can change from software product to product)[47]

Table 7-7. Asset Standardization Areas

- Invoking, controlling and terminating the function
- Error handling
- Help
- User interface (e.g., common user dialogue)
- Communication (e.g., common access to networks)
- Documentation information and format such as including standardized preamble fields to describe the asset in terms of name, author, date created, version number, parameter descriptions, data definitions, documentation template for different types of assets
- Conforming to analysis and design modeling standards such as OMG's UML
- Naming conventions
- Query processing
- Asset interface

Documentation is a fundamental component of asset reusability. Asset documentation is discussed further in the next section of this chapter. Table 7-8 provides some general guidelines to follow when creating an asset to ensure its reusability.

Table 7-8. General Asset Development Guidelines

- Before building a new asset from scratch, make sure that it does not already exist. If it does, make every effort to reuse rather than re-invent the asset.
- Follow naming conventions.
- Use a consistent design style and a style that is compatible with the design principles (e.g., GUI design standards) used in the organization's asset acceptance and certification procedures.
- Use templates from the Reuse Library/Catalog to create new assets to ensure that the assets adhere to a standard format and are complete.
- Practice information hiding by using object technology. An object encapsulates its data and provides only operations necessary for manipulating its data.
- Restrict communication between assets. Assets should be loosely coupled, and they should be highly cohesive.
- Be aware of the organization's asset certification criteria. Follow those criteria as much as possible when creating an asset.
- Make each asset development decision in a way that satisfies the current known requirements as well may satisfy future requirements.
- Make sure the underlying abstraction for the asset is well understood, because abstraction is the basis for reusability. Make the abstraction clean, simple, and amenable to reuse.
- Make the asset as robust as possible to enable it to handle errors and exception conditions.
- Make the asset as efficient as possible.
- Follow the organization's programming, user interface, database, testing, and documentation standards.
- Document the asset in a manner so that someone who is not familiar with it can understand the asset and the context/domain for which it was originally created.
- Capture design decisions along with the design to relate the asset design to its documentation and implementing code; provide links to all related assets that may be reused along with this asset (e.g., link the test scripts to their associated use case so that when the use case is reused, its test scripts can also be reused).

7.5.2 Document and Classify Assets

IEEE Std. 1517 requires that each asset developed or acquired is documented and classified:

8.1.4.2 The asset shall be documented and classified.[47]

Discussion

The asset should be named, documented, and classified in a manner that complies with the organization's standards. The classification scheme developed by the domain asset manager should be used to classify the asset.

Implementation Suggestions

Table 7-9 shows the five types of documentation that are needed to fully describe an asset.

Table 7-9. Types of Asset Documentation

Specification information	1. Purpose: a high-level description of the asset's functionality that describes in a succinct, yet expressive way what the asset does but not how it works
	2. If possible, a formal semantic description of the asset
	3. Abstract: description of the function, input, output, and when and how the asset can be used
Declarative information	1. Preconditions and post-conditions: assertions for valid use of the asset
	2. Events or conditions that cause the asset to change state
Quality/Certification information	1. Reliability information such as defect density based on lines of code or function points
	2. Warranties that describe responsibilities for defect corrections and the mechanisms for solving problems with the asset
Reuse information	1. Reuse history: number of times used
	2. Software products in which the asset has been used
	3. Reuse guidelines for using the asset to build a software product
Detailed information	1. Performance documentation
	2. Interface requirements
	3. Algorithms used
	4. Design decisions, tradeoffs considered and underlying rationale
	5. Creation information including the domain for which the asset was created
	6. Limitations (e.g., licensing, legal constraints, disclaimers)
	7. Test plan, test cases, test data, test results
	8. Relationships to other assets
	9. Traceability information
	10. Outstanding problems and defects and recommendations for improving the asset

7.5.3 Evaluate Assets

IEEE Std. 1517 requires an evaluation of assets that are developed or acquired for the purpose of reuse in the domain:

> *8.1.4.3 The domain engineer shall evaluate the asset in accordance with the organization's asset acceptance and certification procedures. The results of the evaluation shall be documented.*[48]

Discussion

Including an evaluation of the asset as part of its development or acquisition gives the reuse consumer a high degree of confidence in the overall quality and reusability of the asset. This will ensure that the asset is actually used by software developers to build software products and that the investment the organization makes in the asset pays off.

Implementation Suggestions

The asset should be evaluated in terms of its ability to satisfy the requirements of the organization's acceptance and certification procedures to ensure it will be accepted into the organization's reuse catalog and/or reuse library.

7.5.4 Conduct Asset Reviews

IEEE Std. 1517 requires a formal review of the assets developed or acquired during the Domain Engineering Process:

> *8.1.4.4 The domain engineer shall conduct asset joint review(s) in accordance with the IEEE/EIA Std 12207.0-1996 Joint Review Process.*[49]

Discussion

The purpose of conducting asset reviews is to ensure that assets produced by the domain engineering process are of value to the organization in the sense that they meet the organization's standards and they are reusable.

Implementation Suggestions

This standard uses the IEEE/EIA 12207 Standard Joint Review Process to specify the requirements for asset reviews. Technical reviews, as defined by the IEEE/EIA 12207 Joint Review Process, should be used to demonstrate that the assets are complete, comply with the organization's standards, and are ready to be used as building blocks in the development of software products. Also, usage information about when the asset is needed, how many times it potentially can be reused, and in what specific projects or software products it can potentially be used should be reviewed to assess the asset's reusability value to the organization.

7.5.5 Submit Assets

IEEE Std. 1517 requires that assets developed or acquired and approved during the Domain Engineering Process be submitted to the asset manager responsible for their management:

8.1.4.5 The domain engineer shall submit the asset to the asset manager.[50]

Discussion

The responsibilities for managing the asset and providing access to the asset are assigned to the asset manager for the domain.

Implementation Suggestions

Assets should be submitted for inclusion in the organization's reuse catalog and/or reuse library where they can be accessed by software developers for use in building software products and where they can be updated and maintained over their lifetime.

7.6 Asset Maintenance Activity

The purpose of this activity is to specify the requirements for maintaining all types of domain assets, including domain models and domain architectures. IEEE Std. 1517 requires that the domain engineer use IEEE Std. 1517 Maintenance Process when modifying an asset for the purposes of correcting a deficiency in the asset or meeting new requirements. The IEEE Std. 1517 Maintenance Process specifies the requirements for maintaining software products developed with assets.

Figure 7-7 shows the activities that comprise IEEE Std. 1517 Maintenance Process. When this Maintenance Process is applied to the maintenance of an asset, rather than a software product, it is assumed that the user of the standard may tailor the process to create a "mini" version that is more appropriate for asset maintenance efforts. In addition, in this activity IEEE Std. 1517 adds the reuse-related tasks that pertain especially to the maintenance of assets.

7.6.1 Analyze Asset Modification Requests

IEEE Std. 1517 requires a reuse-based analysis of a request to modify an asset.

8.1.5.1 When analyzing requests for asset modification and choosing implementation options, the domain engineer shall consider

- *conformance with the domain models and the domain architecture*

- *impact on the systems that use the asset*

- *impact on future users of the asset*

- *impact on the reusability of the asset*[51]

Discussion

Because of its multiple-use capability, any change made to an asset has broader implications than changes made to a single-use software part. The impact of the change must be considered not only in the context of software products for which the request was made, but to all other current and future software products in the domain. For example if a change is made to an asset that comprises its conformance with the domain models and the domain architecture, it may be difficult to use the asset in building future software products in the domain because the modified asset no longer fits easily into the domain architecture. Or, if a change is made to an asset that adversely affects its generality or adaptability, its reusability may be diminished.

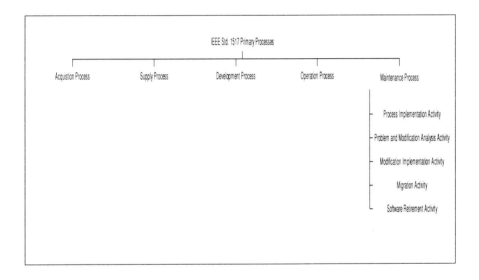

Figure 7-7. Activities in the IEEE Std. 1517 Maintenance Process

Implementation Suggestions

Asset acceptance and certification procedures should be used as the basis for analyzing the appropriateness of an asset modification request and choosing how to satisfy the request. One option for satisfying an asset modification request that should be considered is rejection of the request. A request should be rejected if this is the only way to preserve the reusability of the asset and to protect the integrity of software products using the asset.

7.6.2 Obtain Approval for Asset Modification

IEEE Std. 1517 requires formal approval of an asset modification plan before modifying an asset:

> *8.1.5.2 The domain engineer shall obtain approval for the selected implementation option, schedule, and plans to modify the asset.*[52]

Discussion

This task implies that a plan for modifying an asset is created. Components of the plan include the implementation approach selected and the schedule for modifying the asset. This task also implies that approval for the plan must be obtained before the asset is modified. However, the task does not specify from whom the approval is to be obtained because the standard does not address the asset ownership issue.

Implementation Suggestions

The user of IEEE Std. 1517 is given full discretion in choosing who has ownership authority over domain assets. For example, it may be assigned to the domain engineer who developed the asset, the asset manager who manages the asset, or to the user of the domain software products. The choice depends on how the organization is structured, who supplies the funding for domain engineering and asset management activities, and any legal restrictions regarding asset ownership.

7.6.3 Notify Asset Manager

IEEE Std. 1517 requires a notification of the asset manager concerning how the asset modification request is to be addressed:

> *8.1.5.3 The domain engineer shall notify the asset manager who sent the asset modification request about whether the asset modification was approved and the plans and schedule for those approved modifications. When a modification request is not approved, it shall be recorded and entered into the Problem Resolution Process, as specified in the IEEE/EIA Std. 12207.0-1996.*[53]

Discussion

The purpose of this task is to assure that the asset manager is kept in the communication loop about any plans to modify an asset.

Implementation Suggestions

Asset users receive information (perhaps via e-mail) about the status of an asset, outstanding problems or issues concerning the asset, and new versions or implementations of the asset through the asset manager, not the domain engineer. The role of the asset manager is to serve as a communication link between domain engineers and asset users.

7.6.4 Modify the Asset

In this task, the domain engineer implements approved asset modifications:

> *8.1.5.4 After approval is obtained, the domain engineer shall enter the Domain Engineering Process (clause 8) to implement modifications to an asset.*[55]

Discussion

Although IEEE Std. 1517 requires the domain engineer to use the Domain Engineering Process to implement the approved modifications to an asset, it is assumed that only a subset of the activities defined in the Domain Engineering Process will be needed when modifying an asset. For example, the asset modification plan will not need to be as comprehensive as a domain engineering plan for a full domain engineering project including the development of domain models, domain architectures, and other types of domain assets. In most asset modification efforts, the domain models, domain vocabulary, and domain architectures will not need to be created, documented, classified, and evaluated, since they will already exist.

Implementation Suggestions

The user of this standard should select the necessary activities and tasks in the Domain Engineering Process to form a "mini" version of domain engineering to implement the asset modification.

7.6.5 Submit the Modified Asset

> *8.1.5.5 The domain engineer shall send the completed asset along with any usage instructions and test assets to the asset manager who sent the asset modification request.*[56]

Discussion

The domain asset manager is responsible for managing the asset and providing access to the modified asset.

Implementation Suggestions

When an asset is modified, its associated documentation and classification information should be updated to reflect any changes in the asset's functionality, performance requirements, limitations, usage, and so forth. Also, it is important to package the asset with an updated set of test data, test cases, and test procedures that can be used by the asset consumer to retest the asset. Reusing the associated test data, cases, and procedures along with the asset can result in a great deal of time and cost savings.

7.7 Summary

The Domain Engineering Process is a cross-project life cycle process specified in IEEE Std. 1517 software life cycle process framework whose function is to supply a set of highly reusable assets for use in building software products in the domain. As shown in Figure 7-8, the Domain Engineering Process specifies the activities needed to practice producer reuse. Figure 7-8 also shows the major deliverables produced by the Domain Engineering Process. The party responsible for the Domain Engineering Process is the domain engineer. Figure 7-9 summarizes the areas of responsibility for the domain engineer.

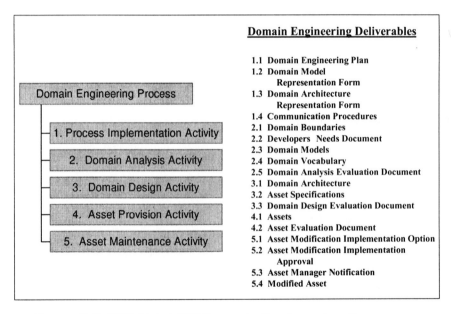

Figure 7-8. IEEE Std. 1517 Domain Engineering Process
Activities and Deliverables

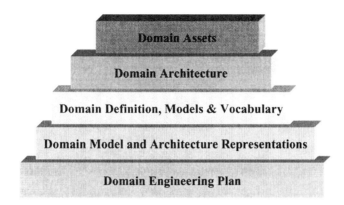

Figure 7-9. Responsibilities of the Domain Engineer

7.8 References

1. *IEEE Std. 1517, Standard for Information Technology—Software Life Cycle Processes—Reuse Processes*, IEEE, Piscataway, N.J., 1999.

2. Ibid.

3. Ibid.

4. K. Kang et al., Feature-Oriented Domain Analysis Feasibility Study, tech. report CMU/SEI-90-TR-21 ESD-90-TR-21, Software Engineering Institute, Carnegie Mellon Univ., Pittsburgh, Pa., Nov. 1990.

5. R. Prieto-Diaz, "Issues and Experience in Software Reuse," American Programmer, vol. 6, no. 8, Aug. 1993, pp. 10–18.

6. *Domain Analysis and Design Process*, DISA/CIM Software Reuse Program, Arlington, Va.

7. *IEEE Std. 1517, Standard for Information Technology—Software Life Cycle Processes—Reuse Processes*, IEEE, Piscataway, NJ, 1999.

8. Ibid.

9. Ibid.

10. Ibid.

11. Kang et al, *Feature-Oriented Domain Analysis Feasibility Study*, pp. 35–45.

12. Ibid., pp. 47–57.

13. *UML Summary,* Version 1.1, September 1, 1997, Rational Software Corporation, Santa Clara CA, Rational Web Page: rational.com.

14. *IEEE Std. 1517, Standard for Information Technology—Software Life Cycle Processes—Reuse Processes.*

15. Ibid.

16. Ibid.

17. Kang et al, *Feature-Oriented Domain Analysis Feasibility Study*, pp. 31–34.

18. Ibid., pp. 31–34.

19. *IEEE Std. 1517, Standard for Information Technology—Software Life Cycle Processes—Reuse Processes.*

20. Ibid.

21. Ibid.

22. Ibid.

23. Ibid.

24. Ibid.

25. Ibid.

26. Ibid.

27. Ibid.

28. Kang et al, *Feature-Oriented Domain Analysis Feasibility Study*, pp. 47–52.

29. R. Prieto-Diaz, "Issues and Experience in Software Reuse," pp. 10–18.

30. R. Prieto-Diaz and G. Arango, Editors, *Domain Analysis and Software System Modeling*, p. 66.

31. *IEEE Std. 1517, Standard for Information Technology—Software Life Cycle Processes—Reuse Processes.*

32. Ibid.

33. Ibid.

34. Ibid.

35. Ibid.

36. Ibid.

37. *ISO/IEC 12207–1996 Standard for Information Technology—Software Life Cycle Processes*, International Organization for Standardization & International Electrotechnical Commission, Geneva, Switzerland, 1996.

38. I. Jacobson, *Object-Oriented Software Engineering: A Use Case Driven Approach*, Addison Wesley Longman, Reading, Mass., 1992, p. 275.

39. *IEEE Std. 1517, Standard for Information Technology—Software Life Cycle Processes—Reuse Processes.*

40. E. Leinfress, "Managing Class Libraries Takes Discipline," *Client/Server Computing Software Magazine*, June 1993, pp. 15–21.

41. E. Leinfress, "Managing Class Libraries Takes Discipline." Jacobson, Ivar, *Object-Oriented Software Engineering*, p. 296.

42. I. Jacobson, *Object-Oriented Software Engineering*, p. 296.

43. M. Griss and W. Tracz, "WISR'92: 5th Annual Workshop on Software Reuse Working Group Reports," *ACM SIGPLAN Software Engineering Notes*, vol. 18, no. 2, Apr. 1993, pp. 74–85.

44. Jacobson, Ivar, *Object-Oriented Software Engineering*, p. 303.

45. Jacobson, Ivar, *Object-Oriented Software Engineering*, p. 293.

46. D. Coleman et al., *Object-Oriented Development: The Fusion Method*, Prentice-Hall, Upper Saddle River, N.J., 1994, p. 220.

47. Ibid., p. 218.

48. *IEEE Std. 1517, Standard for Information Technology—Software Life Cycle Processes—Reuse Processes.*

49. Ibid.

50. Ibid.

51. Ibid.

52. Ibid.

53. Ibid.

54. Ibid.

55. Ibid.

56. Ibid.

Part 3.
Application

Chapter 8.
Application of IEEE Std. 1517

8.1 Purpose of IEEE Std. 1517

IEEE Std. 1517 is about reuse—but more to the point, it is about *systematic reuse*. As the standard explains, "systematic reuse is the practice of reuse according to a well-defined, repeatable process."[1] The fundamental purpose of this standard is to specify the software life cycle processes, activities, tasks, and software infrastructure that enable the practice of systematic reuse.

IEEE Std. 1517 specifies the practice of systematic reuse from two perspectives:

1. *Consumer Reuse*: The development, operation, and maintenance of software systems and products with the use of assets.

2. *Producer Reuse*: The development, management, and maintenance of assets.

Assets are software life cycle deliverables that are designed for reuse and that are used as building blocks to create software products and their associated deliverables.

8.2 Users of IEEE Std. 1517

The user of IEEE Std. 1517 may be an individual or an organization that is interested in learning about or adopting the best-known systematic reuse practices. Users of this standard are expected to be familiar with the concept of software life cycle and examples of software life cycle models, such as the waterfall or iterative models, and are expected to have access to the IEEE/EIA Std. 12207.0-1996.[2] Since the design of IEEE Std. 1517 is based upon the IEEE/EIA Std. 12207.0 software life cycle framework, like the 12207 Standard, this standard may be used by many different types of users for many different purposes. In general, expected users include both managers and technical persons involved in the acquisition, supply, or development of software applications and systems or reusable assets. Table 8-1 lists common types of users of IEEE Std. 1517.

8.2.1 Usage Views of the Standard

How this standard is viewed depends upon the type of user. For example, if the user is a software development project team that wishes to develop a software product with the use of assets, then the view of usage is software engineering. Under the software engineering view, the software development project team uses principally IEEE Std. 1517 Development Process along with the related 12207 Standard supporting and organizational processes to implement the technical and management aspects of a software life cycle appropriate for the project. As another example, if the user is a reuse program manager who is responsible for establishing an organizational-level reuse program, then the view of usage is a management view. The reuse program manager uses the IEEE Std. Reuse Program Administration Process along with the 12207 Standard Management, Infrastructure, Training and Improvement Processes to establish and manage a formal reuse program.

IEEE Std. 1517's usage views are based upon the 12207 Standard usage views, which include: contract view, management view, operating view, engineering view, and supporting view. However, there are slight differences in the usage views of these two standards because of IEEE Std. 1517's focus on reuse. Table 8-2 summarizes the principal usage views of IEEE Std. 1517.

Table 8-1. Common Types of IEEE Std. 1517 Users

Technical Users

- Software professions
- Software engineering students
- Software development project teams
- Software maintenance project teams
- Domain engineering project teams
- Software librarians
- Software quality assurance teams
- Software configuration managers

Management Users

- Software project managers
- Software organization managers
- Reuse program managers

Table 8-2. IEEE Std. 1517 Usage Views

Contract	Acquisition Process Supply Process
Software Engineering	Development Process Maintenance Process
Domain Engineering	Domain Engineering Process Asset Management Process
Operation	Operation Process
Management	Reuse Program Administration Process Management Process Infrastructure Process Training Process Improvement Process

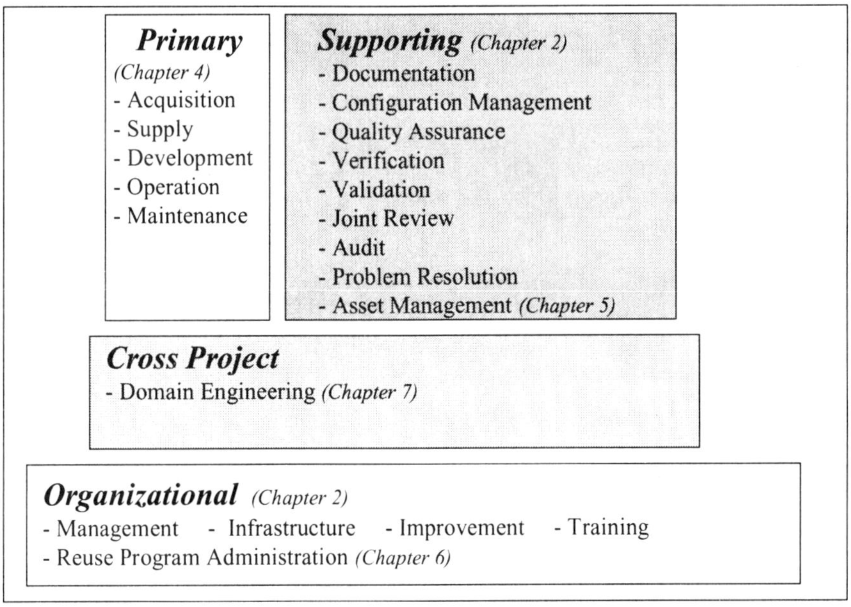

Figure 8-1. IEEE Std. 1517 Processes

8.3 Conformance Options of IEEE Std. 1517

Depending upon the use, the standard may used as a whole by implementing all its required processes, activities, and tasks; or may be used in part by implementing all the required activities and tasks in the pertinent process(es). Figure 8-1 shows the processes included in IEEE Std. 1517.

8.3.1 Full Conformance

If the standard is implemented as a whole, then every required process, activity, and task specified in the standard must be implemented by the user. The user is then said to be in *full conformance* with IEEE Std. 1517.

A required IEEE Std. 1517 task is indicated by the words "shall" or "will" appearing in the text. For example, in the user's model of the software development process, preliminary test requirements must be created using applicable existing test assets in order to implement the following IEEE Std. 1517 required task:

> *5.3.5.5 Preliminary test requirements shall be created reusing applicable test requirements if any exist.*[3]

If the user's life cycle model implements every required process, activity, and task defined in IEEE Std. 1517, then the life cycle model is in full compliance with IEEE Std. 1517 and also with IEEE/EIA Std. 12207.0-1996.

However, the user of this standard may also choose to implement only a of subset of the required processes, activities, and tasks in the user's software life cycle model. For example, this is the case when a user chooses to implement only one reuse perspective in the software life cycle model or when the user is performing a reuse project.

8.3.2 Reuse Projects

There are several reasons for performing a reuse project. Some reasons are to:

- Define the major domains in an organization
- Create a reuse library
- Establish a reuse program
- Assess an organization's reuse readiness
- Conduct a reuse pilot project
- Define an organization's reuse strategy

For example, when initiating a reuse program in an organization, a reuse project is often performed to define the major domains in the organization. The domain represents a segment of the organization where practicing reuse can potentially provide significant benefits to the organization. Domains are used as the basis for deciding how and where reuse will be practiced in the organization. To perform a domain definition project, the user of this standard should implement IEEE Std. 1517 Domain Identification Activity requirements in the Reuse Program Administration Process.

As another example, consider the need for an inventory of highly reusable, high quality assets to succeed with reuse. The asset inventory must be organized so that the assets are easy to find and understand. A reuse library definition project is frequently performed to define the mechanisms, procedures, and tools for storing, organizing, managing, and retrieving assets. To perform a reuse library definition project, the user of this standard should implement IEEE Std. 1517 Asset Management Process requirements.

Finally, consider establishing a reuse program. Since it typically requires three-to-five years, establishing a reuse program at the organization level is often treated as a reuse project. When viewed as a project, the reuse program is likely to be better planned, funded, managed, and monitored. To perform a reuse program project, the user of this standard should implement IEEE Std. 1517 Reuse Program Administration Process requirements.

8.3.3 Selective Conformance

When a user of this standard implements all the required activities and tasks in a particular IEEE Std. 1517 Process, then the user can claim *selective conformance.* For example, if the user implements all the required tasks in the Domain Engineering Process, then selective conformance to the Domain Engineering Process is achieved.

8.4 Uses of IEEE Std. 1517

There are several ways a user may choose to use this standard. Some common uses are to:

- Integrate reuse into the software life cycle
- Improve the software life cycle with respect to reuse
- Measure the reuse capability of the organization
- Establish a reuse program in an organization
- Facilitate the use of assets to develop, operate, and maintain a software system or product
- Facilitate the development, management, and maintenance of assets
- Contract for the acquisition and supply of assets
- Contract for the acquisition and supply of software systems and products developed with assets
- Implement a component-based development approach

8.4.1 Integrate Reuse into the Software Life Cycle

The primary use of IEEE Std. 1517 is to direct the integration of reuse into the user's software life cycle model. The standard specifies the reuse processes, activities, tasks, and deliverables that minimally must be present in a software life cycle model to enable the practice of systematic reuse. It not only specifies what must be present, but also where it must be inserted into the life cycle.

A user who has an existing software life cycle model may use IEEE Std. 1517 to determine what must be added to the model to support reuse. A user who is developing a new software life cycle model intended to support reuse may use IEEE Std. 1517 to define the reuse-related elements of the model. The user may use the standard in its entirety to implement both perspectives for practicing systematic reuse in the life cycle or may selectively use the standard to implement the practice of reuse from only one perspective or in only a subset of the model's processes.

8.4.1.1 Adopting Reuse in Stages

Experience has shown that often the safest and most cost-effective way to adopt reuse is by following an evolutionary approach where reuse is introduced in stages into the organization. This approach lessens the possibility of culture shock from the changes that practicing reuse brings and lessens resistance to the concept of reuse. Evolving in graduated, well planned steps towards the adoption of systematic reuse as a standard software practice minimizes the risk of failure of a reuse program and any negative impact from reuse.

One way in which to stage the adoption of reuse is to first introduce the consumer reuse perspective into the software life cycle model, followed later on with the introduction of the reuse producer perspective. Implementing consumer reuse in the software life cycle model entails, at a minimum, implementing IEEE Std. 1517 Development Process requirements. (Recall that the Development Process was presented in Chapter 4.) In addition, if the development of the software system or product in the organization normally requires the development of a Request-for-Proposal (RFP), a formal contact, and the designation of a separate party to supply the software system or product, then the IEEE Std.1517 Acquisition Process and Supply Process should also be implemented as part of the consumer reuse perspective

The advantage such a staged approach offers is that consumer reuse is generally easier to adopt than producer reuse. It requires less reuse skills, effort, and resources and less change to the organizational structure. Also, it can be practiced without lengthening software project schedules. The safest course is to introduce the consumer perspective in software projects by expecting the project team to use a software life cycle model that directs them to use available assets, but does not direct them to create new assets. After the organization gains experience with consumer reuse, producer reuse can be introduced. Also, this approach allows an organization to see some of the benefits from reuse in a shorter time as well as to reduce the risk for failure.

8.4.2 Improve the Software Life Cycle with respect to Reuse

Another important use of IEEE Std. 1517 is as an aid to improve the software life cycle with respect to reuse. IEEE Std. 1517 specifies the reuse requirements for a life cycle that supports the practice of systematic reuse. To improve an existing model, the user can map each IEEE Std. 1517 reuse requirement to the user's software life cycle model. Requirements that are not implemented in the model show the user specifically where the model is deficient in terms of its ability to support reuse, and therefore exactly how to improve the model. For example, IEEE Std. 1517 requires that the reusability of a software design be evaluated as part of the general design quality review. If the user's current model does not provide for evaluating the reusability of a software design, then one way to improve the model is to add reusability criteria to other software design quality review criteria such as completeness, consistency, traceability to requirements, and compliance to standards.

8.4.3 Measure the Organization's Reuse Capability

Models such as the Capability Maturity Model (CMM) from the Software Engineering Institute at Carnagie Mellon University are often used to measure the software engineering capability of an organization in terms of the maturity of an organization's software life cycle processes.[4] Software process maturity is considered of great importance to an organization because the more mature its software processes are, the more likely they will produce better quality software deliverables.

The typical reasons for measuring software process maturity are either to improve the software life cycle or to assess the capability of a vendor to supply high quality software products.

The maturity of a software process typically is described by a set of characteristics, such as the inclusion of activities for project planning, that enable the process to produce high quality software deliverables. The maturity of a software process is measured by the presence of these characteristics. The maturity of a software life cycle model is measured in terms of the maturity of its processes. The capability of the vendor is assessed based upon the maturity of the vendor's software life cycle.

Reuse maturity is measured for the same reasons and in the same manner as software process maturity, except that the focus is on reuse maturity. IEEE Std. 1517 specifies the processes that must be included in the software life cycle to support reuse and explicitly describes the reuse characteristics of each process in terms of a set of reuse-related tasks. Therefore, the reuse maturity of a software life cycle can be measured by determining the extent to which the software life cycle includes all the required processes and the extent to which all the required reuse-related tasks are implemented by each required process. For example, a software life cycle that fully supports the practice of systematic reuse must include a domain engineering process and, within the domain engineering process, all the required reuse-related tasks must be implemented by the software life cycle.

8.4.4 Establish a Reuse Program

IEEE Std. 1517 guides the user in the practice of reuse at the individual software project level and at the organization level. At both levels, an infrastructure including hardware, software, tools, techniques, standards, metrics, and facilities that support reuse is needed. However, the infrastructure needs are obviously greater at the organization level. A formal reuse program is needed to handle planning, managing, controlling, and implementing reuse practices across the software projects in an organization. Therefore, another important use of IEEE Std. 1517 is to guide the establishment of a formal reuse program. The user who wishes to establish a formal reuse program at the organization level should implement the requirements specified in IEEE Std. 1517 Reuse Program Administration Process. (See Chapter 6 for more detail regarding the Reuse Program Administration Process.)

8.4.5 Facilitate the Use of Assets

The most fundamental reason for practicing reuse is to avoid needlessly redeveloping the same software deliverables over and over again. With reuse, the software developer is expected to assemble software deliverables, such as software designs or software test requirements, from existing assets. Since this is a significantly different approach to software development than usually employed by software developers, reuse of assets in all likelihood will not happen unless the software life cycle model supports the practice of consumer reuse.

Another common use of IEEE Std. 1517 is to facilitate the use of assets by defining the software life cycle requirements for finding, selecting, and using appropriate assets to produce software deliverables during the software development, operation, and maintenance processes. When the reason for using this standard is mainly to facilitate the use of assets, implementing the reuse-related tasks specified in IEEE Std. 1517 Development Process, Operation Process, and Maintenance Process will be of primary importance. (These processes are discussed in Chapter 4.)

8.4.6 Facilitate the Development, Management, and Maintenance of Assets

While facilitating the use of assets focuses on consumer reuse, facilitating the development [and maintenance] of assets focuses on producer reuse. The end product of consumer reuse is a software product that may or may not be reusable in whole or in part. On the other hand, the end product of producer reuse is a product whose primary purpose is reuse; that is, an asset which is reusable. Because the end products of consumer reuse and producer reuse have substantially different functions, the software life cycle requirements to support the practice of consumer reuse and producer reuse are also quite different. In fact, they are viewed as so different that producer reuse is seen as a different and separate life cycle. The life cycle for producer reuse is called *domain engineering*.

Thus, domain engineering is the life cycle of an asset. Although like a software product life cycle, domain engineering addresses analysis, design, implementation, and maintenance, each phase has distinct differences from its counterpart software product phases because of the reusability characteristics inherent in assets. For example, in the software product life cycle, analysis is performed to define the requirements of the software product to be developed. In the domain engineering life cycle, domain analysis is performed to define the common requirements shared by a set software products that are classified in a common group called a domain. The common requirements shared by the software products in the domain are represented in a domain model.

The way in which assets are managed also differs from the way in which software products are normally managed. Because of their multi-use capability, asset management presents unique and often more extensive access, security, configuration management, change control, and notification requirements.

When the reason for using this standard is to facilitate the development and maintenance of assets, the Domain Engineering Process specifies the most important software life cycle requirements that the user must implement. (The Domain Engineering Process is discussed in Chapter 7.) In addition, to handle the special asset management requirements, the requirements specified in IEEE Std. 1517 Asset Management Process must be implemented in the user's software life cycle model. (The Asset Management Process is discussed in Chapter 5.)

8.4.7 Contract for Reuse

IEEE Std. 1517 may be used to create a formal contact between two or more organizations or an informal contract within an organization. The terms of the contract address the acquisition requirements and supply requirements for a software product(s) or asset(s). For example, the contract may involve the development of a new software product based on the reuse of assets or it may involve the supply of a set of assets that meets the organization's general quality and reusability criteria.

In the case of a formal contract, IEEE Std. 1517 assumes that software acquirer and supplier are separate organizations. In the case of an informal contract, the standard assumes that they are in the same organization.

The requirements specified in one or more of the processes defined in the standard may be used to create the terms of the contract. Because process tasks have been expressed in contractual language in the standard, it is relatively straightforward for the user to include them directly in the contract.

8.4.8 Implement CBD Approach

Recall from Chapter 1 that *component-based development* is an assembly approach to software development in which software products are constructed by means of assembling components. What is necessary to adopt a CBD approach? Most often, the focus is on the acquisition of the components themselves and supporting software tools. Certainly, components and tools are essential but they are not sufficient to practice CBD. CBD requires a disciplined approach to software development that emphasizes organization-level planning, management, and coordination across software projects and products. A well-defined, reuse-based software process is needed to provide this discipline.

8.4.8.1 Characteristics of a CBD Process

More particularly, the characteristics of a CBD process must be:

- Well-defined, repeatable

- Based on modularization and information hiding

- Scalable to develop large, complex software applications

- Reuse-based

First, to manage reuse and sharing of components among developers and projects, a CBD process must be a well-defined, repeatable process. Repeatedly using the same development process by different project teams to produce multiple software products enables the reuse of tools and components, thereby leveraging the organization's investment in components, software tools, and training.

Second a CBD process must be based on the concepts of structured programming, modularization and information hiding to decompose/compose the system into independent, reusable, and replaceable chunks of functionality (Table 8-3).

Table 8-3. Software Engineering Concepts Underlying CBD

Structured Programming:	A programming technique that standardizes the program structure by imposing rules for program modularization and documentation with the objective of controlling program complexity
Modularization:	A technique for dividing a system into units, called modules, with the objective of increasing program modifiability, reusability, and maintainability
Information Hiding:	A modularization approach in which design decisions about data structures and sequences of events are hidden within a module, with the objective of minimizing the amount of design information revealed to other modules that use this module (in this way, changes to the internal structure of a module will only affect that module)

Third, a CBD process must have the capability of supporting the development of large, complex software systems. Furthermore, a CBD process must be able to deal with components expressed as a wide range of abstractions, including design-level abstractions.

Finally and most importantly, a CBD process must be a reuse-based process. Because reuse lies at the very heart of this development strategy, it must be guided by reuse principles and practices. The reuse-related activities and tasks that are essential to using a CBD approach include the following:

- Reuse planning is included in strategic systems planning and software project planning

- Software development decision making is governed by reuse considerations such as reusing existing components or creating new components

- Analysis and design are broadened from addressing one software product at a time to a set of related software products

- Commonality and variability analysis are integral to analysis and design

- Composition and decomposition techniques, guided by architectural rules for building and using components, are used to assemble productsfrom new and existing components

- Software life cycle is viewed from two perspectives: consumer reuse and producer reuse

8.4.8.2 Adopting a CBD Approach

A user of this standard who wants to adopt a CBD process at the organizational level should attempt to acquire or build a software life cycle model that is in full conformance to this standard. A user who adopts a CBD approach for use in a particular project should attempt to achieve selective conformance to the reuse processes most pertinent to the project.

8.5 Final Advice for Using IEEE Std. 1517

It is important to keep in mind that the reason for using this standard should always go beyond simply some aspect of practicing software reuse. Software reuse is not an end in itself. It is a means to accomplish a goal. Although improving the software life cycle may be seen as a legitimate reason for adopting reuse, it may not be adequate to succeed with reuse. Often, the goal must go beyond technology and into the business realm to gain sufficient support for the establishment of a reuse program and to sustain interest in reuse over a multi-year adoption period. A business goal, such as reducing the time to market, will strengthen management's commitment to reuse. Without a firm commitment, a reuse program—no matter how technically correct or appropriate—is likely to fall by the wayside.

It is also important to keep in mind that the decisions of whether to use this standard and how to use this standard should be based upon economic considerations. The intent of the standard is that it will be applied in a cost-effective manner that brings positive economic benefits to the user.

Finally, it is important to keep in mind that the user of IEEE Std. 1517 should strive to conform not only with the requirements of the standard but also with the spirit of the standard. A reuse initiative at any level will not fully succeed unless the reuse spirit is present.

The reuse spirit is embodied in a willingness to recognize that reuse is a different software paradigm and a willingness to change to embrace a new way of working. Communication and sharing must form the foundation for performing software work based on a reuse approach. Traditional boundaries between software projects and software products must be set aside and time lines between the past, present, and future must be disregarded in the interest of maximizing reuse opportunities.

Although it may seem that practicing reuse requires a radical departure from traditional software engineering practices, quite the opposite is true. The changes needed to adopt reuse suggested this standard are evolutionary not revolutionary in nature. The spirit of IEEE Std. 1517 is to guide the user on an evolutionary path of extending widely accepted and proven software life cycle models to include the best known reuse practices.

8.6 References

1. *IEEE Std. 1517, Standard for Information Technology—Software Life Cycle Processes—Reuse Processes*, IEEE, Piscataway, N.J., 1999.

2. *ISO/IEC 12207—1996 Standard for Information Technology—Software Life Cycle Processes*, International Organization for Standardization & International Electrotechnical Commission, Geneva, Switzerland, 1996.

3. *IEEE Std. 1517, Standard for Information Technology—Software Life Cycle Processes—Reuse Processes*, IEEE, Piscataway, N.J., 1999.

4. *Capability Model Summary*, Software Engineering Institute, Carnegie Mellon Univ., SEI Web Page: sei.cmu.edu.

Chapter 9.
Relationship to the SEI
Capability Maturity Model

9.1 Measuring Software Process Maturity

The Capability Maturity Model (SW-CMM or CMM) is a widely accepted and widely used method for evaluating the maturity of an organization's software development and maintenance processes. Since its original publication in 1989, hundreds of organizations worldwide have used CMM, making it a *de facto* industry standard for improving their software processes.

Organizations use the CMM primarily for two purposes:

1. Assessment of the organization's software processes for the purpose of improving the software processes

2. Evaluation of the software processes used by a vendor for the purpose of determining the capability of the vendor to produce quality software

9.2 History of CMM

At the request of the US Department of Defense, the Capability Maturity Model was developed by Carnegie Mellon University's Software Engineering Institute (SEI) as a method to assess the capabilities of software contractors.[1] The SEI's work on software maturity models resulted in the following capability maturity models:

- CMM for Software

- SE-CMM for System Engineering

- SA-CMM for Software Acquisition

- P-CMM for People

- IPD-CMM for Integrated Product Development

- Capability Model Integration

The SEI's goals in developing these capability maturity models are to:

- Address disciplines that have an impact on software

- Provide an integrated process improvement reference model

Level 5: Optimized

Level 4: Managed

Level 3: Defined

Level 2: Repeatable

Level 1: Initial

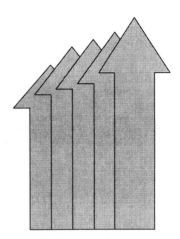

Figure 9-1. CMM Levels of Maturity

- Establish industry consensus on software processes
- Harmonize with official standards, such as *ISO/IEC DTR 15504 Software Process Improvement and Capability Determination Standard*

The focus of the discussion in this chapter is on the SEI CMM for Software. The current version of CMM is Version 1.1 released in 1993.[2] A revision to CMM, which is open to public review, is ongoing and is expected to result in Version 2.0.[3] This CMM revision work is sponsored by the US Department of Defense. At the time of writing, the Office of the Under Secretary of Defense for Acquisition and Technology has halted the release of CMM Version 2.0 until the Common CMM Framework for integrating the use of multiple CMMs is approved.

9.3 CMM Framework

The CMM framework describes the software life cycle in terms of five maturity levels. As Figure 9-1 shows, each successive level represents a more mature software process. Maturity levels are based on activities that an organization performs to improve its software process. Table 9-1 describes each CMM maturity level.[4]

The CMM framework links maturity of the process to the quality of the software products that it produces. As espoused by the Deming principles of total quality management (TQM), the CMM concept of process maturity is based on the assumption that a more mature software process is likely to produce better quality software, which in turn can lower software development and maintenance costs as well as reduce the risks of project failure.

Empirical evidence from industry has shown that the benefits expected to be derived from using a more mature software process as defined in the CMM are predictability, effectiveness, and control.[5] In particular, one study using data from 52 US Air Force software projects found improved cost and schedule performance when more mature software processes were used. While projects that used software processes rated as CMM maturity level 1 overran time schedule and budget, projects that used a software process rated as CMM maturity level 2 or level 3 much more closely met schedule and budget estimates.[6]

Organizations typically follow an evolutionary path of software process improvement by using the CMM maturity levels as successive steps in continuously improving their software processes. Surveys indicate that most US corporations are at the first level of maturity, often well on their way to the second, but few organizations have reached the third level or higher.[7] Figure 9-2 shows the results of a recent maturity status survey.[8]

9.4 Key Process Areas

The CMM framework uses key process areas (KPAs) to describe the features that a software process exhibits at each level of maturity. The KPAs represent the requirements that must be achieved to reach a level of maturity. An organization can use the KPAs to rate its software processes and to determine where to focus process improvement efforts to advance the maturity of its software processes.

Table 9-1. The CMM Framework

CMM MATURITY LEVEL	DESCRIPTION
Level 1: Initial	The software process is mainly ad hoc, left to the discretion of the individuals performing it
Level 2: Repeatable	The software process includes project management processes to track cost, schedule, and functionality. Disciplines are in place that make the software process repeatable in multiple projects
Level 3: Defined	A standardized, documented software process is developed for the organization and is used, perhaps in a tailored form, on all projects in the organization
Level 4: Managed	Measures of the software process and the software products produced by the process are defined and used to collect data that is used in the management and control of both the process and its products
Level 5: Optimizing	Continuous process improvement is achieved by using feedback from process and product measures and by identifying, piloting, and adopting appropriate new technologies and ideas

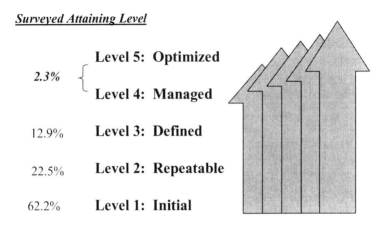

Surveyed Attaining Level

Level 5: Optimized

2.3% {

Level 4: Managed

12.9%   **Level 3: Defined**

22.5%   **Level 2: Repeatable**

62.2%   **Level 1: Initial**

Figure 9-2. 1997 Survey of the CMM Level Attained by 628 Organizations

A KPA is described in terms of key practices that define the infrastructure and activities for implementing the KPA. The key practices for a key process area are grouped into five features: commitment to perform, ability to perform, activities performed, monitoring implementation, and verifying implementation. The KPAs related to each CMM level of maturity for versions 1.1 and 2.0 are listed in Table 9-2.[9] Note that Level 1 has no KPAs.

9.5 CMM Version 2.0

CMM Version 2.0 (an enhancement and update of Version 1.1) is in draft form at the time of writing this book. Draft C is the most current draft and is available for public review.[10] The CMM is being updated to:

- Respond to change requests from its users to correct defects in the CMM

- Incorporate additional good software practices for different KPAs

- Introduce new KPAs to expand the scope of CMM

- Revise the architecture of the CMM from a staged to a continuous model

Some of the major changes expected between CMM Version 1.1 and Version 2.0 include the following:

- Software Project Tracking and Oversight (a Level-2 KPA) has been renamed as Software Project Control

- Software Subcontract Management (a Level-2 KPA) has been expanded to include off-the-shelf and custom-supplied software and has been renamed as Software Acquisition Management

- Intergroup Coordination (a Level-3 KPA) has been renamed as Project Interface Coordination

- Training Program (a Level-3 KPA) has been renamed as Organization Training Program

- Software Product Engineering (a Level-3 KPA) has been expanded to include all software life cycle processes from requirements elicitation through delivery, installation, and support

- Quantitative Process Management (a Level-4 KPA) has been rewritten to require the use of rigorous statistical techniques and has been renamed as Statistical Process Management

- Organization Software Asset Commonality has been introduced as a new Level-4 KPA

9.6 Comparing CMM and the 12207 Standard

The 12207 standard is the Standard for Information Technology—Software Life Cycle Processes[11] (see Chapter 2). Recall that there are two versions: 1) the international version: ISO/IEC 12207 and 2) the US version: IEEE/EIA 12207. This discussion applies to both versions.

The CMM uses the term "software process" to refer to the software life cycle, which includes both software development and maintenance activities and describes the management and technical aspects. The 12207 standard uses the term "software life cycle" and defines it as the comprehensive set of processes for acquiring, supplying, developing, operating, and maintaining software products as well as supporting and managing processes.

The CMM and the12207 standard are similar in several ways. They both are frameworks for software life cycle processes. They both are requirement-level specifications. They describe software life cycle process requirements but not the implementation details for software processes. They both can be applied to an individual software project and to an entire enterprise (or organization).

On the other hand, they also differ in some significant ways. First, although the purposes for using the CMM or the 12207 standard may be similar (e.g., vendor selection or process improvement), they describe the software process requirements from two different perspectives. The CMM describes the requirements from the perspective of properties that characterize maturity in a software process. The 12207 standard describes the requirements from the perspective of a set of minimum requirements needed to achieve compliance to the standard. CMM requirements are used to rate the maturity of an organization based on the software life cycle it uses. An organization achieves compliance to the 12207 standard by using a life cycle model that contains the processes and their corresponding activities and tasks as required by the standard. The 12207 standard is used to establish a common, well-understood baseline of what minimally should be included in a software life cycle process model. For example, the 12207 standard can be used by two parties who wish to enter into a legally binding contract where one party agrees to use compliant software processes to perform software services or provide software products to the other party.

Table 9-2. CMM Version 1.1 and 2.0 Key Process Areas

CMM MATURITY LEVEL	VERSION 1.1 KEY PROCESS AREAS	VERSION 2.0 KEY PROCESS AREAS
Level 1: Initial	None	None
Level 2: Repeatable [KPAs focus on establishing project management controls]	2.1 Requirements Management 2.2 Software Configuration Management 2.3 Software Project Planning 2.4 Software Product Tracking and Oversight 2.5 Software Quality Assurance 2.6 Software Subcontract Management	2.1 Same 2.2 Same 2.3 Same 2.4 Software Project Control 2.5 Same 2.6 Software Acquisition Management
Level 3: Defined [KPAs focus on institutionalizing software process across all projects in the organization]	3.1 Integrated Software Management 3.2 Intergroup Coordination 3.3 Organization Process Definition 3.4 Organization Process Focus 3.5 Peer reviews 3.6 Software Product Engineering 3.7 Training Program	3.1 Same 3.2 Project Interface Coordination 3.3 Same 3.4 Same 3.5 Same 3.6 Same 3.7 Organization Training Program
Level 4: Managed [KPAs focus on quantitative measures for the software process and software product]	4.1 Quantitative Process Management 4.2 Software Quality Management	4.1 Statistical Process Management 4.2 Organization Process Performance 4.3 Organization Software Asset Commonality
Level 5: Optimizing [KPAs focus on implementing continual and measurable process improvement]	5.1 Defect Prevention 5.2 Technology Change Management 5.3 Process Change Management	5.1 Same 5.2 Organization Process and Technology Innovation 5.3 Organization Improvement Deployment

There are differences between the CMM framework and the 12207 standard framework. The CMM organizes processes into a maturity framework. The 12207 standard organizes software processes into the life cycle framework to show the context in which the processes operate and how they relate to one another. Another difference is that the CMM is a *de facto* standard, while the 12207 standard is a *de jure* standard.

9.7 Using CMM to Rate a 12207-Compliant Software Process

CMM is used to measure the software capability of an organization in terms of the maturity of its software process. Suppose the organization uses a 12207-compliant software life cycle process model, what would its CMM maturity rating be?

The IEEE/EIA 12207-compliance can be applied at the project level or at the organization level. In addition, at each level, compliance can be absolute or tailored. Absolute compliance at the organization level means that an organization's life cycle contains the minimum set of processes, activities, and tasks that are specified as mandatory in the standard. Absolute compliance also can be claimed for a single process (e.g., Development, Configuration Management).

Tailoring is done to enable the standard to better meet the needs of a specific project or a particular organization. Tailored compliance is achieved when the organization's life cycle model contains all the processes, activities, and tasks selected by the tailoring process in accordance with the standard. The "spirit" of the tailoring process suggests that an organization use tailoring to properly scope the work for a contract (e.g., software maintenance, not software development), rather than as a way to "water-down" the standard's requirements.

Table 9-3 shows the mapping of the CMM Version1.1 KPAs to the corresponding 12207 Standard Processes. As shown by this mapping, an organization that achieves absolute compliance to 12207 would probably merit a CMM Level 5 Maturity rating. An organization that claims tailored compliance to the 12207 standard may only achieve a lower level of CMM maturity, depending upon what 12207 standard processes were deleted by the organization's application of the tailoring process.

9.7.1 Mapping 12207 Processes to Other CMMs

Some 12207 processes can be mapped to other CMM maturity models, namely:

- The 12207 Acquisition Process can be mapped to the SA-CMM
- The 12207 Training Process can be mapped to the P-CMM

9.7.2 Advantages of Achieving 12207 Compliance

The advantage of achieving 12207 compliance is that this important international standard is the cornerstone of the IEEE SESC Standards Collection. The ISO/IEC 12207 Standard is the reference model for the software life cycle process framework in software engineering standards.[12] Many software engineering standards are being revised to show a clear relationship with the 12207 Standard framework. For example, the ISO 9003 Standard, which is the interpretation of the ISO 9001 Standard for software, has committed to recognize the ISO 12207 Standard as the software life cycle process standard. The ISO 9000 standards are recognized as the worldwide standard for quality programs. Note that the CMM is aimed at general software process improvement, while ISO 9000-3 is aimed specifically at software quality process improvement.

Table 9-3. CMM Version1.1 KPAs Mapped to 12207 Standard Processes

CMM KPAS	12207 STANDARD PROCESSES
Level 1: Initial	
Level 2: Repeatable	
2.1 Requirements management	• Development process • Software requirements analysis activity
2.2 Software configuration management	• Configuration management process
2.3 Software project planning	• Supply process • Planning activity • Management process • Planning activity
2.4 Software project tracking and oversight	• Management process • Execution and control activity • Problem resolution process
2.5 Software quality assurance	• Quality assurance process • Audit process • Verification process • Validation process • Joint review process • Problem resolution process
2.6 Software subcontract management	• Acquisition process
Level 3: Defined	
3.1 Integrated software management	• Acquisition process • Request-for-proposal activity • Supply process • Planning activity • Management process
3.2 Intergroup coordination	• Management process • Infrastructure process
3.3 Organization process definition	• All of 12207 standard processes
3.4 Organization process focus	• Improvement process
3.5 Peer reviews	• Joint review process
3.6 Software product engineering	• Development process • Maintenance process
3.7 Training program	• Training process
Level 4: Managed	
4.1 Quantitative process management	• Improvement Process • Management Process • Review and evaluation activity • Problem resolution process

Table 9-3 Continued

4.2 Software quality management	<ul><li>Validation process</li><li>Verification process</li><li>Quality assurance process</li><li>Problem resolution process</li></ul>
Level 5: Optimizing	
5.1 Defect prevention	<ul><li>Validation process</li><li>Verification process</li><li>Problem resolution process</li><li>Quality assurance process</li></ul>
5.2 Technology change management	<ul><li>Improvement process</li></ul>
5.3 Process change management	<ul><li>Improvement process</li></ul>

Table 9-4. Examples of Software Standards

STANDARD NUMBER	STANDARD NAME
IEEE Std 1074-1995	Standard for developing software life cycle processes
IEEE Std 1008-1987	Standard for software unit testing
IEEE Std 1042-1987	Guide to software configuration management
IEEE Std 1219-1992	Standard for software maintenance
IEEE Std 1420.1-1995	Software reuse—data model for reuse library interoperability: basic interoperability data model (BIDM)
IEEE Std. 1420.1a-1996	Supplement to software reuse—data model for reuse library interoperability: asset certification framework

Another advantage of using the 12207 standard is that while the CMM describes only the characteristics of software processes, the 12207 standard provides for more detailed software process specifications. The 12207 standard references other standards that provide software process implementation details, as well as information about data (products) produced by the software life cycle processes and best practices. Examples of other standards for the software life cycle and individual life cycle processes are shown in Table 9-4.[13]

9.8 SPICE

Commonly known as SPICE, the *ISO/IEC DTR 15504 Software Process Improvement and Capability Determination Standard* is an ongoing international collaboration to develop a software process assessment standard.[14] The objective of ISO 15504 is to establish a common framework for software processes capability ratings. It also will provide a migration path for existing models, such as the CMM, to become 15504-compliant. A joint technical committee of the ISO (International Standardization Organization) and the IEC (International Electrotechnical Commission) was officially formed in 1993. The 15504 standard is currently in draft form and is expected to be complete in the 1999-2001 time frame. An objective of the ongoing revision CMM work is to make CMM 15504-compliant.

9.9 CMM Support for Reuse

Since reuse is the central topic of discussion in this book, it is important to explore the question of how well does the CMM support the practice of reuse in an organization. For example, can the CMM measure the software reuse capability of an organization's software life cycle processes?

With respect to CMM version 1.1, the answer is that the CMM can only indirectly measure reuse capability. CMM version 1.1 KPAs do not explicitly describe the reuse characteristics of processes. However, CMM Version 1.1 does, of course, describe the characteristics of a mature process. The more mature a software process, the more likely it is able to support systematic reuse. A well-defined, repeatable software process that has been institutionalized across the organization provides an excellent foundation upon which to add reuse-specific process characteristics. But unless reuse-specific characteristics (e.g., reuse-related activities and tasks) are covered by the KPA practices, the CMM cannot effectively measure reuse maturity.

9.10 Organization Software Asset Commonality

CMM Version 2.0 is attempting to correct the reuse deficiencies of Version 1.1. A new Level-4 KPA called Software Asset Commonality has been included in to draft for Version 2.0. Its purpose is "to exploit commonality among software products to achieve cost, quality, and cycle benefits."[15] According to Draft C, a common software asset has the potential to be used across projects in an organization. A common software asset is defined as "a description of a partial solution (such as a code unit, a sub-system, or a design document) or captured knowledge (such as a requirements database or test procedures) that can be used to build or modify software products." Software requirements, designs, code units, test cases, and documentation are listed as examples of common software assets in Draft C.

Organization Software Asset Commonality involves practices for:

• Defining common asset requirements

• Establishing and maintaining a set of common assets

• Deploying the common assets across the organization

The key practices for this KPA are listed in Table 9-5.[16] Table 9-5 also maps the Organization Software Asset key practices to the reuse processes specified in IEEE Std. 1517. The mapping shows that both the CMM and IEEE Std. 1517 in general cover the same aspects of software reuse. However, there are two major differences in their coverage. First, IEEE Std. 1517 provides more implementation detail in the official body of the standard than does the CMM. Many of the specifics of reuse are captured only as sub-practices or examples in the CMM. For example, the CMM Asset Development key practice explains:

> *This activity typically includes: 1. Developing and documenting a software domain architecture for each product line as appropriate; 2. Obtaining existing software assets from internal and external sources., etc.[17]*

Table 9-5. Organization Software Asset Commonality Key Practices

KEY PRACTICE	KEY PRACTICE DESCRIPTION	STD.1517 REUSE PROCESS
Commitment to Perform		
Policy	Senior management establishes and maintains the written organizational policy for establishing and deploying common software assets	Reuse Program Administration Process
Sponsorship	Senior management sponsors the activities for establishing and deploying common software assets across the organization	Reuse Program Administration Process
Ability to Perform		
Plan	Establish and maintain the plan for establishing and deploying common software assets	Reuse Program Administration Process
Resources	Allocate adequate resources and funding for establishing and deploying common software assets	Reuse Program Administration Process
Responsibility	Assign responsibility and authority for establishing and deploying common software assets	Reuse Program Administration Process
Training	Train the people performing or supporting organization software asset commonality as required and needed	Reuse Program Administration Process
Activities Performed		
Perform	Perform the activities for organization software asset commonality to support quantitatively managed processes	Reuse Program Administration Process
Commonality	Analyze software products across the organization to identify common attributes	Domain Engineering Process

Table 9-5 Continued

Asset Development	Develop and maintain common software assets for use across software projects as appropriate	Domain Engineering Process
Deploy Assets	Deploy common software assets across the organization	Asset Management Process
Feedback	Provide feedback on the use and evolution of common software assets to the developers and users of the assets	Asset Management Process
Measurement and analysis		
Insight	Define, collect, and analyze measures to provide insight into the performance of the activities for Organization Software Asset Commonality	Reuse Program Administration Process
Process Assurance	Objectively review designated activities of establishing and deploying common software assets for adherence to specified requirements, plans, processes, standards, and procedures	Reuse Program Administration Process
Product Assurance	Objectively review designated software work products of establishing and deploying common software assets for adherence to specified requirements and standards	Domain Engineering Process
Senior Management Reviews	Review the activities for establishing common software assets with senior management periodically and as needed	Reuse Program Administration Process

In comparison, consider the following excerpt from the specification for the Reuse Program Administration Process in IEEE 1517 standard:

> *5.3.5.1 The developer shall derive a software architecture that is based on selected, applicable domain architectures. If no such domain architectures exist, the developer may define an architecture for this software product that is consistent with the domain models and that describes the structure of the software product and the software components that comprise this structure. The developer shall allocate software requirements to this architecture following the domain models that correspond to the selected domain architecture, if it exists. The software architecture shall be documented reusing applicable documentation assets, if any exist. (This task defines reuse-related requirements in addition to those requirements specified in IEEE/EIA Std. 12207.0 – 1996, task 5.3.5.1)[18]*

The second major difference is that the1517 standard focus is on conformance to a standard framework for reuse processes to establish a common understanding of reuse across the industry; while the CMM focus is on features of software processes for assessment and reuse processes improvement purposes. The 1517 software life cycle framework, which is based on 12207 framework, fits reuse processes, activities, and tasks into the context of the whole life cycle. This context information adds much value and guidance to the user.

The Organization Software Asset Commonality KPA is the most controversial change being considered in CMM Version 2.0.[19] Many concerns have been raised. One concern is that reuse is expressed at too abstract a level to be of value to those interested in implementing good reuse practices. Another concern voiced by some Level 4 and 5 organization's is that defining Organization Software Asset Commonality as a Level 4: Quantitatively Managed KPA makes it too rigorous for even them to meet. In Draft C of CMM Version 2.0, a Quantitatively Managed Process is defined as "a process that is controlled using quantitative, typically statistical techniques," and a Defined Process as "a repeatable process that is defined at the organizational level or tailored from the organization's set of standard processes."[20]

Developers of IEEE Std. 1517 agree with these concerns. Their general opinion is that when an organization achieves CMM Level-3 Maturity, it is ready to successfully institutionalize systematic reuse.

9.11 Harmonizing CMM and 1517

There is a chance that, because it is so controversial, Organization Software Asset Commonality will not be included in the final release of CMM Version 2.0. This would be very unfortunate indeed. It would be valuable to industry if along with their attempts to "harmonize" the CMM with the 12207 standard, the developers of CMM Version 2.0 could also "harmonize" the CMM reuse practices with the IEEE 1517 Reuse Processes Standard.

9.12 References

1. *Capability Model Summary*, Software Engineering Institute, Carnegie Mellon Univ., SEI Web Page: sei.cmu.edu.

2. M. Paulk et al., *Capability Maturity Model for Software*, Version 1.1, SEI CMU/SEI-93-TR-24, Carnegie Mellon Univ., Pittsburgh, Pa., 1993.

3. *CMM* , Version 2.0, Draft C, October 1997, SEI, Carnegie Mellon Univ., SEI Web Page: sei.cmu.edu.

4. *CMM Summary.*

5. Ibid.

6. P. Lawlis, R. Flowe, and J. Thordahl, "A Correlation Study of the CMM and Software Development Performance," *CrossTalk*, Sept. 1995, pp. 21–25.

7. E. Gottesdiener, "What is Your Development Maturity?" *Application Development Trends*, Mar. 1996, pp. 60–74.

8. J. Bulter, "A Report card: Assessing the Assessor," *Managing SystemDevelopment,* Feb. 1998, pp. 8–10.

9. *The Capability Maturity Model for Software*, SEI, Carnegie Mellon University, SEI Web page: sei.cmu.edu.

10. *Draft C of SW-CMM* ,Version 2.0, October 22, 1997, SEI, Carnegie Mellon University, Web page: sei.cmu.edu.

11. IEEE/EIA Std. 12207.0-1997, *Standard for Information Technology—Software Life Cycle Processes.*

12. IEEE SESC Policy Statement, *SESC First Annual Meeting*

13. *Letter,* Leonard Tripp, September 24, 1997.

14. Moore, James, *Software Engineering Standards: A User's Roadmap*, IEEE CS Press, Los Alamitos, Calif., 1998, pp. 37–39.

15. *Spice*, SEI, Carnegie Mellon University, SEI Web Page: sei.cmu.edu.

16. "Organization Software Asset Commonality," *SW-CMM SM*, Version 2.0, Draft C, October 22, 1997, SEI, Carnegie Mellon University, SEI Web Page: sei.cmu.edu.

17. Ibid.

18. Ibid.

19. *IEEE Std, 1517 Standard for Information Technology—Software Life Cycle Processes— Reuse Processes.*

20. *Draft-C of SW-CMM*, Version 2.0, October 22, 1997, SEI, Carnegie Mellon University, SEI Web Page: sei.cmu.edu.

21. Ibid.

Chapter 10.
Relationship to the OMG
Unified Modeling Language

10.1 Overview of UML

The Unified Modeling Language is a nonproprietary, open "standard" from the Object Management Group. On November 17, 1997, the OMG announced its adoption of the UML into the Object Management Architecture as a means of giving object-oriented software developers working in all programming languages and on all platforms a common modeling language for building distributed objects. At the time of writing this book, the current version of UML is Version 1.1. The following discussion is based on this UML Version.[1]

Like the IEEE 1517 Reuse Processes Standard, the UML supports the world trade of software, down to the component level. An important objective of UML is to provide sufficient notation and semantics to model frameworks, distributed systems, and component-based systems. Another important objective is to facilitate model interchange across tools.

The UML offers a common notation and semantics for describing software systems and, in particular, software analysis and design models. According to the UML Summary document, the UML is "a language for specifying, visualizing, and construction artifacts of software systems, as well as for business modeling. The UML represents a collection of 'best engineering practices' that have proven successful in the modeling of large and complex systems."[2] The UML defines an artifact as "a piece of information that is used or produced by a software development process."[3] The focus of the UML language is a metamodel for specifying an object model.

The notations in the UML include several graphical diagrams such as Use Case, Class, Activity, and Sequence. Table 10-1 lists the graphical diagrams included in Version 1.1 of the UML Standard.

10.2 History of UML

In 1995, Grady Booch and Jim Rambaugh combined the Booch and Object Modeling Technique (OMT) object-oriented methods to create the first draft of the UML, which they called the Unified Method.[5] Later in 1995, Ivar Jacobson incorporated Object-Oriented Software Engineering (OOSE) in the Unified Method. In 1996, Booch, Rambaugh, and Jacobson combined the semantics and notations used in each of their three methods to produce an object-oriented analysis and design notation, which was called UML Versions .9 and .91. Also in 1996, a consortium of

UML Partners, including representation from several different corporations was formed to incorporate the ideas of a wide variety of experts. The UML Partners produced UML Version 1.0. In 1997, UML Version 1.0 was submitted to the OMG in response to the OMG Analysis and Design Task Force Request for Proposal. After receiving feedback from industry at large, UML Version 1.1 was produced and subsequently adopted by the OMG in 1997.

Table 10-1. UML Graphical Diagrams[4]

Use Case Diagram	A diagram that shows the relationships of actors and use cases within a system; derived from OO SE use-case diagrams
Class Diagram	A diagram that shows a collection of declarative (static) model elements, such as classes, types, and their contents and relationships; derived from class diagrams used in various object-oriented methods, including OMT and Booch
Behavior Diagrams:	
Statechart Diagram	A diagram that shows a behavior that specifies the sequences of states that an object or an interaction goes through during its life in response to events, together with its responses and actions; based on statecharts of David Harel with minor modifications
Activity Diagram	A special case of a state diagram where all or most of the states have an internal action and one or more outgoing transitions involving the completion of an internal action; similar to work-flow diagrams
Interaction Diagram:	
Sequence Diagram	A diagram that shows object interactions arranged in time sequence; derived from object-oriented diagrams such as interaction, message trace, and event trace diagrams
Collaboration Diagram	A diagram that shows object interacts organized around the objects and their links to each other; forms the basis for patterns
Implementation Diagrams:	
Component Diagram	A diagram that shows the organizations and dependencies among components; derived from Booch process and module diagrams
Deployment Diagram	A diagram that shows the configuration of run-time processing nodes and the components, processes, and objects that live on them; derived from Booch process and module diagrams

10.3 OMG

The Object Management Group was formed to create a component-based software marketplace. Its charter emphasizes the creation of guidelines and object management specifications to enable the development of a heterogeneous computing environment across all major hardware platforms and operating systems.

The OMG defines object management as:

> *software development that models the real world through representation of objects. These objects are the encapsulation of attributes, relationships and methods of software identifiable program components. Object management results in faster application development, easier maintenance, enormous scalability, and reusable software.*[6]

The OMG, an industry consortium based in Framingham, MA, currently is composed of over 800 member companies including many hardware and software vendors. Established in 1989, the OMG promotes the theory and practice of object technology to support and enable the development of distributed computing systems. Its goal is to enable object-oriented software system portability and interoperability.

In 1990, the OMG issued its first set of object interoperability specifications. The main focus was to provide a common architectural framework for distributed computing. Since 1990, OMG has defined vendor-independent terminology, interface specifications, and a framework for distributed computing. The framework, called the Object Management Architecture (OMA), is a comprehensive specification that incorporates CORBA, the UML, and object services, and also includes specifications for interaction between ActiveX and JavaBeans. The OMA includes an Object Request Broker (ORB) through which objects interact. Objects, which may be any element in a distributed system, make requests and get responses through the ORB. The Object Request Architecture (ORA), a type of peer-to-peer model, specifies how objects interact via an ORB.

The Common Object Request Broker Architecture (CORBA) is the OMG's specification of the interfaces that compliant objects must support to use a CORBA-compliant ORB. Interfaces are described in the OMG's Interface Definition Language (IDL).

As a final note about OMG, it is important to point out that the OMG is an industry consortium, not an official standards body. Although commonly referred to as "standards" in the literature, the OMG specifications are actually vendor-independent *de facto* standards arrived at through consensus of its members.

10.4 UML Users

Corporations, software developers, software methodologists, and software tool vendors can all benefit from using the UML. Corporations that are committed to the UML can protect their organizations from needlessly wasting time and resources and experiencing the confusion that comes from dealing with multiple modeling languages. Software developers can use the UML diagrams to express their object-oriented analysis and design models in a form that ensures a common interpretation of the models by both human developers and automated tools. Methodologists can use UML to guide their selection or development of software life cycle methodologies by including UML semantics and notation in their methodology selection criteria and development requirements. Tool vendors can use the UML semantic metamodel as a tool metamodel to produce tools that enable interoperability.

10.5 UML Compliance

Tools comply with the UML by producing diagrams expressed in the UML notation. UML compliance enables tool interoperability; i.e., tools that comply to the UML can share information. Typically, compliance is on a diagram-by-diagram basis since tool vendors often elect to support only a subset of the standard UML diagram set. Tool vendors can increase the marketability of their products by using UML compliance to demonstrate the property of interoperability in their tools.

10.6 Where is the Process?

One frequently cited shortcoming of the UML is that it is a notation standard without a process. Users of the UML must supply their own software life cycle processes. However, in defense of the UML, it should be noted that it never was the intention of the UML developers to develop a process standard. Their position is that, although they recognize the importance of following a well-defined and well-managed process when developing software, different organizations and different domains require different processes. At this time, they believe that there is not enough industry consensus for standardizing the software life cycle. Furthermore, they believe that there may never be a consensus because the very nature of the life cycle requires that it be tailored for use in a particular context. What is more likely to occur, according to the developers of the UML, is the creation of a framework standard for the software life cycle rather than a process standard.

The developers of the ISO 12207 Software Life Cycle Processes Standard and the IEEE 1517 Reuse Processes Standard could not agree more. The purpose of these two standards is to provide a framework for the software life cycle. ISO 12207 defines the minimum requirements for a software life cycle presented in the form of a specification for the processes, activities, and tasks that must be included in the life cycle. IEEE Std. 1517 adds the required reuse processes, activities, and tasks to the 12207 framework. Because neither the 12207 nor the 1517 standard defines how to implement these requirements, both standards may be applied to all types of software life cycles, including methods that support object-oriented development and component-based development. The software life cycle framework is used by mapping the processes, activities, and tasks in a particular life cycle model to the framework.

The ultimate goal of the UML is to bring a well-defined, repeatable discipline to software engineering. However, the UML alone cannot accomplish this goal.[7] It must be applied in the context of a process. According to the UML, "a process 1) provides guidance as to the order of a team's activities, 2) specifies what artifacts should be developed, 3) directs the tasks of individual developers and the team as a whole, and 4) offers criteria for monitoring and measuring a project's products and activities."[8]

10.7 Partnering UML and 1517

By partnering with the process standard, the UML can accomplish its goal. UML provides the notation for the artifacts, and the process standard provides a framework for a software life cycle that produces these software artifacts.

Because the UML focus is on object-oriented development and component-based development, which both imply a reuse approach, the life cycle process framework specified in the IEEE Std. 1517 is a more appropriate framework (as compared with the ISO 12207 process framework) to partner with the UML. For example, component-based development includes two types of development processes: 1) a development process for components, and 2) a development process for software systems constructed from components. The IEEE 1517 Std. includes a specification for the two types of component-based development processes.

10.8 References

1. *UML Summary*, Version 1.1, September 1, 1997, Rational Software Corporation, Santa Clara, CA, Rational Web Page: rational.com.

2. Ibid.

3. *UML Glossary*, Version 1.0, January 13, 1997, Rational Software Corporation, Santa Clara, CA, Rational Web Page: rational.com.

4. Ibid.

5. *UML Summary.*

6. *History of the OMG*, Object management Group, Framingham, Mass., OMG Web page: omg.org.

7. D. Melewski, "Connecting the Dots," *Application Development Trends,* February, 1998, p.25–32.

8. *UML Summary.*

Sources for Reuse Standards

IEEE Std. 1517—1999 Standard for Information Technology— Software Life Cycle Processes—Reuse Processes

This standard provides the requirements specifications for the processes, activities, and tasks that must be included in the software life cycle to support and enable the practice of systematic software reuse. It also includes the definitions of common software reuse terms. Users of the standard include suppliers and developers of assets and developers and customers of software systems and applications developed with assets.

IEEE/EIA Std 12207.0—1996 Standard for Information Technology— Software Life Cycle Processes

This standard provides the requirements specifications for the processes, activities, and tasks that minimally must be included in the software life cycle. The processes are organized in a software life cycle framework. The standard also includes the definitions of software life cycle terms. Users of the standard include suppliers, developers, users, and customers of software systems and applications.

IEEE Std. 1420.1—1995 Standard for Information Technology— Software Reuse—Data Model for Reuse Library Interoperability— Basic Interoperability Data Model (BIDM)

This standard describes the minimal information that reuse libraries should be prepared to exchange to describe their assets to support library interoperability. BIDM is an abstract data model that describes the data content but not the formations for representations for the data. Intended users of this standard are reuse librarians and asset developers.

IEEE Std. 1420.1a—1996 Guide for Information Technology— Software Reuse—Asset Certification Framework

This guide provides extensions to the BIDM (IEEE 1420.1-1995) that may be used to describe the manner for certifying the quality and other attributes for assets. The intended users of the guide include reuse librarians and asset developers and acquirers.

IE1td 1420.1b Trail Use Supplement to IEEE Standard for Information Technology—Software Reuse—Data Model for Reuse Library Interoperability—Intellectual Property Rights Framework

This trial standard specifies extensions to the BIDM (IEEE 1420.1-1995) that can be used to describe the intellectual property rights, management policies and procedures and associated metadata for an asset in a reuse library. The intended users include reuse librarians and asset developers.

IEEE Std. 1430—1996 Guide for Information Technology—Software Reuse—Concepts for Operations and Inter-operating Reuse Libraries

This guide describes the Reuse Library Interoperability Group (RIG) assumptions for organizing reuse library networks.

Source for Obtaining Standards

IEEE Customer Service
445 Hoes Lane, PO Box 1331
Piscataway, NJ 08855-1331
USA

Phone: +1 800 678 IEEE (in the US and Canada)
+1 732 981 0060 (outside of the US and Canada)

FAX: +1 732 981 9667

http://standards.ieee.org

Index

About the Author

Carma McClure is Vice President of Research at Extended Intelligence, Inc., a Chicago-based company offering reuse methodology services and products. She has lectured about and consulted on software technologies such as maintenance, re-engineering, CASE, repositories and reuse, for major corporations, military and government organizations worldwide. She has written numerous articles and published ten software engineering books.

She served as chairperson of the Reuse Process Working Group of the IEEE Software Engineering Standards Committee which wrote the IEEE Std. 1517 Reuse Processes.

Dr. McClure received a B.A. in Mathematics from Loyola University and an M.S. and Ph.D. in Computer Science from Illinois Institute of Technology. She is a professor at the Illinois Institute of Technology and the Kellogg Graduate School of Management at Northwestern University. She also served as an ACM National Lecturer. E-mail: 73733.2037@Compuserve.com.

IEEE
COMPUTER
SOCIETY